The
and Philosophy

Popular Culture and Philosophy® Series Editor: George A. Reisch

Volume 1 *Seinfeld and Philosophy: A Book about Everything and Nothing* (2000)

Volume 2 *The Simpsons and Philosophy: The D'oh! of Homer* (2001)

Volume 3 *The Matrix and Philosophy: Welcome to the Desert of the Real* (2002)

Volume 4 *Buffy the Vampire Slayer and Philosophy: Fear and Trembling in Sunnydale* (2003)

Volume 5 *The Lord of the Rings and Philosophy: One Book to Rule Them All* (2003)

Volume 9 *Harry Potter and Philosophy: If Aristotle Ran Hogwarts* (2004)

Volume 12 *Star Wars and Philosophy: More Powerful than You Can Possibly Imagine* (2005)

Volume 13 *Superheroes and Philosophy: Truth, Justice, and the Socratic Way* (2005)

Volume 19 *Monty Python and Philosophy: Nudge Nudge, Think Think!* (2006)

Volume 25 *The Beatles and Philosophy: Nothing You Can Think that Can't Be Thunk* (2006)

Volume 26 *South Park and Philosophy: Bigger, Longer, and More Penetrating* (2007)

Volume 30 *Pink Floyd and Philosophy: Careful with that Axiom, Eugene!* (2007)

Volume 31 *Johnny Cash and Philosophy: The Burning Ring of Truth* (2008)

Volume 33 *Battlestar Galactica and Philosophy: Mission Accomplished or Mission Frakked Up?* (2008)

Volume 34 *iPod and Philosophy: iCon of an ePoch* (2008)

Volume 35 *Star Trek and Philosophy: The Wrath of Kant* (2008)

Volume 36 *The Legend of Zelda and Philosophy: I Link Therefore I Am* (2008)

Volume 37 *The Wizard of Oz and Philosophy: Wicked Wisdom of the West* (2008)

Volume 38 *Radiohead and Philosophy: Fitter Happier More Deductive* (2009)

Volume 39 *Jimmy Buffett and Philosophy: The Porpoise Driven Life* (2009) Edited by Erin McKenna and Scott L. Pratt

Volume 40 *Transformers and Philosophy: More than Meets the Mind* (2009) Edited by John R. Shook and Liz Stillwaggon Swan

Volume 41 *Stephen Colbert and Philosophy: I Am Philosophy (And So Can You!)* (2009) Edited by Aaron Allen Schiller

olume 42 *Supervillains and Philosophy: Sometimes, Evil Is Its Own Reward* (2009) Edited by Ben Dyer

Volume 43 *The Golden Compass and Philosophy: God Bites the Dust* (2009) Edited by Richard Greene and Rachel Robison

Volume 44 *Led Zeppelin and Philosophy: All Will Be Revealed* (2009) Edited by Scott Calef

Volume 45 *World of Warcraft and Philosophy: Wrath of the Philosopher King* (2009) Edited by Luke Cuddy and John Nordlinger

Volume 46 *Mr. Monk and Philosophy: The Curious Case of the Defective Detective* (2010) Edited by D.E. Wittkower

Volume 47 *Anime and Philosophy: Wide Eyed Wonder* (2010) Edited by Josef Steiff and Tristan D. Tamplin

Volume 48 *The Red Sox and Philosophy: Green Monster Meditations* (2010) Edited by Michael Macomber

Volume 49 *Zombies, Vampires, and Philosophy: New Life for the Undead* (2010) Edited by Richard Greene and K. Silem Mohammad

Volume 50 *Facebook and Philosophy: What's on Your Mind?* (2010) Edited by D.E. Wittkower

Volume 51 *Soccer and Philosophy: Beautiful Thoughts on the Beautiful Game* (2010) Edited by Ted Richards

Volume 52 *Manga and Philosophy: Fullmetal Metaphysician* (2010) Edited by Josef Steiff and Adam Barkman

Volume 53 *Martial Arts and Philosophy: Beating and Nothingness* (2010) Edited by Graham Priest and Damon Young

Volume 54 *The Onion and Philosophy: Fake News Story True, Alleges Indignant Area Professor* (2010) Edited by Sharon M. Kaye

Volume 55 *Doctor Who and Philosophy: Bigger on the Inside* (2010) Edited by Courtland Lewis and Paula Smithka

Volume 56 *Dune and Philosophy: Weirding Way of the Mentat* (2011) Edited by Jeffery Nicholas

Volume 57 *Rush and Philosophy: Heart and Mind United* (2011) Edited by Jim Berti and Durrell Bowman

Volume 58 *Dexter and Philosophy: Mind over Spatter* (2011) Edited by Richard Greene, George A. Reisch, and Rachel Robison-Greene

Volume 59 *Halo and Philosophy: Intellect Evolved* (2011) Edited by Luke Cuddy

Volume 60 *SpongeBob SquarePants and Philosophy: Soaking Up Secrets Under the Sea!* (2011) Edited by Joseph J. Foy

Volume 61 *Sherlock Holmes and Philosophy: The Footprints of a Gigantic Mind* (2011) Edited by Josef Steiff

Volume 62 *Inception and Philosophy: Ideas to Die For* (2011) Edited by Thorsten Botz-Bornstein

Volume 63 *Philip K. Dick and Philosophy: Do Androids Have Kindred Spirits?* (2011) Edited by D.E. Wittkower

Volume 64 *The Rolling Stones and Philosophy: It's Just a Thought Away* (2012) Edited by Luke Dick and George A. Reisch

Volume 65 *Chuck Klosterman and Philosophy: The Real and the Cereal* (2012) Edited by Seth Vannatta

Volume 66 *Neil Gaiman and Philosophy: Gods Gone Wild!* (2012) Edited by Tracy L. Bealer, Rachel Luria, and Wayne Yuen

Volume 67 *Breaking Bad and Philosophy: Badder Living through Chemistry* (2012) Edited by David R. Koepsell and Robert Arp

Volume 68 *The Walking Dead and Philosophy: Zombie Apocalypse Now* (2012) Edited by Wayne Yuen

Volume 69 *Curb Your Enthusiasm and Philosophy: Awaken the Social Assassin Within* (2012) Edited by Mark Ralkowski

Volume 70 *Dungeons and Dragons and Philosophy: Raiding the Temple of Wisdom* (2012) Edited by Jon Cogburn and Mark Silcox

Volume 71 *The Catcher in the Rye and Philosophy: A Book for Bastards, Morons, and Madmen* (2012) Edited by Keith Dromm and Heather Salter

Volume 72 *Jeopardy! and Philosophy: What Is Knowledge in the Form of a Question?* (2012) Edited by Shaun P. Young

Volume 73 *The Wire and Philosophy: This America, Man* (2013) Edited by David Bzdak, Joanna Crosby, and Seth Vannatta

Volume 74 *Planet of the Apes and Philosophy: Great Apes Think Alike* (2013) Edited by John Huss

Volume 75 *The Good Wife and Philosophy: Temptations of St. Alicia* (2013) Edited by Kimberly Baltzer-Jaray and Robert Arp

Volume 76 *Psych and Philosophy: Some Dark Juju-Magumbo* (2013) Edited by Robert Arp

In Preparation:

Boardwalk Empire and Philosophy (2013) Edited by Richard Greene and Rachel Robison-Greene

Futurama and Philosophy (2013) Edited by Courtland Lewis and Shaun P. Young

Ender's Game and Philosophy (2013) Edited by D.E. Wittkower and Lucinda Rush

Frankenstein and Philosophy (2013) Edited by Nicolas Michaud

How I Met Your Mother and Philosophy (2014) Edited by Lorenzo von Matterhorn

Jurassic Park and Philosophy (2014) Edited by Nicolas Michaud

Justified and Philosophy (2014) Edited by Rod Carveth

For full details of all Popular Culture and Philosophy® books, visit www.opencourtbooks.com.

Popular Culture and Philosophy®

The Walking Dead and Philosophy

Zombie Apocalypse Now

Edited by
WAYNE YUEN

OPEN COURT
Chicago and LaSalle, Illinois

Volume 68 in the series, Popular Culture and Philosophy ®, edited by George A. Reisch

To order books from Open Court, call toll-free 1-800-815-2280, or visit our website at www.opencourtbooks.com.

Open Court Publishing Company is a division of Carus Publishing Company.

Copyright © 2012 by Carus Publishing Company

First printing 2012
Second printing 2013
Third printing 2013

All rights reserved. No part of this publication may be reproduced, stored in a retrieval system, or transmitted, in any form or by any means, electronic, mechanical, photocopying, recording, or otherwise, without the prior written permission of the publisher, Open Court Publishing Company, a division of Carus Publishing Company, 70 East Lake Street, Suite 300, Chicago, Illinois 60601.

Printed and bound in the United States of America.

Library of Congress Cataloging-in-Publication Data

The Walking dead and philosophy : zombie apocalypse now / edited by Wayne Yuen.
     p. cm. — (Popular culture and philosophy ; v. 68)
   Includes bibliographical references (p.   ) and index.
   ISBN 978-0-8126-9767-4 (trade paper : alk. paper)
   1. Kirkman, Robert. Walking dead. 2. Walking dead (Television program) 3. Graphic novels—United States. 4. Zombies in literature. I. Yuen, Wayne, 1978-
PN6727.K586W39 2012
741.5'973—dc23
                                                        2012009582

*For Bogo and Fizzgig
I promise I won't eat you in a zombie apocalypse.*

Contents

Acknowledgments ix

Spoilers Warning xi

Philosophy for the Dead xiii
WAYNE YUEN

This Sorrowful Life 1

1. Are You Just Braaaiiinnnsss or Something More?
   GORDON HAWKES 3

2. Can *You* Survive a Walker Bite?
   GREG LITTMANN 17

3. What Your Zombie Knows
   RICHARD GREENE 29

4. Walking Contradictions
   ROBERT DELFINO AND KYLE TAYLOR 39

5. I'm Gonna Tell Them about Wayne
   MARTY MCKENDRY AND MICHAEL DA SILVA 53

What We Become 65

6. A Stagger-on Role to Die For
   DAVE BEISECKER 67

7. What's Yours Still Isn't Mine
   JASON WALKER 81

8. Women in a Zombie Apocalypse
   ASHLEY BARKMAN 97

9. Dead ~~Man's~~ Party
   DANEE PYE AND PETER O'SULLIVAN 107

Miles Behind 117

10. Better Off Undead
    RACHEL ROBISON-GREENE 119

11. Realistically, Nice Guys Finish Last
    SI SHEPPARD 129

12. The Optimism of *The Walking Dead*
    BRANDON KEMPNER 141

13. The Horror of Humanity
    JULIA ROUND 155

14. Monsters of Modernity
    STEPHEN BRETT GREELEY 167

The Heart's Desire 177

15. People for the Ethical Treatment of Zombies (PETZ)
    JEFFREY A. HINZMANN AND ROBERT ARP 179

16. The Only Good Walker Is a Dead Walker
    FRANKLIN ALLAIRE 195

17. I Don't Think Those Rules Apply Anymore
    ADAM BARKMAN 207

18. Dead Ends
    ELIZABETH RARD 217

19. Babes in Zombie Land
    TAURIQ MOOSA 231

20. What's Eating You?
    WAYNE YUEN 243

We Are the Walking Dead! 253

Index 259

Acknowledgments

I'd like to first and foremost thank Robert Kirkman for the fantastic comic book series and television series that makes this work possible. I'd also like to thank series editor George Reisch for saying yes to this volume and giving me the opportunity to edit it. To all the contributors who made the bulk of this volume, I appreciate your hard work, patience, and polite tolerance of my irritating demands, cajoles, and suggestions. Finally, to my wife Tiffany, thanks for being there when I'm a zombie at night from working my crazy hours.

Don't Open: Spoilers Inside

The Walking Dead is both a very successful television show, and graphic novel series. The television series has been finding its own story to tell, that is independent of the events of the graphic novel storyline. However, this doesn't mean that the events in the graphic novels won't happen in the television series (confused yet?).

This book will cover the events of both the graphic novels and the television series, and as such, may contain spoilers for those who have only watched the television series, and not read the graphic novels. If you're a fan of the television series, and don't want spoilers, I would highly encourage you to pick up the graphic novels, as they are fantastic! Conveniently, the graphic novels have a compendium out that collects Issues #1–48, and there are trade paperbacks and hard cover editions that can help you catch up to Issue #90, which will cover any reference you'll find in this book.

Philosophy for the Dead

WAYNE YUEN

The end of the world rarely is the end, at least in popular culture. Instead, it's the beginning of a new world, a world that is devoid of strong central government and traditional social institutions, and is populated with tougher than nails survivors. Oh yeah, and zombies.

Okay, so zombies don't exist. So why think about zombies in a philosophical way? Why take so seriously, something that's merely meant to entertain and scare us?

For every author in this book, there might be a different reason. You might say that we're fans and we're philosophers. It's natural to combine the things you love together. You might point out that zombies are philosophically interesting because they represent our fear of death, or the inscrutability of the human mind. Maybe it's just as much fun to think about zombies philosophically, as it is to watch people fight them off. Even the CDC is getting in on the fun. Recently it published a document to help people prepare to survive a zombie apocalypse, because preparing for zombies turns out to be excellent preparation for things like hurricanes and earthquakes as well.

The CDC recommends that people have survival necessities like water, food, and shelter. But everyone knows that packing a survival pack for a zombie apocalypse requires multi-functional tools that the CDC and FEMA left out, like shotguns (for hunting wild game), chainsaws (for firewood gathering), flamethrowers (for cooking), and katanas (for decapitating walkers). In the first episode of *The Walking Dead*,

Morgan reflects on his wife's decision to take photo albums, rather than useful supplies. What good are photos going to be in this new world that they live in? For Morgan, what they left behind is just as important as what they took. In the event of a zombie apocalypse, what we leave behind might only be intangible things like the way we lived our lives, or our philosophy.

The Walking Dead is philosophically exciting, because unlike a zombie movie, we get to really explore what it means to live in a world overrun with zombies. How should we treat one another? How should we divide the labor? Without support from things like government, law enforcement, and political correctness, are we all really equal? Can we take whatever we find? Does private property still even exist? Is the world going to be "nasty, brutish, and short" or will it be simply different from ours, with its own problems and hardships, coupled with its joys and triumphs?

And we can't forget those shambling corpses out to consume our flesh. Zombie Ontology, Metaphysics, Basic Ideas Embodied into zombies. What are they? Can they exist? In some ways, they're only a supporting cast, but without them running, crawling, stumbling, or herding towards Rick, Lori, Carl, Andrea, Glenn, and all of the survivors we get to meet, we wouldn't have such compelling characters and circumstances.

I don't doubt that if I were faced with a walker, I would either run or try to kill it, but shouldn't that give me pause? Is killing a walker wrong? What if it's a consciously aware thing like a panda bears or a dolphin, just less cute? Can I keep one as a pet or does it have a right to be free? I suppose it might all boil down to what exactly is going on in a walker's mind.

It might be surprising to most people, but philosophers have been talking about zombies for quite some time, even before it became a pop-culture phenomenon. René Descartes describes mindless automatons that look like humans, but have no internal mental life. Although he didn't call them zombies, it's a pretty close description to what most people think zombies are today. Within philosophy though, the best known use of zombies is probably David Chalmers's work arguing against the idea that human minds can be reduced to nothing but physical matter, namely our brains. These P-zombies might be the majority of people around us!

So with great humility and humbleness to the works of Rene Descartes and David Chalmers, I've brought together a rag-tag bunch of survivors, to continue the great tradition of philosophy and zombies. We're not survivalists or sheriffs. We may not have the most practical skills to help fight off the walkers, but perhaps our ideas will help us find a place in the world, after the zombies rise.

Did I mention that I own a katana?

This Sorrowful Life

1
Are You Just Braaaiiinnnsss or Something More?

GORDON HAWKES

It may come as a surprise to some readers that leading philosophers—men and women with PhD's from the likes of Oxford, Harvard, and Yale—take the possibility of zombies very seriously. The question, "Are zombies possible?" has sharply divided philosophers. On one side are those who say, "Yes. It's just obvious," and on the other side those who say, "Do I look undead to you . . . ? Of course not!"

Hundreds of academic articles, and even several whole books, have been written in attempts to settle the dispute. To mention just one example, the philosopher Robert Kirk (not to be confused with *The Walking Dead* creator Robert Kirk*man*) wrote the book *Zombies and Consciousness* to show the impossibility of zombies.

Yet not one of these books or articles so much as mentions *The Walking Dead* comics or the TV series! This sad case of neglect has nothing to do with poor taste among contemporary philosophers—this book itself is evidence against that. The zombies that philosophers discuss are not quite the same as the ones in *The Walking Dead*. They are, shall we say, slightly more abstract and philosophical than the standard Romero-esque versions envisioned by Robert Kirkman. For this reason, these philosophical zombies have been labeled . . . wait for it . . . philosophical zombies (or P-zombies for short) in order to differentiate them from their pop-culture cousins.

P-zombies are not, as you might expect, versions of the undead that lurk around university campuses and libraries, looking for helpless, unsuspecting victims to debate on weird topics. They are actually indistinguishable from normal human beings in every respect. They speak and act the same as ordinary people, and they are physically identical down to the last molecule. The distinguishing feature of a P-zombie, and what makes it different from you and me, is that it lacks consciousness. Although it speaks, acts, and looks the same as a human, it lacks the inner experience that you and I have of the world. For a P-zombie, all is dark inside.

Why does it matter so much to philosophers whether P-zombies are possible or not, and what does their possibility have to do with *The Walking Dead*?

The possibility of P-zombies is directly connected to a very significant metaphysical question: Is there something in a human being that isn't physical? Is there some part of a human that can never be eaten by a walker? Is there some immaterial essence or soul that humans possess, or are they just solid, edible matter all the way through? Philosophers agree that if P-zombies are possible, it means that there's something non-physical about humans, namely *consciousness*. If they are possible, it means, at the very least, that there is more to a person than just the flesh-and-bones body that gets reanimated by the zombie infection. This is precisely the position that Rick Grimes takes in the *Walking Dead* series.

You Can Eat My Body, But You'll Never Eat My Mind!

While it doesn't seem likely that Rick has read much philosophy, let alone heard of such a thing as a philosophical zombie, he clearly believes that there is something over and above the physical body. Consider what he tells Morgan Jones when he discovers that Morgan's son, Duane, has become a walker, and that Morgan has been killing people to feed to him: "Morgan, you know that's not your son. Your son died. . . . That's just his body—there's nothing of your son left in there. He's gone. Let him go" (*The Walking Dead* issue #58).

Rick's advice presupposes that there is something more to Duane than "just his body." Even though Duane's body is present, Rick says there's nothing of Duane "left in there." Therefore, there must have been some immaterial or non-physical part of him which is no longer present. This view, that humans are both physical and non-physical, is called dualism.

The French philosopher René Descartes famously argued for dualism in his *Meditations on First Philosophy*. He believed that the mind and the body are distinct, and ultimately that the mind can exist without the body. Most people are familiar with Descartes's famous phrase, "I think, therefore I am," which comes from the idea that you can doubt everything and anything—"Is the physical world actually real? Is 2 plus 2 actually equal to 4?"—except for the fact that you are thinking right now. If nothing else, you know that you're a thinking thing.

Descartes claimed that we can conceive of ourselves as thinking things that take up no space, or in his words, that are not "extended." We can conceive of our minds, the part of us that we refer to as "I," as completely separate from our physical bodies. In contrast, we can conceive of our bodies as physical things that don't do any thinking. You can imagine being an immaterial mind (taking up no physical space) looking down on your physical body, while it is being eaten by a horde of walkers. Therefore, according to Descartes, you are distinct from your body, and you can exist without it. For both Descartes and Rick, Duane is not his body, and, in Rick's view, Duane's immaterial mind is no longer a part of the body which Morgan has been feeding.

In holding to dualism, Rick takes the intuitive, commonsense view that most people today believe in. Also, the vast majority of people in history have believed in dualism, as almost every society and culture in history has had some notion of an essence or soul that survives a person's body after death. While belief in an afterlife is not essential to dualism, dualism appears to be essential for an afterlife, as it's not clear how life after death would be possible if there were no immaterial part of a human to carry on.

Certain characters in *The Walking Dead* indicate that they might believe in an afterlife (which would also imply dualism). Michonne speaks to her dead boyfriend. Andrea appears to speak to Dale, after he's died, through his hat (*The Walking Dead* issue #91). Rick himself talks to Lori, after she's dead, on a rotary phone. However, it's not entirely clear whether any of them believe they are actually talking to the dead person, or if it is just a coping mechanism. Michonne and Rick agree to keep their habits secret; Andrea decides to stop talking to the hat; and Rick says of his dead wife, "Lori, . . . you're not even real" (#81). Regardless of whether there is an afterlife, it's no surprise that most people hold unquestioned assumptions that imply dualism. The mind, the "I" that you think of, does not *seem* to be the same as the body you're in, the thing that walkers want to make a meal of.

Up until the time of Descartes, almost every major philosopher was a dualist of some sort. Ironically, it was Descartes's precise formulation of dualism, where the immaterial mind is utterly distinct from the physical body, which provoked the strongest criticisms. If the mind is a thinking, immaterial thing and the body is a non-thinking, material thing, they appear to have nothing in common. As physical matter, the body must obey the laws of physics and chemistry, whereas the mind, a non-physical substance, is free of them. For this reason, the twentieth-century philosopher Gilbert Ryle mockingly labeled Descartes's view "the ghost in the machine." Ryle saw, as Descartes himself saw, the problem that arises when we consider that our minds can affect our bodies (you can will yourself to blink right now), and our bodies can affect our minds. As Steven Pinker put it in his book, *How the Mind Works*, "How does the spook interact with solid matter?" This problem, along with others, has led most philosophers to reject dualism.

The most natural response a dualist could offer is that the *how* question is a sort of misunderstanding. Assuming that immaterial substance could affect material substance—like a soul moving a body—it wouldn't do so through physical contact, like one billiard ball crashing into another. Furthermore, there are many instances of things—for example, the force of gravity, the wave/particle nature of light, the existence of subatomic particles—where we are able to say *that* it is so without being able to say *how* it is so. Another response, given by David Chalmers in *The Conscious Mind*, is that the physical and non-physical interact based on fundamental "psychophysical laws," which are a fundamental part of the universe in the same way as the law of gravitation.

You're Just Tasty Meat All the Way Down

So there's a sharp difference between what most people, including Rick, believe and what most philosophers and scientists believe. The large majority of academics who study the mind reject dualism in favor of materialism, the belief that the entire universe and everything in it, including the human mind, is physical. *The Walking Dead*, both in the comics and the TV series, accurately reflects this difference of opinion between the man on the street and the academic. Both Dr. Edwin Jenner in the television series and Dr. Stevens in the comic—who can be taken to represent academics and scientists in general—are clearly materialists.

With his dying words after being bitten by a zombie, Dr. Stevens, the Governor's personal doctor, tells his assistant, Alice: "Think of it scientifically. I'm just evolving into a different—worse life form. I'll still exist . . . in some way" (#32). He believes there's nothing more to him than his physical body, so it's logical that he thinks he'll still exist ("in some way") as long as his body still exists. Also, in "TS-19," Dr. Jenner, while showing the group an "enhanced internal view" of Test Subject 19's brain, states that the "electric impulses in the brain that carry all the messages,"—that is, the *physical* signals—are "everything." He adds, "Somewhere in all that organic wiring, all those ripples of light . . . is you—a thing that makes *you* unique, and human." In other words, the thing that makes us human, according to Dr. Jenner, is something physical in the brain. He even specifies a location, the neocortex, as containing "the *you* part."

Thus, Jenner disagrees with Stevens's belief that a person still exists after becoming a zombie. Concerning death, he says, "Everything you ever were or will be . . . Gone." Both Stevens and Jenner are clearly materialists, but Dr. Jenner places human identity in the function of the neocortex. Once that stops functioning, the person no longer exists.

The human mind, according to materialists like Jenner and Stevens, is nothing over and above the brain. It just is the brain. If materialism is true, you're just tasty meat all the way down.

The predominance of materialism is relatively recent in the history of ideas. Its rise in popularity has coincided with the dramatic and rapid rise of science during the last century to a position of supremacy as the means by which we gain knowledge, not only about the world around us, but also, more importantly, about ourselves. Science, through empirical research, has succeeded in explaining mystery after mystery—from how disease is caused by micro-organisms to how DNA can replicate itself. The sciences have succeeded in explaining the physical world to such an extent that it seems, given enough time, scientists will be able, at least in principle, to explain most everything (perhaps even what causes walkers, provided they don't accidentally incinerate all their samples like Dr. Jenner did). As a result, most philosophers believe that the workings of the human mind will eventually be explicable in physical terms, in the same way as photosynthesis, digestion, or even a computer program.

The 'You' Part: Edible or Inedible?

The mind, or the "you" part, is nothing more than the brain for a materialist, so once we figure out how the brain works, we'll have figured out how we're able to think and act and experience the world the way we do. As Dr. Jenner says, speaking of the physical processes in the brain, "They determine everything a person says, does, or thinks from the moment of birth to the moment of death." In contrast with Descartes and Rick Grimes, Jenner and Stevens do not believe that you are an immaterial self; rather, you are just a collection—albeit an incredibly complex collection—of electric impulses and organic wiring, which function as a complex system that generates all your thoughts, beliefs, feelings, and actions.

It's obvious the brain is intimately connected to the mind—neither materialists nor dualists deny this. But, if your mind is just your brain, how can that grey, lumpy zombie delicacy in your skull account for everything your mind is capable of? There are many features of your mind that remain deeply mysterious.

Consider that, right now, you're looking at small, black marks on a white page. Yet these small black marks are nothing like the *meanings* that you understand in your mind. With my keyboard I make the marks "p" and "a" and "g" and "e," and when you read them together as "page" those four black marks are understood by you as referring to the rectangular sheet of paper (or screen on an e-reader) that you're now looking at. Your thought is *about* the page in front of you. This "aboutness" of your thoughts is what philosophers call *intentionality*, and, at present, it is still an unexplained feature of your mind.

Furthermore, as you read these sentences, you understand them and can judge whether they make sense or not, or whether they are true or false. For example, the sentence "Walkers smell like the color green!" makes no sense, and the equation "1 walker + 3 walkers = 17 walkers" is clearly false. You are able to perceive the sense and the truth or falsity of these sentences through your ability to reason. You possess what philosophers call *rationality*, another unexplained feature of your mind.

Perhaps the most curious and fascinating feature of your mind, though, is that you *experience* the world around you. Even now, it feels a certain way for you to be looking at these black letters on a white background. When I point out that you're breathing, you become aware that there is *something it is like* to take a breath of air. You feel this book in your hands, its weight, the smoothness of its cover. When you read an issue of *The Walking Dead*, or watch an episode, there is an internal, private, subjective experience that you have. Perhaps you feel anger at the Governor's rape of Michonne; sadness when Lori is shot; pity, like Rick, when you see Hannah, the bicycle girl, reanimated as a legless walker; or shock when Sophia walks out of the barn.

In all of these examples, you experience the world in a way that only you have access to. No one else knows exactly what it's like for you to be reading these words, or to feel this book in your hands or to read and watch *The Walking Dead*. This subjective inner experience that you have is what philosophers call *consciousness*.

If materialists could explain these features of the mind, then dualism would be forlorn indeed. However, there is by no means any sort of consensus as to how a physical configuration of neurons in the brain can be "about" anything, or how neurons firing can be "true" or "false." These mysteries seem to lend support to Rick's belief in an immaterial mind. While dualism is an unpopular, minority position, it's like a walker that just won't stay dead, and materialists have been unable to put a bullet in its brain. The last mystery mentioned, consciousness, has proven especially difficult, and it has led some contemporary philosophers, with the aid of philosophical zombies, to side with Rick and conclude that there must be something non-physical in the mind.

Will My P-Zombie Twin Bite?

If there's any philosopher who should be mentioned in a book on philosophy and zombies, it's David Chalmers. The Australian philosopher has done for zombies in philosophy what George Romero did for the undead in pop culture. In his book, *The Conscious Mind*, Chalmers lays out what has come to be known as the Zombie Argument, an argument that consciousness is not physical, and, consequently, that materialism is false.

If Dr. Jenner is right and consciousness is physical, then consciousness will be entirely dependent on the physical structure of the brain. Any change in conscious experience will be nothing more than a change in the physical arrangement of molecules in the brain. Since consciousness would just be the configuration of molecules in the brain, it would be logically impossible for two physically identical creatures to have different conscious states.

When Test Subject 19 (who it turns out is Dr. Jenner's wife, Candace) has her brain scanned by the CDC's "MRI virtual camera," it records changes down to the level of individual neurons. Suppose that at the ten-minute mark of her brain scan, she was in extreme pain from the zombie fever. If, at the twenty-minute mark, her brain was in an identical configuration, down to the last molecule, she would have to be having the exact same conscious experience of pain. It wouldn't be possible for her to be having any other conscious experience, since that would mean that consciousness doesn't depend on the physical configuration of the brain. If materialism is true, consciousness *just is* the physical configuration of the brain.

This is where P-zombies come in. Try to imagine a P-zombie, a creature physically identical to a human being, but which lacks consciousness. Now, I can imagine my own P-zombie twin, a physically identical creature to myself, which is the same in every respect, except it lacks the subjective inner experience that I have. When it lies down and has its brain scanned by Dr. Jenner's supercomputer, every last neuron is identical to my own. It is just as much a fan of *The Walking Dead* as I am. It looks like me, walks like me, and talks like me. It reads comics and philosophy the same as I do. However, when my P-zombie twin stubs its toe, it might yell and rub its foot, but there is no inner experience of pain. For my P-zombie twin, all is dark inside.

David Chalmers argues that because we can conceive of P-zombies, and nothing contradictory or incoherent is part of their description, they are logically possible. And if P-zombies are possible, then consciousness isn't entirely dependent on the physical facts, since my P-zombie twin is physically identical to me, yet has no consciousness. Therefore, if P-zombies are possible, consciousness is not physical and materialism is false.

Mile-High Comic Book Covers Just Seem Obvious

Materialists obviously don't believe that P-zombies are possible. Susan Blackmore, making use of a rare, technical term in philosophy, calls the whole idea "daft."[1] However, when Chalmers argues that P-zombies are possible, he is not claiming that P-zombies could actually exist in our world. He is claiming that they are *logically* possible. A *logical* possibility is not the same as an *actual* possibility. For instance, it's logically possible that Tony Moore and Charlie Adlard could create a mile-high comic book cover, but it is doubtful that it is actually possible (Tony Moore probably wouldn't be able to complete it by deadline). Thus, logically possible things are not always actually possible. How can we prove that a mile-high comic book cover is logically possible? There's no way to prove it. If we can conceive of it, and there is no inherent contradictions (like in a square circle), then it would seem that it is logically possible. The onus is on the person who thinks it isn't logically possible to show why.

Logical possibility isn't important only in philosophy, though. It's essential for our enjoyment of *The Walking Dead*.

---

[1] Susan Blackmore, *Consciousness: A Very Short Introduction*. For those who don't speak the Queen's English, 'daft' means 'crazy', or in this case, 'total garbage'.

When we watch the show and read the comics, we are, without realizing it, putting aside questions of actual possibility and reveling in the world of logical possibility. For instance, could Rick *actually* survive for weeks unattended in a hospital without food or water after a severe gunshot wound? Would it *actually* be possible for him to just get up and walk out of there? Well, frankly, we don't care. It's logically possible and, more importantly, asking questions like that ruins the fun.

The Walking Dead, then, presents an example of the nature of the dispute over whether P-zombies are possible. We can conceive of Robert Kirkman's zombie apocalypse scenario quite easily and there doesn't appear to be anything incoherent or contradictory about it. Is it logically possible? It certainly seems to be, although there isn't really any way to argue for that claim. The same is true for P-zombies, which is why dualists like Chalmers end up saying, "It just seems obvious."

Open Up That Barn, Chalmers, and Let Me at Those P-Zombies!

Many materialists agree that zombies are conceivable, they just don't agree that they're possible. They disagree, then, that there is a necessary link between the conceivability of zombies and their possibility. However, there are some materialist philosophers who view philosophical zombies in the same way that Shane views the walkers in Hershel Greene's barn: they're an evil menace to be destroyed.

One philosopher who wants to take a shotgun to the P-zombie's head once and for all is Daniel Dennett. To him, the very thought of a P-zombie is "unimaginably preposterous."[2] "When philosophers claim that zombies are conceivable," he writes, "they invariably underestimate the task of conception (or imagination), and end up imagining something that violates their own definition." Dennett emphasizes that P-zombies must talk, behave, and think just like us if they are to be true to their definition. That means, if you asked one if it was conscious, it would say, "Of course I'm conscious. Why would you ask me that?"

---

[2] Daniel Dennett, *Brainchildren: Essays on Designing Minds*. 'Unimaginably preposterous' is a rough American translation of 'daft'.

For Dennett, if something talks, behaves, and thinks exactly like it's conscious, then it's conscious! Daniel Dennett's view of P-zombies is the same as Herschel Greene's view of walkers: "They're not zombies. They're human!" (Obviously Dennett wouldn't appreciate the comparison if he was a fan of *The Walking Dead*. Unlike Hershel, there is no love lost between him and zombies.)

In an attempt to demonstrate the absurdity of P-zombies, Dennett came up with the "zimbo," a twist on the zombie thought experiment. A zimbo is a creature that lacks consciousness. However, it is capable of "higher-order" thoughts, which is to say that it can reflect on its own thinking. In fact, there's no limit to its ability to monitor what's going on inside itself. You could ask a zimbo whether it likes Tony Moore or Charlie Adlard's artwork better. After it gave you an answer, you could ask it why it felt that way. (I'm not saying which the zimbo prefers. If you want to know, you'll have to ask it yourself.)

It would be able to reflect on its own thought process and see that it felt Moore's drawings were crisper, more detailed, but Adlard's were darker, more ominous. It could reflect even further and see that it didn't really know why it preferred the one over the other. You could ask it what it 'felt' when it watched Shane shoot Otis in the knee to save his own life ("Save the Last One"), or read about Michonne torturing the Governor (#33), and it could reflect on those 'feelings.' (This whole time, though, we are supposed to be imagining the zimbo as only having unconscious thoughts.) The zimbo would become more and more reflective, eventually to the point that it would think that it was actually conscious, and that it had real feelings and real experiences—only, by definition, the zimbo would be wrong. But, Dennett thinks, that's preposterous. Neither we nor the zimbo would ever be able to discover in what way the zimbo was unconscious.

What Is It Like to Be a Walker?

When it comes down to it, Dennett and Chalmers are divided by an intuition, by something that can't really be argued for—you either see it or you don't. The intuition can be illustrated in the following way.

Imagine that you're a walker shuffling through the streets of Atlanta. Your insides are burning with a cruel, visceral hunger. Your gums feel like they've been slit with razor blades. Your vision's blurry and your mind is dull and foggy, like you're almost asleep. . . . Then suddenly you smell something. Fresh meat! The hunger rages inside you and you try to scream, but all that comes out is, "Nnnnngggghhhh!" You want to run, but your feet feel like they weigh a hundred pounds. Oh, if you could only get a bite . . .

It seems possible that there could be "something it's like" to be a walker. There could be an inner experience of pains and . . . well, more pains. We don't know one way or the other. Axel, one of the prisoners that Rick and company find in the prison, thinks there is. He wonders whether it hurts to come back as a walker, then answers his own question, "I bet it hurts real bad. That's why they moan so much" (#22). Dr. Jenner, on the other hand, doesn't think so. The walkers are "just a shell driven by mindless instinct," he says.

But for us, we know first-hand that there is "something it is like" to be ourselves because that's what we experience every moment of our lives. There is "something it is like" to taste an orange, smell a rose, feel wet grass on our feet, hear a dog bark, or see a sunset. Now, when Test Subject 19 (Candace) is still alive, we can see from her brain scan everything going on in her brain as she's suffering from the zombie fever. Yet after we've described all the physical structures and functions of her brain—all of the "electric impulses" and the "organic wiring"—it seems as if there's still something more that we haven't described: the "what it's like" to have the fever. And after she reanimates, we see all the details of her diminished brain activity, but we can still ask, *"What is it like* to be a walker?" These questions of "What is it like?" point to the intuition that Chalmers and Dennett disagree on.

The intuition is the notion that there is *something more* to be described over and above the physical details of the brain, that no matter what configuration or arrangement of neurons one describes, there will always be the *"what it's like"* left out. No amount of information that we can get from enhanced internal views of TS-19's brain will tell us what it's like to have the zombie fever. Chalmers thinks the intuition is correct. He believes the "what it's like" needs explaining, and this leads him to believe consciousness is not physical. Dennett, however, thinks the intuition is completely false. He believes that the notion of a *"what it's like"* over and above the physical details is an illusion. For him, once we've described the physical reasons for why we act, think, and behave the way we do, we'll have also described consciousness.

It may seem that we've reached an impasse. However, if *The Walking Dead* teaches us anything, it teaches us that sometimes we have to make hard choices. Thankfully for us, the choice we're faced with here has nothing to do with chopping off limbs or executing cannibalistic hunters or killing a loved one who has become an undead monster. The choice is between dualism and materialism.

So are P-zombies possible? Is consciousness more than just a physical function of the brain? Is there some part of us that can't be eaten by the walkers? I, for one, am going to side with Rick Grimes and his affirmation that we are more than just our body. He may very well be mistaken—he is in opposition to most philosophers today—but, for me, when it comes down to it, the possibility of zombies just seems obvious.

2
Can *You* Survive a Walker Bite?

GREG LITTMANN

What's going to happen to you when the cannibal undead apocalypse comes? Most people, I suppose, will end up as walker dung, a substance I imagine to be like raw hamburger. However, let's say that you are among the "lucky" few who survive the initial outbreak. When the dead rise up to eat us all, you get to your car in time, or find a cellar to hide in, or are just fortunate enough to be temporarily overlooked like Sheriff's Deputy Rick Grimes lying in his hospital bed.

What do you do now? Can you make it through city streets that are crowded with shambling corpses hunting for living flesh? Will you be able to find one of the tiny bands of human survivors, hiding in the ruins?

For the vast majority of the uneaten, the answer will be "No". *You* don't end up as one of a courageous band of human survivors fighting to stay alive against the odds. *You* get bitten by a walker and become infected. Almost all of the uneaten do—the "resurrected" uneaten in *The Walking Dead* outnumber the living uneaten by a huge margin. That's hardly surprising—all it takes to join the shambling masses is one nip. And walkers can be *quiet!* You just have to lose yourself in your thoughts for a second and one will sneak up right behind you. *Tag—you're "it"!*

So, you get bitten by a walker. You're going to die. The fever will burn you up in short order. Now things *really* get interesting. What will happen to you and all the rest of the bite victims? Is it the end of you? Or will you continue to exist? Will you and all of the other bite victims be *gone*, or do you simply change form and take to a new life, one that involves less paperwork and more rending of flesh with your teeth? This is a question that you're going to care about as the fever courses through your system: whether you regard the existence of a walker to be a hellish fate or a welcome alternative to regular, non-ambulatory death.

The protagonists of *The Walking Dead* certainly *speak* as if the walkers *are* the people who were bitten. Just before Rick puts a bullet in the head of the half-woman whose bicycle he steals in the very first television episode "Day's Gone Bye", he tells her "I'm sorry this happened to you", as though the woman she once was, who was riding her bicycle down the street when a walker bit her, is still there. Similarly in "Wildfire," Andrea addresses the ferocious corpse of her sister Amy by name and gently tells it "I love you," making it clear that she thinks that her sister Amy is still around, just in a new, rotting, cannibalistic form (until she shoots her in the head).

Investigating the issue of the necessary conditions for personal survival is not just a self-indulgent excuse to think about the universe of *The Walking Dead*. The problems that arise here, and the answers that we give here, may have ramifications for real-world cases in which philosophical judgments about personal identity must be made. Questions about the treatment of individuals suffering from brain injury or mental degeneration, the rights of artificial intelligences, even the ethical treatment of animals may hang on what we take the conditions for personal survival to be.

But for right now, let's get back to you—you with the teethmarks on your shoulder and the feeling that your blood is on fire. Are you soon to be gone from this world, or will you be stumbling freely over the ruined highways long after Rick, Lori, Shane and the others have become somebody's lunch?

The Life of a Corpse

The easiest way to try to track personal survival over time is to identify people with their bodies. We certainly use bodily identity to keep track of people—when Ryan finds Lori and Cody again, he recognizes them by the physical resemblance between the bodies he sees and the bodies his wife and son have always had. If people *are* their bodies, then it seems that *we*, the bitten but uneaten masses, will survive the apocalypse (a walker bit me too—bastard ripped my ear off). Of course, we will not have survived *medically speaking*—Dr. Jenner confirms in "TS-19" that the bitten die before becoming walkers.

However, in undead fiction, biological death need not entail non-survival in the sense that really concerns us—whether *we* will still exist. When we become walkers, our bodies not only still exist, they are at least as lively as they were before we died—probably more so if you work at a desk. After the process that Dr. Jenner calls "resurrection," they wander around all day and all night, eat people and other animals, and moan like herds of cattle. In other words, our bodies continue to act very much like biological organisms and continue to function in more or less the same way that they did before. The absence of a heartbeat and the rot setting into our bodies' flesh is a change, but our bodies march on. It seems fair to say, then, that if we are our bodies, we continue to exist after becoming walkers.

Everything You Ever Were or Ever Will Be—Gone

Are you satisfied that you and I and the other bite victims will survive? I'm not. We can tell that people aren't their bodies from the fact that mere bodily survival is not enough for personal survival. Our fear of death is rooted not in the fact that our body will not move any more but that it will not *think* and *feel* anymore. *That* would be non-existence. A person can't survive as a *mindless* walking corpse any more than we can survive as a regular corpse, one that rots motionless in the grave instead of wandering the streets. If a walking corpse thinks nothing and feels nothing—if it is not *conscious*—then we do not survive death and "resurrection," when we become a walker, no matter how active our mortal remains are. When our fever kill us, we won't exist anymore and *we* will never be walkers.

Dr. Edwin Jenner takes this view of death and walker "resurrection." In his opinion, we *don't exist* after we have died from the fever. In "TS-19" he makes his reasoning explicit, "The brain goes into shutdown, then the major organs. Then death. Everything you ever were or ever will be—gone." Showing the survivors images of the inside of a living woman's brain, lit up with electrical activity, he tells them: "That's a person's life—

experiences, memories, it's everything. Somewhere in all that organic wiring, in all those ripples of light, is *you*." Then as he shows them the brain die and go dark, only to have the brain stem start glowing red with walker juice as the corpse resurrects, he adds "The frontal lobes, the neocortex, the *human* part—that doesn't come back. The *you* part."

Given Jenner's reference to "the *human* part", we could interpret him as saying that walkers have merely *animal* intelligence, rather than that walkers aren't *conscious*. However, *that* interpretation doesn't jibe with his certainty that we can't survive as walkers. It's a horrible truth that people can and do suffer damage that severely impairs their intelligence, even to the animal level, but we do not generally doubt that these people have survived. I take it, then, that the thing that Jenner thinks walkers lack, which prevents them from being "you," is conscious awareness. *That's* why the bitten are "gone" once they die—they have no consciousness.

If Dr. Jenner's right, then having been bitten by walkers, we face certain annihilation. But perhaps this outlook is too optimistic. How can Jenner possibly judge whether the walkers are conscious or not? They may not use their frontal lobes and neocortex as we do, but they certainly act like conscious animals. Walkers behave as though they are aware of their environment and act so as to get what they want. They seem to spend their days and nights hunting through the obstacle course of the city in search of food. They appear to be able to tell the difference between other walkers and live humans (unless humans cover themselves in walker guts) and seem to greet the presence of live humans with groans of desire and excitement, getting, as Morgan Jones puts it, "all riled up and hungry." If he's right, if they really are "all riled up and hungry," then they are conscious.

Are Walkers Conscious?

Is there any reason to favor Jenner's view, that walkers are *not* conscious, over Morgan's view that walkers *are* conscious? Are there grounds for arguing that though the walkers *act* much like creatures of animal intelligence, they nevertheless perform these actions mindlessly, without true thoughts or feelings or experiences?

One reason we might have for resisting ascribing even animal consciousness to walkers, even though they behave much like conscious animals, is that walkers and animals are such *different* sorts of systems. For a start, walkers are composed of *dead* tissue, which means that however they make their body function, it is *radically* different from the way that living animals make their bodies function. Just getting by without blood circulation is a wonder of engineering. Furthermore, walkers don't possess brains, or at least, nothing like brains as we know them. As Dr. Jenner demonstrates, when the walker infection resurrects a human body, the only part of the brain that it restarts is the brain stem – the rest is just ordinary dead tissue.

Tasks for which the human brain stem has sole responsibility tend to be very simple—for instance, it can monitor breathing, heart-rate, and blood-pressure, the sort of thing that your conscious mind doesn't even notice. If the walker infection has found a way to use *our* brain stem to produce behavior appropriate for mammalian (or even reptilian) levels of intelligence, then it has found an entirely new way to build a complex computer out of neurons that it found lying around in our heads. Just walking around without falling over is a miracle of computation and adjustment. The walkers may look clumsy, but considering that they are running on a brain stem, they are incredibly graceful creatures.

Of course, we all know that since the walkers are fictional creatures, there is no fact of the matter as to how their "biology" works. That's beside the point. By examining hypothetical cases like the walkers, we test the consistency of our beliefs about how to regard creatures who are not like *us*.

A worry we might have about the above argument against walker consciousness is that it seems to favor systems that happen to be physically similar to ours. Is being more willing to ascribe consciousness to a creature that is physically similar to us a sensible case of reasoning from analogy or a prejudice against those who are unlike us, being artificial or inorganic or simply undead? Dr. Jenner claims that the walkers are driven by "mindless" instinct, but how can he know if they have minds or not? Is he just being a livingist bigot? After all, if we met a living person who behaved like a walker, we would pity (and fear) them, but we wouldn't conclude that they are literally "mindless" and would object if they were treated as an object.

Intelligence Test of the Dead

One standard that we might turn to in the interests of judging various systems objectively is philosophical behaviorism. Philosophical behaviorism, in its simplest form, is the view that mental states (such as beliefs and emotions) simply *are* the behavior that we associate with them. So, for instance, if someone's actions are the actions appropriate to being terrified of walkers, then that person *is* terrified of walkers as a matter of logical necessity, since the terror just *is* the appropriate behavior—screaming, running away, crying "Oh God, don't eat me!" or what have you. Using philosophical behaviorism as our standard for whether a system has conscious mental states has the advantage of not favoring any particular type of creature, such as living organic ones, just because that is what *we* happen to be. Besides, it's only by observing behavior that we can tell what mental state a fellow living human is in, so behavior observation is already a standard we use for ascribing mental states.

If we apply this standard to walkers, then they seem to have an active, if limited, mental life, one we can perhaps imagine having ourselves. Like many animals to which we ascribe mental lives, walkers behave as though they are extremely hungry and sometimes, very angry. They act as though they can distinguish between other walkers and living human beings, understand that living humans are food, and know how to go about getting that food into their mouths. Thus, on this model, we must conclude that walkers genuinely are frequently hungry, sometimes angry, can distinguish between walkers and humans, and know that humans are food on legs, there for the biting.

Extremely simple forms of philosophical behaviorism like the one just sketched above are insufficient for accounting for much of human behavior. It cannot, for instance, account for *pretending*—for the fact that someone exhibiting fear behavior might not really be afraid, but might be an actor faking fear. More sophisticated forms of behaviorism can ameliorate this problem by careful specification of how behavior is to be interpreted. However, most modern philosophers with behaviorist leanings have moved on to a view descended from behaviorism and inspired by advances in computing—*functionalism*.

According to the functionalist model, a mental state is a function that relates stimuli, other mental states, and behavior. So, for instance, the mental state of being afraid of walkers is a function that might take you from the stimulus of seeing a walker coming towards you, together with other mental states you have such as believing that you can run faster than a walker, to the behavior of running away screaming. Being a function, the same mental state may result in all sorts of different behaviors. So, for instance, the mental state of being afraid of walkers might also relate the stimulus of hearing a walker in the next room, together with other mental states such as the belief that the walker has not yet heard *you*, with the behavior of standing absolutely still and quiet. Like behaviorism, functionalism appears to have the virtue of impartiality. A system is judged by neither its composition nor arrangement, but only by its functional role. As for walkers, since they function like animals with conscious mental states, they themselves have conscious mental states. Judged by functionalist standards, the walkers are conscious.

Are you satisfied that you and I and the other bite victims will survive? I'm not. Going by behaviorist and functionalist models, it's impossible, even in principle, for a system to consistently act like a conscious being without actually being conscious. Yet this isn't impossible at all. In fact, it can be demonstrated that behaving like a creature with mental states does not require having those mental states. This can be seen by considering a particularly disgusting hypothetical situation. The argument here is based on a very influential one presented by Daniel Dennett,[1] but *this* version has *walking dead* in it.

A Revoltingly Foul Thought Experiment

I want you to imagine a hypothetical future of the world of *The Walking Dead*, a future in which the human survivors learn not only how to fight back against the undead hordes, but how to exploit them as beasts of burden. It is dangerous to harness the hungry dead, of course, but the survivors need food and food means farming. Given that the horses and oxen have long

---

[1] Dennett, Daniel, 'Toward a Cognitive Theory of Consciousness', *Brainstorms: Philosophical Essays on Mind and Psychology* (1978).

ago been eaten by walkers, the survivors find that there is nothing left to haul a plow but the walkers themselves. In many ways, granny's angry cadaver makes an excellent farm animal. She'll pull left if you dangle the meat on a string to her left and right if you dangle it to her right, she'll walk indefinitely without food and she never gets tired. (Keep away from the mouth, though. If she nips you, there's an axe on the side of the plow, but you'd better be *quick*).

Now, the walker-plowed farms flourish, producing enough food to feed the militias required to keep the wandering undead at bay. As humanity rebuilds civilization, protected by heroes like Rick Grimes, new uses are found for the free power the walkers provide. Milling the corn is easier when you strap Uncle Joe's shambling remains to the millwheel. Building is less hassle when you can move bricks by loading up the cart and putting what's left of mom and dad in yokes and collars.

Eventually, some bright spark who ought to be plowing, or milling, or out on walker patrol, realizes that you can harness walkers to perform simple computations. She starts by placing a walker in a concrete tank with a high window at either end. Meat is dangled in front of one or the other of the windows. The windows are too high for the walker to reach, but seeing the meat causes the walker to move to one end of the tank or the other. Our enterprising survivor can now move the walker to either of two positions. If we name the first position "1" and the second position "0", the walker now describes one "bit" of information (one state of *on* or *off*, one *yes* or *no*).

Yet all any modern computer does is relate bits of information—usually eight bits to a byte, with a million bytes to a megabyte. As long as you have a system to relate bits, you have a computer. So, for instance, you could build a simple computer by arranging several walker tanks together and attaching ropes to the walkers, such that as a walker moves to one end of their tank or the other, the rope attached to them will cause a piece of meat to rise or lower at the window of another walker's tank. The complexity of such a computer system is limited only by your supply of walkers and rope. If you happen to get your hands on eight million walkers, you have yourself a megabyte to play with. A computer constituted of eight million walkers would be a slow and clunky one (not to mention a smelly and dangerous one), but it *would* be a working computer.

Let's allow that the human survivors manage to build such monstrous computers out of stray walkers and bitten relations. Let's also allow that, like people today, they always want a better and more complex computer. So they labor to hunt down the herds of wild corpses and to manufacture ever more rope and pulleys, constantly upgrading their old system by adding more dead people to the memory. Inevitably, as these stinking machines grow more complex, some people decide that they want to build a walker-machine so complex that it can function like a human brain. There is no doubt that, given enough walkers and enough rope, such a machine could be built. We *know* that it is possible for there to be a machine that functions like a human brain because that's exactly what the human brain *is*—a machine that functions like a human brain. The computer in your head is built out of organic tissue, but any computational system that you can build out of one substance can be functionally replicated by a computational system built out of anything else—circuit-boards and wires, pigeons carrying letters, or violent carcasses in rows of cement tanks.

Now, somehow the survivors overcome the staggering logistical problems involved with building a mind-replicating computer out of walkers and rope. They construct a vast and hellish walker-computer containing so many dead human beings roped to pulleys that it is complex enough to replicate the functioning of a human brain. It isn't as *fast* as a human brain, of course. A human could tell you at once what the sum of seven and three is, or what they think caused the walker apocalypse, or how it felt to watch the kids being eaten alive by a pack of infected nuns. A functional copy of a human brain composed of walkers in tanks, on the other hand, would take vastly longer to produce the same output. Still, there is no output that you could get from a human brain that you couldn't get from a walker-computer, given enough time.

As you will recall, on the behaviorist and functionalist models, a mental state simply *is* its associated behavior or functional role, so any system that produces that behavior or fulfils that functional role just *is* that mental state. What this means is that under a behaviorist or functionalist model, the massive walker-computer described above does not simply give the same output as a conscious mind—rather, the massive walker-computer *is* a conscious mind. It *must* be conscious on the model, since it functions like a conscious system. It would be strictly *impossible* for the machine to function like that *without* being conscious.

However, I put it to you that it is at least *conceivable* that such a device constructed out of corpses and rope is not conscious at all. It seems at least *conceivable* that the masses of bound walkers understand *nothing* of what they are doing. That is, it seems conceivable that the whole groaning, rotting system goes through the *motions* of producing the responses that a conscious mind would produce, without having genuine thoughts and emotions—without really knowing what the sum of seven and three is, or having opinions about the cause of the apocalypse, or tortured memories of rampaging nuns and screaming children.

Yet if our mental states truly were just behaviors or functions, it should be *inconceivable* for a system that functions like a human mind *not* to be conscious. Stories about such a system should be *incoherent*. After all, if mental states just *are* behaviors or functions, then asking you to imagine a system that functions like a human mind but has no experiences would be self-contradictory. It would be like asking you to imagine a walker who both has legs and does not have legs, or both stinks of decay and doesn't stink of decay, or both is and isn't creeping up behind you right now. The walker-computer thought experiment shows us that whatever being conscious is, we can't know that a system possesses it just by the way that the system behaves or functions. *That* means that we can't know from observing walkers' behavior that they are conscious.

So, Can You Survive a Walker Bite or Not?

So where does that leave us and the rest of the walker-bitten masses? It leaves us dying in ignorance, burning up from the infection, not knowing if we are about to be plunged into oblivion or doomed to walk the Earth as a hungry, rotting killer. We know that we aren't our bodies, and we know that we aren't a collection of behaviors or functions, but there is no way to know whether we are about to be annihilated by our walker bites or whether we will rise in hideous undeath. Too bad for us. Not every story has a happy ending.

Meanwhile, I think that there are important lessons to be learned here. Most importantly, *we cannot know whether a system is conscious*. This negative result may be important to keep in mind in our interactions with systems that are not human, including animal systems and artificial intelligences. How we treat such non-human systems frequently depends on beliefs we have about their consciousness, or lack thereof. If we really can't know whether a system is conscious, then we might decide to err on the side of caution in our treatment of them.

One of the reasons I like walkers so much is because they are so damn serious. Sometimes, in the long history of the cannibal undead apocalypse genre, the grim and realistic tone of George Romero's seminal *Night of the Living Dead* has been relaxed for something more tongue-in-cheek. And there is nothing wrong with that—Peter Jackson's *Dead Alive* is hilarious, as is Edgar Wright's *Shaun of the Dead,* and the many *Return of the Living Dead* movies would be so much less without their zombie's delightful hunting cry of "braaains." Yet there is a special pleasure to be gained from the serious undead, undead like the *walkers*, who are too dedicated to the horrific task of *eating living human beings* to be distracted by jokes.

There have been a few jokes in this chapter, but that must not distract us from the serious philosophical task at hand, to discover our own fundamental nature. As philosophers hunting for the truth, we must be as serious and relentless as walkers hunting for living flesh. Hunting for truth, like hunting for living humans, is an endless and difficult process, with many obstacles and false leads. Yet it is only by inexorably shambling after the screaming human of truth that we can sink our teeth into the living and bleeding flesh of answers.

3
What Your Zombie Knows

RICHARD GREENE

One thing that makes zombies fun is that they seem kind of dumb. Undoubtedly, they are very scary—especially in large numbers, and they represent the greatest possible threat: annihilation of the human race, but yet, they appear to be really stupid. Thick as bricks! Seemingly, if you had even the smallest matter to be worked out, you just might be better off asking for help from a houseplant, than you would be in consulting a zombie. Appearances, however, at times, can be deceiving.

If It Walks Like a Zombie . . . ?

What evidence do we have for thinking that zombies are dumb? Just how dumb are zombies? What, if anything, do zombies know? Perhaps before addressing these questions we'd better get a clearer idea of what sort of zombies we're talking about.

In Dan O'Bannon's *The Return of the Living Dead* the zombies seem to have whatever intelligence they had prior to becoming zombies. In one scene Freddy (a zombie) offers the following argument to his girlfriend, Tina (not a zombie): "See? You made me hurt myself again! I broke my hand off completely at the wrist this time, Tina! But that's okay, Darlin', because I love you, and that's why you have to let me EAT YOUR BRAAAAAAAAAAAAIIIIIIIIIIIINS!"

In another scene a very clever zombie climbs into an emergency response vehicle, appropriates the radio, and says, "Send more paramedics." Clearly, we're not talking about complete blithering idiots here, although, Freddy's reasoning is suspect.

The upshot is that the zombies of *The Return of the Living Dead* are not typical. They make for a fun parody of more traditional zombie films, such as *Night of the Living Dead* and its sequels, but they don't jibe with our normal conceptions of what zombies are "really" like. You can't converse or reason with a zombie or expect a zombie to try to converse or reason with you.

Another type of zombie can be found in Victor and Edward Halperin's classic movie, *White Zombie*. Here the zombies—victims of evil practitioners of Voodoo—are not quite as clever as those in *The Return of the Living Dead*, but still seem more akin to pre-zombie humans than do paradigmatic zombies, as they are able to follow complex orders and to serve a master. The heroine of the story and a zombie herself, Madeline, is ordered by her master Murder Legendre to kill the hero of the story, Neil, which she attempts to do by wielding a knife. This type of zombie, along with having lost its life, has lost any independent will, but has not lost much, if any, cognitive abilities (even though such abilities are mostly suppressed most of the time).

At the other end of the zombie intelligence spectrum is the philosophical zombie. The philosophical zombie, of course, has no mental life whatsoever. Since, philosophical zombies are discussed in great detail elsewhere in this book,[1] it will suffice to say that they also fail to adequately line-up with our standard conception of what it is to be a zombie—they actually have too little on the ball to count as "true" zombies.

So what we need in order to best address our questions about zombie intelligence (or lack thereof) is a set of zombies that are not as intelligent as the zombies of *The Return of the Living Dead* or *White Zombie*, but have more going on than, say, philosophical zombies. This criterion, I maintain, makes the walkers of *The Walking Dead* ideal for our inquiry.

Paradoxically, these zombies are perfect, not because they are particularly interesting *qua* zombies, but because they are not particularly interesting. That is, they don't seem too terribly different from how we've come to conceive zombies over the past fifty years or so. This is not to say that our conception of zombies is fixed or static; rather, the walkers of *The Walking*

---

[1] See Chapter 1, "Are You Just Braaaiiinnnsss or Something More?"

Dead capture perfectly the way zombies are conceived today. *The Walking Dead* walkers are not too smart, as were the aforementioned zombies of *The Return of the Living Dead* and *White Zombie*. They don't move too quickly, as did Danny Boyle's zombies in *28 Days Later*. They don't play video games like Ed did in Edgar Wright's *Shaun of the Dead*. They can't be domesticated as the eponymous hero was in Andrew Currie's *Fido*.

Even George Romero's zombies have, in recent times, been a bit out of sync with our expectations of what zombies are capable of thinking about or knowing. In his 2005 *Land of the Dead* the zombies, led by a zombie named "Big Daddy," after ensuring that the humans are no longer a threat to them, cease to be aggressive. Instead they seem focused on carving out an existence for themselves that to some extent approximates their prior existence. They're no longer operating on the same base level as the zombies of Romero's earlier movies. These zombies appear to understand something akin to détente. This is in stark contrast to the grunting, slobbering, staggering, lumbering zombies who will eat your brains and flesh at any cost that we've all come to know and love. *The Walking Dead* walker is just that zombie.

If I Know Now What I Knew Then

The next step in getting clear on what zombies know is to get a little clearer on knowledge itself. Philosophers working on questions pertaining to knowledge—known as "epistemologists"—make a distinction between different kinds of knowledge. For our purposes, the most interesting varieties of knowledge are: propositional knowledge—knowing that something is the case (sometimes this is called "knowledge that"), and practical knowledge—knowing how to do something (sometimes this is called "knowledge how").

Police officer Shane Walsh purports to have propositional knowledge about whether or not fellow police officer and good friend Rick Grimes died in the hospital (recall that he led Lori Grimes to believe that he did, prior to Rick's connecting back up with them). Dale Horvath has practical knowledge of how to repair a radiator using only duct tape. In assessing zombie intelligence we'll be interested in both types of knowledge. To keep it simple, we'll treat them as being the same thing, as arguably practical knowledge is just a specific form of propositional knowledge—knowing HOW to fix a radiator with duct tape, for example, is simply a matter of knowing THAT first, you do A, followed by B, and so forth.

Epistemologists do not agree much on what knowledge is. They do agree that in order to have propositional knowledge (and by extension practical knowledge) you must believe something and that thing must be true. For Rick to know that Merle Dixon is a threat to the rest of the group (and to T-Dog, in particular) Rick must both believe that it is the case and it must be true that Merle is, in fact, a threat to the rest of the group. This, however, is not enough for knowledge. In other words, true belief is necessary for knowledge, but not sufficient for knowledge. Something must be added to true belief to get knowledge.

To see why, consider what Rick knew prior to connecting up with the rest of the group. Upon leaving the hospital he wondered whether his wife and son survived the zombie attack. Suppose, quite plausibly, that Rick had a strong feeling that they were alive (assume that he's just naturally optimistic, many people choose to think the best until they learn otherwise). Suppose further that this optimistic feeling at some point turned into an actual belief—he strongly believed that his wife and son were alive. Moreover, as we learn a bit later in the series, they were, in fact, still alive. Certainly we don't want to conclude that Rick knew they were alive (even though he satisfied both the truth and belief condition for knowledge). Rick's belief could just have easily turned out to be false. Often when people feel strongly about something it turns out to wrong.

There is no consensus whatsoever amongst epistemologists about what you need to add to true belief to get an instance of knowledge. Here we hit a real roadblock. Some maintain that we need good evidence for a belief. Others hold that we need a good reason for holding a belief. Others reject both of these approaches altogether choosing instead to focus on the reliability of the process that brought about the belief, or the reliability of the mechanism that produced the belief, or whether the person that holds the belief was virtuous in some way or other in attaining the belief.

The first set of approaches—the evidence/good reasons approaches—tend to be internalist in nature. In other words, they require the knower to be thinking about what they know in the right sort of way. The second set of approaches—the reliability/virtue approaches—tend to be externalist in nature. That is, they don't make any claim about what the knower must be thinking about in order to be a knower.

A problem that is often raised for internalist approaches is that unsophisticated thinkers, such as children, non-philosophers, the very elderly, or animals, are not thinking about the right kinds of things in order to be considered knowers. But it seems right to say that these people are do know things. This, of course, is going to apply to zombies, as well. Certainly, zombies aren't weighing evidence as they come to believe things. So if zombies have knowledge, an externalist account of knowledge must be correct.

Moreover, the very possibility of zombie knowledge actually strongly supports our cashing out knowledge on externalist grounds, even if no zombies really exist (shudder at the thought!). Here's why: if zombies are incapable of doing things such as having higher order thoughts (thinking about their thoughts) about the nature of the evidence for some proposition or the relationship between the evidence and someone's belief, then internalism fails to account for a possible kind of knowledge—zombie knowledge. The internalist account of knowledge would not be tough enough.

This helps us in our enquiry into zombie knowledge in two ways: 1. we do not need to concern ourselves with the details of what constitutes knowledge beyond saying it is appropriately acquired (reliably produced or some such) true belief and 2. we don't need to worry about what is going on in zombie's minds apart from saying that they have beliefs, which seems acceptable, on the same grounds that justify us when we attribute beliefs to certain animals.

The Zombie as Sergeant Schultz

What reason is there for thinking that zombies don't know anything (apart from their just seeming really stupid)? One bit of evidence for this position comes from an account given by Dr. Edwin Jenner in "TS-19." Dr. Jenner is a research scientist at the CDC. During a presentation of what happens to a human brain as it becomes infected and ultimately becomes a walker brain, Dr. Jenner states (of whatever it is that infects humans), "... It restarts the brain stem ... It gets them up and moving ... The human part doesn't come back." The body, says Dr. Jenner, is "just a shell driven by mindless instinct."

According to Dr. Jenner the cerebellum and the cerebrum do not function at all. Walkers have no mental activity beyond pure instinct (and possibly sensory functions such as vision). This account leaves no room for things such as beliefs. If zombies don't have beliefs, then they can't have knowledge. Instincts and capacities are not the same thing as knowledge.

The problem with this account as it stands is in direct contradiction to what we witness when we observe walker behavior. Sure, we see plenty of mindless instinctual behavior from *The Walking Dead* walkers, but, at times, we see much more. In fact, right at the very beginning of the first episode "Days Gone Bye" we see a little girl looking for and finding her stuffed rabbit. Rick walks up to her, calling "little girl." She slowly turns around revealing, of course, that she is a walker. This type of behavior goes well beyond what can be accounted for by instinct. Acting on a desire to find something, recognition, choosing to pick up that item, acting on that choice, turning around in the slow deliberate fashion employed by the little walker girl are all things that exceed "mindless instinct."

This point is also nicely made by another event in "Days Gone Bye." When Rick stays with Morgan Jones and his son, Duane, Morgan's wife, Jenny, now a walker, comes to the door of the house where they were staying, and more importantly, the house she was in when she died. Jenny actually tries to open the door—she turns the handle several times. It's clear from the context that this is not an unusual occurrence. Jenny is going well beyond pure instinct. She knows something like that she used to live in that house (or at least that she was there prior to her dying). She knows how to open a door. It may even be the case that she knows that she belongs (or belonged) there. Also in this episode it's revealed that walkers recognize certain loud noises, such as gunshots, as indicative of the presence of humans.

In "Guts" we get a number of other good examples of zombie knowledge. We see walkers using a tool (a rock) to break a shop window where living folks were hiding inside. We see that walkers know how to climb fences (and fairly quickly). Most importantly, walkers can distinguish other walkers from the living via smell. It seems clear that it is not mere instinct that allows the walkers to make this kind of distinction, as in certain instances (like when Rick and Glen have covered themselves in "eau de zombie" to fool the walkers) the walkers are staring in an evaluative way for an extended period of time before making a determination. Their behavior clearly indicates deliberation of some sort. Beyond mere instinct, there is a kind of processing going on in each of these cases.

The payoff of these considerations is that contrary to what Dr. Jenner claims about walkers being "driven by mindless instinct," walkers have quite a bit of both practical and propositional knowledge. How these things are to be reconciled is a matter for the writers of the show to sort out. It's not entirely bad if it turns out that the scientist is just wrong. Alternatively, it could be written into the show that there is more to a walker's mental life than what shows up on a neurological scan. However it works out, it's clear that walkers are not completely without knowledge.

What Zombies Don't Know Won't Hurt You

We've established that walkers know things. They know lots of things and lots of different types of things. There are, however, lots of things they don't know, as well. For example, at the end of "Days Gone Bye" Rick loses a stockpile of guns. He is forced to leave it outside the tank he is hiding in. Walkers are walking all around the bag of weapons. Clearly using guns would provide a great advantage to the walkers in their quests to kill humans and feed themselves, but they don't appear to know what the guns are for or how they are used.

This raises an interesting question: why are zombies able to know some things, such as how to open a door, but not others, such as how to operate a machine gun? One temptation is to draw a comparison between zombies and higher non-human animals. In other words, the temptation is to say that zombies "become" animals (in the metaphorical sense) upon becoming zombified. My dog, Ranger, for example, has learned how to open a door, but will never learn how to operate a machine gun. This temptation, however, should be resisted. Ranger has figured out how to open a door after several attempts over a long period of time. She lacks the cognitive ability to operate a machine gun, in part because she lacks the relevant concepts related to killing (though she would gladly kill the neighbor's annoying cat if given a chance).

Morgan's wife didn't figure out how to open a door after becoming a walker, she already knew it. It was a matter of recollection, just as it is for pretty much anyone. The little girl at the beginning of "Days Gone Bye" appears to recognize her stuffed animal. The walker in "Guts" that smashed in the window with a rock knew from experience that a rock would be an effective tool for that job.

So why doesn't the past experience of zombies tell them things such as how to operate a machine gun or how to drive a car or that by working together they can be more effective at capturing humans, or how to communicate (they may lack the motor skills to speak, but they certainly could communicate much better than they do), and so forth? We might expect that if recollection played a central role in what zombies know, then zombies would know much more than their behavior tends to indicate. Something in the process of turning humans into zombies severely limits the types of things they remember and hence the types of things they know. It can't just be a matter of familiarity as the example with the little girl walker and Morgan's wife would suggest, as experiences such as driving a car, trying to communicate, or shooting a gun are quite familiar to a great number of people.

It has to be cashed out in terms of complexity. Zombie knowledge, whether it be propositional or practical, derives from past experience and is limited by the complexity of the thing known or the type of task under consideration. The more complicated it is the less apt a zombie is to know it.

Answers

We now have everything needed to answer our three questions, and we've already given some answers:

1. **What evidence do we have for thinking that zombies are dumb?**

2. **Just how dumb are zombies?**

And

3. What, if anything, do zombies know?

Our evidence for thinking that zombies are dumb is that they are pretty freaking dumb. They grunt, they are slow to determine the simplest of things, their knowledge is limited to simple things they recall from their past, such as how to open doors, and recognizing where they used to live. The more complex something is, the less likely it is that a zombie will know it.

Just how dumb are they? This question is best answered by quoting one of my former professors when asked by a peer to assess my intelligence: "Oh, smarter than some, not as smart as others, I suppose."

4
Walking Contradictions

ROBERT A. DELFINO AND KYLE TAYLOR

For is not philosophy the study of death?
—SOCRATES

Tears flow from his eyes as he attempts to aim the sniper rifle on her face. He wants to pull the trigger, but it's hard to kill the woman you love—the wife who bore you a son. The fact that she's now a walker only makes it slightly easier.

Nagging questions remain. Is there a chance that she could be cured and become his wife again? Is she still the same person he married? Is she even a person at all—or, rather, a monster that he should destroy? These are the kinds of philosophical questions that must weigh on the mind of Morgan Jones.

If we put ourselves in Morgan's shoes, we realize that the question of whether walkers are persons is an important one, not only because it's an interesting metaphysical question, but also because it has ethical implications. The answer to this question will help determine if shooting your zombified wife is tantamount to murder or merely akin to shooting an animal.

After all, most people would agree that there's a moral difference between intentionally shooting a person and intentionally shooting a grizzly bear. Philosophers such as Peter Singer have challenged this moral intuition, arguing that such discrimination amounts to *speciesism* (similar to racism). However, the view that, morally speaking, persons should be treated differently than non-persons has been and still is the dominant position in western philosophy.

Throughout history, the most dominant view of what persons are is that they are intelligent, living beings. Included in this understanding of persons is the view that persons have the capacity to make free choices and thus they are morally responsible beings. "Individual substance of a rational nature" was the definition of person given by the ancient Roman philosopher Boethius.[1] And it has long been held that intelligence is rooted in our soul, the spiritual, non-material side of human beings.

"Man is said to be the image of God by reason of his intellectual nature," argues St. Thomas Aquinas, for it is through our mind, not our bodies, that we can most imitate God.[2] The philosopher Immanuel Kant, who believed in the immortality of the soul, argued that persons possess an intrinsic dignity that others should respect. Certainly, much of the dignity accorded persons in contemporary culture and law can be traced back to the view that humans are intelligent, spiritual beings.

But fear not, those of you who are skeptical of souls and all things spiritual. Even most materialists would agree that in order for something to be a person it must be alive and intelligent. We have yet to meet anyone who would consider a corpse or a non-living object such as a piece of metal to be a person. Similarly, everyone agrees that bacteria are living beings, but no one to our knowledge has ever argued that they are persons. (Considering the trillions of bacteria living in your body, we really hope they are not persons!)

What about walkers? Are they persons? Are they even alive? It's not so clear, as the ominous title of the series, *The Walking Dead*, suggests. But philosophy can help us here. First, we need to determine the relationship between some important metaphysical categories, such as "life" and "death." Second, we need to examine how walkers act in the TV series. For it is through studying the actions of a thing that you gain some insight into that thing's nature.

---

[1] Boethius, *Liber contra Eutychen et Nestorium*, p. 85.
[2] Thomas Aquinas, *Summa Theologiae*, I, q.93, a.4.

Matter of Life and Death

Can something be both alive and dead? Does that make any sense? Is it metaphysically possible? Let's begin with something easier. Consider American football. Can a team win and lose the same game? No. This is because winning and losing are mutually exclusive—that is, both cannot be true of the same team in the same game.

Now let's ask a metaphysical question. Can something with mutually exclusive properties exist? Consider a square-circle, which is a geometrical figure that is both a square and a circle at the same time. Is it possible to draw a square-circle on a flat piece of paper? No.

Metaphysicians call things such as square-circles "impossible beings." Something is an impossible being if its very nature contains a contradiction. And it's the contradictory nature of a square-circle that prevents its existence in the real world—the world outside of our mind. It is possible to draw a circle on a piece of paper, and it is possible to draw a square on the same piece of paper. However, it's impossible to draw on a flat piece of paper one figure that is both a square and a circle. It's only in the mind that a person can "think" (loosely speaking) about a square-circle.

Because life and death are mutually exclusive it makes no sense to claim that a walker is both alive and dead. That would be like claiming that the same geometrical figure is both a square and a circle, which is impossible. But there is another possibility. In football a team cannot win and lose the same football game precisely because winning and losing are mutually exclusive. However, a tie is possible in a regular-season football game if neither team scores in overtime. So while winning and losing are mutually exclusive, winning and losing are not *jointly exhaustive* in football. That is, there is another possibility not covered by winning and losing, namely, a tie.

But what about life and death—are they jointly exhaustive? Or is being a walker an alternative to being alive or dead? Robots, after all, can walk and one could plausibly argue that they are neither alive nor dead. Indeed, we generally don't call things that were never alive, such as a piece of metal, "dead." However, robots were never alive either—they are artifacts created by human beings. In contrast, every walker started off as a living human being before it became infected. Is it possible that the zombie infection transforms a human being into something that can move but something to which the categories "life" and "death" no longer apply—namely, the "quasi-living"? Perhaps ...

But for now we can conclude that there are only two options concerning zombies. On the one hand, zombies might be impossible beings because their nature is contradictory. Stories about zombies are the fruit of human imagination and authors of fiction are free to discuss fantastical beings—even beings that have contradictory natures. On the other hand, it might be the case that zombies are *possible beings*. The nature of a possible being does not contain a contradiction, and thus, in principle, they can exist in the real world, not merely in our minds.

Let's just look at walker behavior in *The Walking Dead* TV series, not in the comic book series or in other zombie films. Examining this behavior will help us determine whether zombies are possible or impossible beings because it's through studying the actions of a thing that you gain some insight into that thing's nature. Examining walker behavior will also help us determine if walkers are persons, an important question that we will consider next.

Braaaiiinnnsss . . .

Walkers don't talk. They moan or growl, but they never engage in a conversation. If they did engage in conversation, we could argue that they're intelligent. While their inability to speak can be explained by a lack of intelligence, alternative explanations are possible. For example, perhaps walkers cannot speak because of damaged vocal chords or some similar physical defect. What we must do, then, is consider the other actions walkers perform and ask the following question. Do any of these actions imply intelligence?

Consider the scene where Morgan's zombified wife Jenny turns the door knob of Fred and Cindy Drake's house. Turning a door knob by itself is not a sign of intelligence. But Morgan tells us that she died in that house, accompanied by her husband and son. So perhaps Jenny is trying to open the door to find them. If Jenny is able to form abstract concepts wherein she recognizes that opening the door is a means to an end (finding her son) then we could argue that she's intelligent. But perhaps Jenny's merely hungry and looking for food. Animal Instinct is enough, in such a case, to explain her activity. After all, Jenny appears to give up fairly easily, which would be uncharacteristic of a mother searching for her son.

Unfortunately, it's hard to know what Jenny's thinking, if anything, in this situation. But what's clear is that in order for Jenny to have the goal of finding her son she must have retained some memories of her family despite becoming a walker. Other scenes, however, cast serious doubt on the view that walkers retain memories of their previous lives. For example, consider the episode "Wildfire" when Amy is turned into a walker, perhaps the most disturbing scene of Season One. As a sorrowful Andrea holds her sister, apologizing for the times she was not there for her, we desperately look for any sign that Amy remembers her sister. We hope that Amy, in raising her hand to Andrea's head, recognizes Andrea and seeks to caress her. But we recoil in horror when we realize that Amy merely sees her sister as food.

The only other activity that walkers perform that seems to imply intelligence is the use of rocks to crack the glass doors of the department store in "Guts." The use of tools has often been seen as a sign of intelligence. But what counts as a tool? Certainly, some tools, for example a chainsaw, are based on abstract thought and principles and therefore imply intelligence. However, in this case we simply have a rock, which is a naturally occurring object, being used to break glass. It's not so clear that this is a sign of intelligence. Instead, it's possible that this kind of activity can be explained solely by sensation, memory, and trial and error.[3]

So far, no walker behavior definitively points to intelligence. But there is evidence that walkers are not, or at least should not be, intelligent. Working for the CDC, Dr. Jenner has studied and recorded the process of zombie infection. While showing a video of his wife reanimating from the dead, he comments on the brain's electrical activity, seemingly taking a materialist view of persons:

---

[3] On the role of trial and error in chimpanzees' use of tools, see Daniel J. Povinelli, *Folk Physics for Apes: The Chimpanzee's Theory of How the World Works* (2003).

> It's a person life—experiences, memories. It's everything. Somewhere in all that organic wiring, all those ripples of light, is you—the thing that makes you unique and human. . . . Those are synapses, electric impulses in the brain that carry all the messages. They determine everything a person says, does, or thinks from the moment of birth to the moment of death. ("TS-19")

A little later he describes how zombie infection occurs:

> It invades the brain like meningitis. The adrenal glands hemorrhage, the brain goes into shutdown, then the major organs... then death. Everything you ever were or ever will be . . . gone. . . . The resurrection times vary wildly. We had reports of it happening in as little as three minutes. The longest we heard of was eight hours. In the case of this patient, it was two hours, one minute. . . . seven seconds. [Lori Grimes: It restarts the brain?] No, just the brain stem. Basically, it gets them up and moving. [Rick Grimes: But they're not alive?] You tell me. [Rick: It's nothing like before. Most of that brain is dark.] Dark, lifeless, dead. The frontal lobe, the neocortex, the human part—that doesn't come back. The "you" part. Just a shell driven by mindless instinct.

If only the brain stem restarts, as Dr. Jenner says, then walkers are not intelligent. The brain stem only controls lower functions such as breathing, heartbeat, blood pressure, and swallowing.[4] Dr. Jenner is quite clear that the other parts of the brain, especially the neocortex remain dead.

She's Not Your Wife Anymore . . .

Given how much of the brain remains dead, it's clear that walkers are not intelligent and therefore they are not persons. This conclusion follows whether we take a spiritual or materialist view of human beings. Since Stage One of the disease completely kills the body we can be assured that the soul of our loved one has gone, hopefully, to a better place. This is because the soul, in both traditional philosophy and theology, is understood as the *cause* of life. As such, the soul cannot be present in a human being that has died.

---

[4] Rita Carter, Susan Aldridge, Martyn Page, and Steve Parker, *The Human Brain Book*, 2009, p. 63.

On a materialist view of persons, what remains after zombification is not enough to be a person either. All that remains is a body that is partially reanimated by the walker infection itself. But as Dr. Jenner laments, "the frontal lobe, the neocortex, the human part—that doesn't come back." Thus we are left with "just a shell driven by mindless instinct." And he seems to have no doubts about this, as he shot what was his wife in the head.

The moral implication is clear. Morgan Jones should shoot that walker. She's not his wife anymore. In fact, she's not even a person—she's a walker and a danger to every human being left on our planet. Incidentally, it would be a mistake to conclude that our view about killing zombies during a zombie apocalypse implies anything about aborting human fetuses or killing comatose human beings in present times. Unlike the aforementioned, zombies are violent and capable of exterminating the entire human population.

Believe it or not, mathematicians have calculated that "a zombie outbreak is likely to lead to the collapse of civilization, unless it is dealt with quickly. . . . the most effective way to contain the rise of the undead is to hit hard and hit often" using "extremely aggressive tactics."[5] No zombie should be spared.

Even so, we understand why Morgan hesitates to shoot. It's difficult to kill something that still looks like the wife you love. Indeed, it's a crazy situation—a situation that no one would want to face. And it's natural to wonder if such circumstances are truly possible or merely the stuff of nightmares. This leads us back to our earlier question: Are zombies possible or impossible beings?

Impossible Beings?

Earlier, we mentioned that it's through studying the actions of a thing that you gain some insight into that thing's nature. This is because, metaphysically speaking, actions are rooted in

---

[5] Philip Munz, Ioan Hudea, Joe Imad, and Robert J. Smith?, "When Zombies Attack!: Mathematical Modelling of an Outbreak of Zombie Infection," in *Infectious Disease Modelling Research Progress*, edited by J.M. Tchuenche and C. Chiyaka, 2010, p. 146. Yes, the question mark is officially part of Robert's name.

nature. Put another way, *nature* has priority over *action* because it's the nature of a thing that determines the kinds of actions it can perform.

One implication of this is that a being cannot do things that are incompatible with its nature. For example, unlike birds, Humans cannot fly using their bodies because wings and the ability to fly are not contained in human nature. Therefore, if we can find zombies performing actions that contradict their nature, we will be able to argue that zombies are impossible beings. So, let's review the kinds of actions that zombies routinely perform.

In addition to walking—it is called *The Walking Dead* after all—walkers are able to hunt and eat by making use of at least three of the five senses (hearing, sight, and smell). For example, in "Days Gone Bye" Morgan shoots a walker right in the head just before he meets Rick for the first time. Later while they are barricaded in Fred and Cindy's house, Morgan regrets firing the gun because he knows the sound of the bullet will attract more walkers. "Sound draws them" he laments and "now they're all over the street."

When Rick is about to pull away the curtains, Morgan warns him "Don't do that. They'll see the light." And indeed, walkers must be able to see in order to explain the behavior of the walker formerly Morgan's wife, Jenny. Attempting to look through the door's peephole, and turning the door knob, requires sight. In addition to sight, we know walkers can smell because of "Guts." Remember the scene when Rick and Glenn cover themselves in dead body parts so they can walk past the walkers? This apparently worked because their human scent was masked by the odor of the dead body parts ... that is, until it started raining. If you look very closely exactly thirty minutes into "Guts," one of the walkers uses his nose to sniff Rick.

However, in order for walkers to hear, see, smell, move, and eat it seems that the major organs and systems of the body—including important parts of the brain—must be alive and functioning. Dead eyes do not see and to move one's arms or legs requires functioning muscles and nerves, which cannot function for long without a steady supply of energy delivered to them through the bloodstream. This requires the ability to obtain energy from breathing and eating, which implies functioning respiratory and digestive systems.

Could it be that the major organs of walkers are alive and only the exterior parts of the body are dead? That might solve the whole problem of walkers appearing to be both alive and dead. It is not contradictory for part of an entity to be alive and part to be dead. However, this is not a plausible position for at least three reasons. First, consider the serious wounds and decay of the outer body displayed by many of the walkers in this TV series. Based on what we know from biology and medicine, it does not seem possible that the major organs and systems of the body could live for long with such wounds and covered in such filth and decay. Gangrene would arise and eventually destroy whatever living organs remained. Shane makes this point explicitly in Season Two's "Pretty Much Dead Already."

Second, while some walkers might not look that decayed, some are in an absolutely wretched state. For example, in "Days Gone Bye," Rick comes upon the walker known as bicycle girl, or Hannah. This walker has been cut in half, with the lower part of her body missing. In addition, her ribs are showing and her face is in an advanced state of decay. How this walker could move at all, considering it is missing the organs it needs for nutrition and energy production, defies human biology.

Recall that this particular walker does not have a functioning stomach and intestines and so she could not process food even if she ate it. And consider the medical fact that "without oxygen or glucose [sugar], the brain can last for only about ten minutes before irreparable damage occurs."[6] Yet, despite all of the above, this walker moves herself along the ground and recognizes Rick as a source of food. In addition, she's still moving a day later when Rick shoots her out of pity, saying "I'm sorry this happened to you."

Third, as we have seen, Dr. Jenner is clear that only the brain stem is restarted in walkers. But this is problematic because if only the brain stem reanimates then there is no way that walkers could walk and sense. Again, dead eyes do not see and dead muscles do not move.

But even if eyes, muscles, nerves, and lungs were to reanimate there are still problems. The kinds of movements that

---

[6] *The Human Brain Book*, p. 45.

walkers engage in when they chase down prey, attack, and eat are not possible without the motor cortex and the parietal lobe, which are part of the neocortex. In addition, without the temporal and occipital lobes, which are also part of the neocortex, walkers will not be able to see or hear. However, Dr. Jenner is quite clear that the neocortex does not reanimate, only the brain stem does. Finally, without the limbic system, which is also not part of the brain stem, walkers should not be able to smell as they do in "Guts." Given all of these brain problems, walkers should not be able to walk in any significant way. And because they should not be able to see, smell, or hear either, walkers should not pose much of a threat at all.

Quasi-living Beings?

The evidence that zombies are contradictory and therefore impossible beings, like square-circles, is strong. The only way we can try to avoid this conclusion is to return to an earlier question. Is it possible that the zombie infection transforms a human being into something that can move but something to which the categories "life" and "death" no longer apply? In other words, could zombies represent a new category of beings, the "quasi-living"? You might be surprised to learn that the "quasi-living" is not a new category after all. For example, many scientists and philosophers consider viruses to exist on the borderline of the living and the non-living. As the philosopher Manuel Vargas notes:

> Consider that there are a range of mysterious, "quasi-living" entities that we do not yet understand well. These include viruses and the even less well known viroids. It's unclear whether these entities count as living. At least for some of them, it is possible to introduce conditions that stop all quasi-living functioning but then to change those conditions so that their functioning is restored. If we come to count viruses and viroids as living, then those capable of ceasing and recovering their quasi-living functioning might be candidates for the Undead.[7]

---

[7] Manuel Vargas, "Dead Serious: Evil and the Ontology of the Undead" in *Zombies, Vampires, and Philosophy: New Life for the Undead*, 2010, edited by Richard Greene and K. Silem Mohammad, p. 44.

In fact, you might be surprised to learn that there are fungi that can take over and control the bodies and brains of carpenter ants, turning them into zombie-like beings.[8] And there is evidence that the zombie infection in *The Walking Dead* is caused by a virus—despite the fact that in "TS-19" Dr. Jenner says he does not know whether the infection is "microbial, viral, parasitic, or fungal."

This evidence can be found in "Wildfire." There, while looking through Dr. Jenner's microscope, we saw an infectious agent with no nucleus that was able to inject genetic material into another cell. These are indications it is a virus. If viruses are quasi-living and they are responsible for turning humans into zombies why not regard zombies as quasi-living? We can think of several reasons.

First, while viruses themselves might be quasi-living they can only infect actually living cells. Viruses cannot use dead cells as hosts. Yet it is only some time after death that the virus reanimates the body. Look carefully at Dr. Jenner's video. Seconds after the brain stem has been reanimated by the infection, TS-19's mouth, neck, and shoulders begin to move. But how could dead human tissue move? It can't. Were TS-19's muscles, nerves, and other organs converted into some "quasi-living" substance within the two short hours since her death? This would have to be carried out by an infectious agent that does not need a functioning circulatory system to travel and is able to convert dead cells into quasi-living cells, which seems unlikely. And what about Shane's death in "Beside the Dying Fire"? He was not bitten or scratched by a walker, and yet he transformed into a walker only a few minutes after being stabbed to death by Rick. Part of the explanation comes from Rick, who tells the group, "We're all infected." This is the message Jenner whispered into his ear in "TS-19." But there's still a problem. Presumably, Shane's body was ordinary living tissue—not quasi-living tissue—right before Rick killed him. As such, it would have had to be converted into quasi-living tissue within a few minutes. This does not seem like enough time for such a radical transformation.

---

[8] Brian Switek, "The Scariest Zombies in Nature," October 18th, 2010, <http://www.smithsonianmag.com/science-nature/The-Scariest-Zombies-in-Nature.html>.

Second, even if converting dead cells into quasi-living substance were possible, it seems unlikely that these organs and tissues could function so similarly to when they were alive. For example, the senses (hearing, sight, and smell) function much the same, and the arms and legs move much the same. But human organs have evolved over millions of years to function in a certain way under certain conditions and it seems implausible that their entire way of functioning can be re-written from the cellular level up by an infection.

Third, even quasi-living organs would require a steady supply of energy to keep moving and functioning throughout a walker's existence. We know from the laws of physics that perpetual motion machines can't exist. And yet there are several cases where walkers seem to defy the laws of physics when it comes to energy. Consider the walkers that are locked in the hospital cafeteria in "Days Gone Bye." Remember the spray-painted warning "DON'T OPEN DEAD INSIDE"? Well, those walkers have been locked in there for about two weeks, and yet they are still moving and functioning. (When Shane tries to rescue Rick in the hospital from the zombies, a flashback scene in "TS-19," the flowers in Rick's room look new and Rick's beard is much less grown-in than when he wakes up in "Days Gone Bye." Given this, we can estimate that about two weeks have passed.)

How can this be? To the extent that everything needs energy to continue functioning, walkers that do not get energy for a long time should become dormant like viruses. And recall the walker we mentioned earlier that was cut in half. How is she getting energy to move? Without a functioning stomach and intestines she could not get energy even if she ate. Unless she is photosynthesizing, which is highly unlikely, we see no way to explain the fact that she continues to move and sense. Given all the above problems, it seems that zombies are impossible beings after all.

The Metaphysics of Fear

Although we have argued that walkers in *The Walking Dead* are impossible beings, we realize that our present knowledge of living and quasi-living beings is imperfect and subject to future revision. Additionally, we recognize that some versions of zombies might turn out to be possible beings. For example, when humans are turned into zombies in the movie *28 Days Later* they don't die first and then later emerge as the undead. Instead, they remain living but become insanely violent due to the rage virus. Still, many other movies are similar to *The Walking Dead* in their portrayal of zombies. And have you noticed that in the last decade "zombie media" has exploded in popularity? What could explain this obsession with undead, and most likely, impossible beings?

The answer lies in fear. Zombies, are a projection of some of our worst fears. They represent everything we do not want to be. We're living, they're dead. We're intelligent, they're not. We're civilized, they're cannibalistic beasts. We hope for an afterlife of happiness, they represent an afterlife of horror. If humans are in the image of God, zombies are the reverse image of us—deformed, hideous, and bestial. Zombies force us to contemplate human nature itself and our worst fears about it. That is why zombies fascinate and terrify us. And the idea of a "zombie apocalypse" evokes our fears about the end of the world. It calls to mind a kind of judgment day—"the wrath of God" as Jacqui says.

The contradictory nature of zombies can also be explained by their origin in our fears. Fear and irrationality often go hand in hand. Zombies are dead ... and yet they are alive. This makes little sense until you realize that zombies are a metaphysical projection of our fears. They are the kinds of beings that can only exist in our minds (and on the screen through special effects). Zombies speak to our deepest fears and questions about life and death. Hamlet in Shakespeare's play had it right when he asked the question "To be or not to be?" No one wants to be caught in between the world of being and non-being—the world of *The Walking Dead*.[9]

---

[9] We would like to thank the following people for their suggestions on an earlier draft of this chapter: Wayne Yuen, Rachel Hollander, Roberta Hayes, Tony Spanakos, David Shear, Phil and Stephen Greeley, Joe Jordan, Andrew D'Auria, Jerome Hillock, Thomas Riley, Bill Baker, and Dima Shnaydman of the band *Dead Men Dreaming*. This chapter is dedicated with love to Bruce Campbell, because if anyone can drive back the zombie hordes with a twelve-gauge double-barreled Remington, it's him. Hail to the king, baby.

5
I'm Gonna Tell Them about Wayne

MARTY MCKENDRY AND MICHAEL DA SILVA

Wayne Dunlap. Georgia license. Born in 1979. He had $28 in his pocket when he died. And a picture of a pretty girl. 'With love from Rachel.' He used to be like us. Worrying about bills or the rent or the Super Bowl. If I ever find my family, I'm gonna tell them about Wayne. One more thing . . . He was an organ donor.

—Rick Grimes, *The Walking Dead* "Guts"

Before Wayne was a walker, Wayne was a man. Rick dwells on this point before putting an axe hilt-deep into his decomposing corpse. Rick and Glenn then pilfer rotten sludge from the body to mask their scent from the remaining horde of undead cannibals. Alas, such are the hardships of the post-apocalyptic lifestyle. However Rick's message to his fellow survivors is clear: walkers used to be human and this fact has moral significance. Consider the following argument:

1. **All humans deserve moral respect.**
2. **All zombies are residual humans.**
3. **All residual humans deserve moral respect.**
4. **Therefore all zombies deserve moral respect.**

If this argument is sound—and we will argue that it is—then the survivors must respect Wayne. Indeed, the survivors must respect every walker.

You may be suspicious of our claim that "All residual humans deserve moral respect." Perhaps being a residual human isn't as morally valuable as being a living human. However, we do feel it is right to respect the past wishes of people now dead and we do feel it is right to respect the bodies of the dead. We respect legal wills, graves, and cadavers in part because the deceased person carries on through them. For the same reason, we should respect walkers. Re-animate zombies resemble living humans to a much greater degree than do mere de-animate corpses. If corpses deserve respect, walkers deserve more respect. We will argue that the universal duty to respect zombies translates into a universally-held survivor duty to execute walkers respectfully.

Moral Dignity

In some ways walkers remain human. If you prick them, do they not bleed? If you sever their limbs with chain saws, do they not stumble? There is a glimmer of residual humanity in their wild, innocent eyes. There may even be inherent moral dignity. Indeed, one explanation for why we might accord walkers moral standing is that zombies have dignity.

So, what is dignity? Immanuel Kant defines dignity as the inherent worth or moral value that people possess as rational beings who exercise free will. Free will is the ability that people have to make choices, and free will translates into dignity because beings that can make choices deserve respect. A simple way to think about this concept is to consider the example of ordering off a menu (and let's assume for now that it is one without brains as an option). Everyone who can consider and select from multiple dishes deserves to have their selection respected. If you want the fries, and you have considered the salad, you should be free from the coercion of others to enjoy the fries. Your dignity as a free being should be respected.

This concept of dignity by choice runs through *The Walking Dead*. For example, Rick and Shane respect Jim's choice to stay behind and die because his choice to do so is freely made as a self-aware and infected, yet informed, person.

Another way to explain this idea of dignity is to say that having dignity means you have the right not to be used by other people. The basic idea is that people's universal ability to choose makes them all equals. Since we are rational beings, we cannot treat equals as non-equals. It follows that we must treat equals as equals. In other words, choice gives every person dignity, and we must therefore respect every person. Also, every dignified person must not allow themselves to be used, since you are a dignified person, and we need to treat every person respectfully, including ourselves. Everyone must assert their equality by practicing self-respect. Kant summarizes the idea of dignity:

> Humanity itself is a dignity; for a human being cannot be used merely as a means by any human being . . . but must always be used at the same time as an end. It is just in this that his dignity consists, by which he raises himself above all other beings in the world that are not human beings and yet can be used and so over all things. (*The Metaphysics of Morals*)

Crucially, creatures that cannot exercise choice do not have dignity. This is why, for Kant, people have dignity and animals don't. Accordingly, people may not use other people, but people may freely use and exploit animals. This is because animals act by instinct, not choice. Many thinkers dispute whether this distinction is so clear cut. Indeed, walkers represent a philosophically problematic mix of human and non-human features.

As former humans, walkers remain like people in two respects. First, walkers are human corpses. Corpses are morally governed by the wishes of the deceased persons. This consideration means that survivors must speculate about how deceased persons would reasonably have wanted their zombie selves treated if they had known they could become walkers. It doesn't matter if the deceased person ever actually considered the possibility of becoming a walker. It's enough that the person would have chosen to have their body treated in a certain way had they known their fate. Indeed, issues like this arise all the time when thinking about inheritance and memorial services.

The second way that walkers are like humans—and therefore dignified—is more complicated. Zombies are residual humans. That is, zombies are minimally-sentient human subjects who still act out the personal choices of their former, fully human selves. Hence, walker action is sometimes an exercise of freedom even though walkers are no longer free. Walkers are not conscious, but walkers have been shaped by consciousness. That is, walkers continue to do some basic things that the deceased persons actually chose to do during their lives, like eating.

Kant's rules seem too strict for post-apocalyptic Atlanta. Because people must treat themselves with equal respect, Kant largely forbids selfless sacrifice. Unfortunately, the post-apocalyptic hellscape sometimes demands selfless sacrifice to create the possibility of group survival. If Kant were to come back from the dead, he would disagree with some of the ways we use his concept of dignity. But if Kant were to come back from the dead, we would be forced to give him both barrels. Let's call it a wash.

In short, if zombies have dignity—as we claim—then every survivor in *The Walking Dead* must respect every walker. Moreover, a survivor commits a moral wrong by violating zombie dignity even to save his or her self. Wrongs may be excused, but they are still wrongs. We can imagine Merle dismissing the concept of inviolable zombie dignity with a solemn hork of disapproval. Yet Merle is no philosopher, and a hork is no argument.

Dignifying the Dead?

In *The Walking Dead*, we know that people actually die prior to reanimation as walkers. This point is clear from Dr. Jenner's research in "TS-19." Since walkers are human corpses, if there is a moral duty to respect human corpses, then there is a moral duty to respect walkers. So, we need to know if there is a moral duty to respect human corpses.

We owe rational beings a duty not to use them. That is, rational beings have dignity. But corpses are no longer rational beings. Corpses are the physical remnants of formerly rational beings, so how can they have dignity? When people are alive, they can freely make choices about how they would like their corpses to be treated after death. The moral obligation to respect a person's decision about their corpse binds the actions of rational beings after the person has died. This is the idea behind organ donation. Wayne's choice to be an organ donor means that Wayne determined the purpose for his own corpse which now could reasonably include Rick and Glenn using some of his abdominal sludge. Hence, Rick and Glenn can use Wayne's body as a means because Wayne chose as his end to be used as a means. In this way, they do not treat him as a *mere* means, but respect his chosen end. A Kantian might object that a person cannot morally choose to be used for the benefit of others, but this is where we part ways with Kant in the post-apocalyptic context. We don't think Wayne is a pawn. We think Wayne is hero.

The moral duty that governs people's treatment of human corpses is shaped by the previous choice of the deceased person regarding the fate of their particular corpse. In other words, respecting the dignity of living rational beings entails respecting their wishes regarding their corpses. Generally speaking, people wish that their corpse will be treated as though it retains some of the dignity of the living person. In effect, then, corpses have dignity. This conclusion explains the funeral rites practiced across cultural boundaries and agrees with our moral intuition that it is wrong to disturb a grave or treat a corpse with disrespect.

This conclusion also suggests that the dead should hold *legal* rights. Indeed, Kant recognizes both a legal and a moral duty to respect the rights of the dead to determine inheritance and the fate of other goods they enjoyed in life. Similarly, the German constitutional court has explicitly found that deceased persons continue to hold a right to dignity. This agreement of the Kantian framework with contemporary legal systems further suggests the plausibility of the dead possessing moral dignity.

In *The Walking Dead*, the problem of respecting the dignity of the dead is that the survivors generally do not know what the zombified persons would have wanted done with their corpses. This problem is further complicated by the fact that most persons would not have contemplated the reanimation of their corpses. However, respect extends to hypothetical choices because choices are often implicit and inferred. You can wrong me by not buying enough beer for both of us if you knew I would've wanted beer too. Corpses represent dignified people who existed in the past and would've made choices about their future, so we respect their implicit choices.

In this situation, the survivors must therefore ask, "What would reasonable persons want done with their corpses if they knew the corpses would become walkers?" We hazard that the reasonable person would not want to exist perpetually as an undead cannibal because of the threat that such entities pose to the living, not to mention the aesthetic issues. Recall the pitiful state of Hannah the bicycle girl, the half-zombie that Rick encounters in "Days Gone Bye," and Rick's subsequent respectful execution of the creature. No one would want to live like that creature.

With respect to human corpses, we therefore conclude that the survivors owe the deceased two moral duties. First, the survivors must act on the presumption that deceased persons wanted their corpses treated with dignity and not as mere objects. Second, the survivors must act on the presumption that the deceased persons would not have wanted their corpses to become zombies. This conclusion entails that the corpses be de-animated in a respectful way. The half-zombie Hannah appears to suffer. Ending that suffering in the quickest, least-degrading way possible is morally essential.

Zombie Residue

Zombies also have dignity by virtue of their residual subjectivity, the limited mental functions and personality traits that zombies possess upon reanimation. We know from Dr. Jenner's research on TS-19 that a walker is a deceased human with a reactivated brain stem. We also know that death and reanimation are both caused by an unknown pathogen, and higher brain functions relating to personality and memory do not resume.

Numerous incidents in *The Walking Dead* prove that the reactivation of a walker's brain stems enables functions like walking, growling, and feasting. Of course, the absence of Dr. Jenner's wife's consent (or a reasonable expectation thereof) may suggest we only know these facts about walker brains as a result of Dr. Jenner disrespectful treatment of his wife. It's not surprising that a guy who would treat Rick and co. in such a creepy manner would be the type of guy to treat even his wife with indignity. Perhaps, though, Dr. Jenner's wife would have wanted to make a contribution to science. This is a question of fact that we will not speculate upon. We will give Dr. Jenner the benefit of the doubt.

We know from the example of Morgan's zombified wife, Jenny, that some basic memories and relatively complex functions also resume upon reanimation. Consider that Jenny repeatedly returns to the house where her husband and son are taking refuge. Her repeated return to a spot of personal significance invites the inference that she has some basic memory function. Further, Jenny finds the front door and attempts to gain entry by turning the door handle, a cognitively complex action. Surely these behaviors are the result of intuitive impulses rather than deliberative choice. However, it can't be denied that a remnant of Morgan's wife's mind exists in her zombified form. This remnant of her particular and formerly conscious mind is her residual mind. The residual subjectivity of each walker will be different if we assume that every walker's brain function is physiologically consistent with Morgan's wife's brain function.

Though Kant likely would not agree with us, we think that this residual subjectivity translates into zombie dignity because the ends or goals that human beings once freely determined may still be accomplished, and these ends require respect. Choices freely made by the living may continue to determine zombie ends. In this sense, zombies are purposive beings in that they may fulfill some rudimentary purposes of their deceased physiological precursors. Zombies cannot choose, but they are in part, at a basic level, creatures of choice. And choice demands respect.

If the mind of a person continues to manifest its will, then in some ways that person still exists. Perhaps this is why Morgan found it so difficult to kill his wife—to destroy her brain with his high-powered deer rifle would destroy the little piece of his wife that has carried on. And while walkers are not rational beings, they carry forth the wills of rational beings. Thus, a walker is not a mere object, but is instead a residual subject. It follows that human beings owe zombies a moral duty not to treat them as mere objects, but to consider how the purposive actions of zombies relate to the wills of the deceased persons and act respectfully.

The Implications of Zombie Dignity

So zombies have dignity because they are corpses of rational beings and because they are residual subjects. Our respect for zombies flows from our respect for the choices of their dead precursors. This consideration raises the question of how to deal with zombie-versions of people who formerly expressed a desire to eat people or to return as a zombie after death. Any ethical system that allows for the semi-autonomous dead to eat the conscious living seems perverse.

Luckily, Kant provides us with an easy solution to this problem. Imagine someone chose to become a walker because walkers look "bad ass" and it would be cool, in a sense, to eat other people later on (one's annoying co-worker, say). We would not respect the choice to embrace a walker identity since our right to exercise our autonomy is constrained to the extent that it affects others' ability to exercise their autonomy. Since Dale cannot remain dignified while being eaten alive, Chris cannot choose to become a walker for the sole purpose of eating others.

Fans of *The Walking Dead* aside, most people would not want to be zombies. Hence, there could be a duty to kill zombies in order to fulfill the wishes of their previously living selves. If so, the killing would have to respect the likely wishes of the deceased person. This conclusion creates a problem because, in a Kantian framework, one cannot will one's own death. We would have a moral obligation not to will ourselves to be zombies, since they don't will in a meaningful sense, even if we entertain residual subjectivity. However, we could not will ourselves to cease existing as residual subjects either. Kant would view it as a contradiction. Kant explicitly opposes suicide (contra Dr. Jenner) and likely would not approve of mercy killing. On the other hand, the zombie is already dead, so perhaps you do not truly kill a zombie. Kant may say "Do not kill" and "You cannot will your own death," but he does not say "Do not return the undead to the dead."

Nevertheless destroying or removing a zombie's head destroys its residual subjectivity and thereby hinders that dignified being's semi-autonomous action. So a claim that there is a duty to kill zombies relies on the proposition that the free choices of the living beings about being zombies override the free choices of those same beings that continue to drive zombie action. For example, Jenny's presumptive choice not to remain a walker must override Jenny's previous choice to dutifully return to her family. The essential problem is that zombies are quasi-rational beings that cannot be reasoned with. So in respecting zombie dignity, we must attempt to respectfully resolve the contradictory choices of the former living being. A duty to kill is grounded in the notion that the choices of the living about not being zombies trump the choices they made that continue to manifest through zombie behavior.

So how would Kant treat a cognitively incapable human being who would rather have died than exist as a cognitively incapable human? While Kant would likely not endorse a duty to kill such a person, we wonder if he would be willing to extend "You cannot will your death" into "You must exist forever in a state of undeath." Kant might very well allow that the undead are different than the cognitively impaired. Further, granting individuals the choice to cease being undead does not seem antithetical to future choice in the way that suicide might, since the choices of the undead are so limited. Dignity for a zombie may be different than the dignity of a human being and may thereby lead to different ethical imperatives. Respect for the zombie may entail returning it to its natural state of being: death.

If a human being kills a zombie, however, that person should make every effort to employ a respectful method. Merle's capricious killing of walkers in "Guts" is not only problematic because it endangers his fellow human beings and wastes bullets the survivors "ain't even got," but because it does so both unnecessarily (the walkers he kills pose no real threat when he is killing them) and with a patent display of disrespect for the dignity of the zombies. Merle hunts walkers for sport. He derives amusement from them as objects. It's no surprise that we soon find that Merle shows no respect for the dignity of his fellow man either. His racist language and acts of violence demonstrate a willingness to treat other people as less than human, so it's no surprise that he views walkers as mere objects, whose deaths he can cause for his own pleasure.

Rick, by contrast, demonstrates empathy for the undead and a means of killing them respectfully. He quickly kills both the aforementioned half-zombie and Leon, the zombified deputy at the Sherriff's Department armory, with gunshots to the head. In the latter case, Rick even knowingly takes on the risk of other walkers hearing the shot. Despite the fact that he did not care for the "dumb and careless" living Leon, Rick tells Morgan that he "can't leave him like this." Kant could not have done better himself, though one suspects he would view the wasted ammunition as an irrational expenditure. It is impossible to say with certainty what manual implement Immanuel Kant would have favored for respectful zombie executions, though one hopes he can endorse our survivors' use of baseball bats.

Threshold Cases

If a duty to kill exists, it raises an important practical question: when should we kill an infected person? Season One of *The Walking Dead* provides two interesting case studies: Amy and Jim.

Amy is the first established character in the series to die. She dies and becomes infected after a walker attack at the RV camp in "Vatos." In the television series, unlike in the comic book, she returns from the dead. In "Wildfire," Andrea kills Amy's walker form.

To kill an infected but unturned human being would violate that person's dignity. Andrea does not face this problem because Amy dies quickly as the result of walker-inflicted wounds. Andrea, though, faces the problem of whether to desecrate her sister's body to prevent reanimation. By allowing Amy to become a walker, Andrea may violate another duty. The survivor community becomes disturbed by Andrea's refusal to ensure that Amy will not become a walker. The community's position seems pragmatic and well-grounded. It strikes a compromise between respect for the infected living and security concerns. It ensures the safety of the camp as well as Amy's presumptive wish against reanimation.

There would be something inhuman about forcing Andrea to rush, and it is certainly easier for her to kill walker Amy than to hack up Amy's dead body. Yet we wonder whether Andrea's choice to let Amy become a walker is less respectful than the alternative. Andrea violates Amy's presumptive choice against reanimation and destroys a residual subject (a zombie) rather than an object (a corpse).

Perhaps we could better assess Andrea's decision if we knew Amy's views on whether to become a walker. We certainly know Jim's views on the matter, so his case is helpful here. A walker bites Jim in the attack on the RV camp. Jim's death is slower than Amy's and he feels the onset of the infection. Debate surrounding what to do with him continues throughout "Wildfire." Eventually, Jim expresses his desire to be left behind as the group moves to the CDC. When Dale suggests that Jim has made his decision known and that it deserves respect, both Rick and Shane anguish over the possibility of following through on Jim's wishes. Shane says he doesn't know if he can live with it. Lori, however, points out that "it's not your call, neither one of you." Here the choice of the infected is central. The choice must be an informed one, so Shane once again reminds Jim that "it doesn't need to be like this" before leaving Jim to die by the side of the road in accordance with his choice.

Exposing others to harm by leaving Jim to turn into a walker is troubling, but the survivors cannot violate Jim's dignity to avert this harm. Practically speaking, the danger of one walker in the wilderness is minimal. Jim's decision to die is potentially problematic, but it is not, as in the case of suicide, an active choice between life and death. It is, rather, a choice between a quick death followed by nothing and a slow death followed by zombification. By respecting Jim's choice, the group at least takes the most pressing ethical value into account: Jim's autonomy. The survivors' autonomy cannot violate Jim's own, so they must respect his decision. Lori is right: whether the group should leave Jim to die is not Rick or Shane's call. We can question whether Jim made the right choice. If we think waiting for death while injured is analogous to killing one's self, he made the wrong and unethical choice. One thing, however, is clear: neither Rick nor Shane nor any other survivor has the right to make that decision for him.

Remembering Wayne

In post-apocalyptic society as in present-day society, people respect one choice that living persons make about their death: the decision to save lives. Rick and the survivors respect Wayne's wish and, in so doing, respect his autonomy and dignity in a way that using the body parts of a random walker would not.

It might be objected that Wayne chose to donate his organs rather than to have his organs used as camouflage. Using our own reasoning against us, someone could argue that Wayne would not have agreed to the use of his body in an undignified manner. An ax is certainly not a medical instrument and Rick's surgery fails to meet any standard of care we would expect of a medical professional. Yet we resist the urge to focus on the text of his driver's license instead of the spirit of selflessness that motivated his decision. The utter respect with which Rick and the survivors treat Wayne's body changes an apparent desecration into an act of heroism. The more gruesome the act, the nobler the sacrifice.

We hope Rick will make good on his promise to tell his family about Wayne, though this point is unclear from what we see on *The Walking Dead*. Rick is under a Kantian duty to fulfill his oath because the Kantian concept of dignity demands that we do not lie to each other. Moreover, Rick should tell his family about Wayne because Wayne, in life, made a decision that benefits the survivors. Wayne's choice is doubly respectable both as an exercise of rational autonomy and for the correctness of its content. Wayne chose that his body would save lives. There are few things to be grateful for in a world of undead cannibals, but Wayne is one of them. Somewhere, perhaps, an undead Immanuel Kant is smiling.

What We Become

6
A Stagger-on Role to Die For

DAVE BEISECKER

If y'all were like me, you caught the opening season of *The Walking Dead* as it first came out on AMC, complete with commercial interruptions (no cheating with a DVR!). That means you would have caught that Toyota commercial featuring the Corolla that evades a zombie horde. And you also would have encountered a promotion I find most intriguing.

During the initial broadcast of each episode, AMC revealed a "secret" codeword, which viewers could use to enter themselves in a contest on the series website for a chance at a "stagger-on role as a zombie" (presumably for the filming of Season Two). Of course, many would jump at the chance to participate as an extra in just about any capacity. But I was struck by something more. For the promotion highlighted the fact that one gets to take part *as a zombie*, as if that was supposed to imbue the contest with even greater appeal.

As one who succumbed to the temptation to enter the contest—several times in fact—I can personally attest to this additional appeal. For I doubt that I would have been nearly so enthusiastic to remember those code words, had the contest merely been for some garden-variety extra. Having done nearly a decade in George Romero's home town of Pittsburgh, it's been one of my life (or should I say "death"?) ambitions to play an on-screen role as part of a zombie uprising. Becoming a zombie is on my bucket list. Alas, Romero didn't shoot one of his Living Dead movies while I was in the steel town. Even more tragically, AMC never tabbed me for that coveted "stagger on role" (though if any producers of *The Walking Dead* happen to be reading this, . . . call me. I'm still available . . .).

Just as *The Walking Dead* franchise taps into a broader cultural fascination with all things zombie, this AMC promotion exploited an epidemic sweeping over the globe. Attested by the outbreak of "zombie" walks, proms, and pinup contests all around us, it's clear that many of us are infected with a desire to "impersonate" our zombie twin. Many of us find these activities fun, but what could account for the peculiar appeal of "crossing over," even if only temporarily?

It's built into the very concept of a zombie that the possibility of becoming a zombie is supposed to be one of the most horrible and terrifying fates to contemplate, one that no rational creature would ever wish on either themselves or their remains. In order to underscore the true terror of a zombie apocalypse, those in the horror business deliberately portray zombies in spectacularly (often gratuitously) vile and repulsive fashions. Just think of the pitiful, moaning wretch of a corpse that Rick first encounters while riding through the park. How could anyone ever find it fun to appear as ugly and corrupt as one of *those things*?

Not only do the walking dead typically appear as horribly-mangled, disease-ridden carcasses, their behavior is equally vile and despicable. It's not just that they're single-mindedly bent on cannibalism; it's also the appalling manner in which they carry out the practice, munching and gnawing on their still-living victims while remaining oblivious to their writhing and screaming. Certainly none of the main characters of *The Walking Dead* share any such ambition with us to explore life on "the other side". So this appears to be one of those weird cases in which the audience's desires appear to diverge wildly from the interests of a story's protagonists. Whatever answer to this question we reach, I sincerely hope that it doesn't have to involve the attribution of depravity on the part of those with such desires . . . for by my own admission, such an attribution would squarely boomerang back upon me.

An Enhanced Paradox of Horror

I like to think of the AMC *Walking Dead* promotion as a particularly vivid example of an amplified version of what is sometimes called "the paradox of horror." The aesthetician (and movie aficionado) Noel Carroll first raised this paradox in *The Philosophy of Horror* (1990). Carroll's paradox is trying to explain the delight so many of us take in contemplating the horrific in books, movies, and television.

Carroll characterizes the horror genre in terms of the emotional responses horrific creatures or "monsters" are meant to provoke in their audiences, chiefly fear and disgust. Through its disgusting and threatening nature, the quintessential horror monster serves to terrify audience and protagonists alike. Curiously, however, disgust and terror are both negative emotions which we generally don't find pleasurable. And that's what generates the paradox. Except when it comes to fiction, we shun things that horrify us. Though we might chase other kinds of thrills, we're spooked by the genuinely monstrous, and we voluntarily experience disgust only under duress. Real-life horror is not pleasurable. So why do so many of us enthusiastically seek out the horrific in our entertainment choices? In short, why do we revel in shows like *The Walking Dead* as much as we do?

There is some question about whether audiences can genuinely be afraid of fictional monsters, as opposed to feeling a fear for a story's main characters, or somehow pretending to be afraid. However, our visceral reactions to horrific disgust are more clearly genuine. And so Carroll spends more time emphasizing the disgust or revulsion that an audience is supposed to feel toward horror monsters. He tells us that disgust is a characteristic reaction to what we find impure or otherwise inexplicable.

We typically revile those things that resist categorization or transgress conventional boundaries in a way that defies ready explanation "according to reigning scientific notions." We flinch or shudder at things that are what he calls "categorically interstitial": contradictory, incomplete, or formless (such as The Blob). Kirkman's *The Walking Dead* exemplifies each of these characteristics and so it's a particularly apt test case for any proposed solution to the paradox of horror.

The walkers are both alive and dead. Their maimed, mangled bodies have no business ambulating. With their exposed innards, what should be inside them is on the outside. Their gooey, oozing, decaying bodies lack form and integrity. They are diseased, polluted, their flesh contaminated. In short, you just wouldn't want to touch one if you didn't have to.

So what can possibly explain our enduring fascination with things like zombies that rank so high on the "ick factor"? Carroll himself proposes that simple curiosity explains much of horror's appeal. Our disgust at a monster is fueled largely by its very nature, it is something initially inexplicable according to current science. The pleasure we derive in a good horror story comes from our learning alongside the story's protagonists about the existence of the monster, then about the true extent of the protagonist's peril, and finally about how to remove, neutralize, or otherwise cope with the threat. Horror stories are thus voyages of discovery, which naturally inquiring beings like us find fascinating. And so the pleasure we feel in a good horror story is not a pleasure we take in actually being disgusted or afraid. Rather, it is the satisfaction of discovery and the relief we feel at the removal of a perilous doubt.

I can't resist pointing out that as far as monsters go, there is little in Kirkman's walkers that seem to be all that mysterious. Kirkman's walkers are clearly inspired by the ghouls that George Romero first brought to life in his "living dead" series. Indeed, Kirkman pays homage to Romero in his very first issue. Remember the young kid that smacked Rick in the back of the head with the shovel? His name is Duane Jones, same as the actor who played the male lead in *Night of the Living Dead*. So when we first came to *The Walking Dead, we* already knew from the very outset how to dispatch walkers; you shoot them in the head. Duh! And Kirkman deftly finesses how the survivors managed to figure this out by putting Rick to sleep in the hospital during the crucial discovery phase. Morgan Jones simply tells him all he needs to know shortly after he comes out of his coma.

Despite the similarities between Kirkman's Walking Dead and Romero's Living Dead, there are a few subtle differences. For instance, Kirkman's walkers have a much less discriminating palate. Thankfully for Rick, they are literally hungry enough to eat a horse, a feat that Romero's dead can accomplish only through intense conditioning.

Despite being commonly identified as "zombies," there is little in Kirkman's walkers to connect them with Vodou-inspired forebears. They aren't under the control of any nefarious witchdoctors or bocors; indeed, nothing can control them, not even themselves. Just as Romero is remarkably reticent about the ultimate cause of the zombie rising, so too is Kirkman.

I think this is a good thing. There can be a strong temptation to pin the blame of a zombie outbreak on the morally dubious activities of some individual or organization. Here the usual corporate or military suspects play the role of the overreaching "mad scientist" in what is basically an updated, hackneyed version of the Frankenstein theme. However, such explanations for why the dead have suddenly come back to life threaten to inject a source of evil into the plot that serves only to distract us from the zombies themselves. Witness, for instance, Alice's battles with the Umbrella Corporation in the *Resident Evil* franchise, in which the zombies are relegated to an increasingly marginalized role.

We're not all that curious about the cause of the walker outbreak, and might well be disappointed if the show or series found itself needing to invent one. I'd venture to say we're even less interested in finding a cure for the infection. It would be a surprise indeed if the heroes of the show ever find a way to inoculate themselves, and I daresay an unwelcome surprise at that, for that would truly be the end, the point at which *The Walking Dead* "jumps the shark." Deep down, many of us would rather the series, like the zombies, to come back again and again. We truly wish there to be no way out.

Now my primary focus here is actually an *amplified* version of Carroll's "paradox of horror," which is specifically applicable to the AMC promotion. For it's one thing to be fascinated by and to enjoy things that are, by all accounts, meant to terrify and gross us out, but it's taking it to a whole new level of perversity to find pleasure in actually *being* an irredeemably gross and repellant instrument of the apocalypse, hell-bent on devouring the last vestiges of one's own kind. It's built into the very concept of a zombie that you *wouldn't* want to be one. And that is what it seems like we would be doing, in seeking out a "stagger on role" as a zombie.

Initially, we might be tempted to try to apply Carroll's solution to the original paradox of horror to this amplified version as well. Perhaps zombie activities are akin to re-enactments of historical periods and events, in which we impose certain physical and equipmental limitations on ourselves in order to get a glimpse of a "way of life" that isn't our own. We might, for instance, claim that in taking on the role of a zombie, we thereby satisfy an abiding curiosity about a zombie's "lived experience." I don't think such a simple reply works well, for I find it unlikely that many of us really harbor such curiosity.

The very idea that zombies have any sort of experience at all is open to doubt. Those in the business of studying consciousness even use 'zombie' as a term of the trade for something that lacks conscious experience altogether. But even if we set that concern to the side, and accept that there might be something that it's 'like' to be a zombie, virtually any attempt to learn what that would be like would be doomed to failure. We just can't seriously hope to take on their mental lives at all (at least not as long as we plan to come back from the experience!).

The philosopher Thomas Nagel makes a similar negative assessment about our ever learning what it's like to be a bat. Rooted as we are in our own point of view, we just don't have the cognitive equipment to gain access into the lived experience of bats, even by doing "batty" things such as hanging upside down in dark closets. Similarly, we shouldn't think that we could ever really learn what it's like to be a zombie by staggering around the AMC set for *The Walking Dead*.

Playing a zombie on TV just wouldn't take things far enough for those with a genuine curiosity about experiencing things as a zombie truly would. Mind you, alas, I haven't ever been on the set, but I suspect that it's not nearly as horrible as it "really" would be. I imagine there isn't nearly enough viscera, and I certainly doubt that it reeks quite like it "should." But when you think about it that way, it would be approaching the height of depravity to take things "far enough" to get any semblance of what it really would be like to be one of the walking dead. For who in their right minds are going to be tempted to mangle a limb or two and rip out their entrails just so that they can slip around in their own gore, all in the name of satisfying curiosity? Who'd even go so far as to follow in Glenn and Rick's footsteps and liberally cover themselves with reeking zombie goo? Their decision to engage in their own form of "zombie walk" was driven by desperation, not curiosity, and they undertook the ordeal only under great duress.

So perhaps like bats, what it's like to be a walker is way past the limit of our reasonable comprehension. And perhaps that's just as well. For not only would it seem virtually impossible to learn what it's really like to be a zombie, the whole endeavor of trying to satisfy such curiosity ought to strike one as seriously misguided from both moral and rational points of view. We'd lock anyone up who really acted out of a curiosity to find out what it's like to harbor an insatiable hunger for human flesh, paired with a reckless disregard for one's well-being. The "method" approach for AMC's stagger on role just isn't available, and I wouldn't want a method actor for such a role anyway! In short, the satisfaction of curiosity just doesn't seem to be provide a reasonable answer to this amplified version of the paradox of horror. Curiosity doesn't motivate Jim when he asks Rick and the rest of his surviving companions to be left behind to complete his "transformation." Instead, he only wishes once again to be with family.

Zombie Dreams?

We don't share Jim's motivation for becoming one of *The Walking Dead*, and I trust none of us ever will. Nevertheless, we've yet to uncover just what our own motivations could be, let alone rationally defend them. Our enhanced paradox of horror remains unresolved, and to lend it in an additional air of mystery, let me point out how disconnected the desire to play a zombie is with our own personal fantasies concerning a zombie apocalypse.

Even though no one truly looks forward to the end times, we can still enjoyably play out and explore the consequences of such an occurrence in our fantasy-lives. Indeed, *The Walking Dead* invites such speculation, as do books like *The Zombie Survival Guide*, and the Zombie Hunter's Website. Even the CDC has recently gotten into the game by issuing guidelines about how to prepare for a zombie onslaught. However, in each of these imaginative exercises, we are not taking on the role of the zombies themselves. Despite its title, the *Zombie Survival Guide* is not a handbook for the recently deceased!

If I were to be dropped (à la Bruce Campbell?) into the world of *The Walking Dead* (or walkers to be dropped into my world), I'd much rather prefer to be a survivor than a walker. Should the dead begin to begin to come back to life and start feasting upon the living, I'd much rather take on the role of zombie *killer* than that of zombie. Zombies are the cannon-fodder for our more violent fantasies. Just look at the enduring popularity of zombie-themed first-person shooters.

And the narrative in *The Walking Dead* leads us to identify with (some of) the survivors. We might have a few zombie favorites in the series—it's a particularly nice touch that the television series has some of the walkers play recurring roles. Think of the creepy cadaver who always seems to be lurking around that Atlanta bus. I enjoy seeing him over and over again, and I'd hate it if Glenn or Rick finally succeeded in putting him to rest. However, it would be the height of perversity to identify or to align our sympathies completely with the walkers. While we can pity them, and even cheer them on when some deserving survivor gets what's coming to them, that's just not the way we're supposed to engage the narrative. They're not the home team, and we're not supposed to root for them.

Still, that doesn't mean that we don't. By no means would I deny that we ever harbor dark, transgressive fantasies that we're not "supposed" to have. Of course we do; there's an id in all of us just waiting to be released. And some of our more subversive fantasies can have us taking on the role of villains or monsters menacing the rest (or remnants) of humanity. Wouldn't it be fun to be Godzilla for a day and stomp around on some poor defenseless city? Such fantasies might appeal mostly to our inner twelve-year-old; still, it's understandable why we might like to act out as a monster here and there. So perhaps the very fact that we're not "supposed" to have these fantasies can help to explain their appeal. It's a form of rebellion.

While we all harbor fantasies that we might not like to share, such an attitude seems far more appropriate for, say, *vampires* than the walking dead. Like zombies, vampires have also witnessed an onscreen resurgence, but one that serves only to deepen our paradox.[1] Vampires possess superpowers,

---

[1] The Romero-like conception of the zombie is arguably an offshoot of the vampire family tree, though one that by now has taken on a quite distinct evolutionary path. In confecting his "living dead" Romero was inspired largely by the "vampires" of Richard Matheson's novelette *I am Legend*, who exhibit many features now more commonly associated with modern-day zombies (the flesh-eating rather than blood-sucking, however, is a nod to H.P. Lovecraft's "Reanimator").

which allow them to overcome the limitations of ordinary human embodiment. They can impose mastery over us. And so the cunning and seductive vampire has now become the glamorous cool-kid on the undead block.

The lowly, wretched zombie, by contrast, lacks any such sex appeal. Glamorous actors don't line up to play them, and authors needn't take any such pains in order to convince us of the undesirability of zombification. We can make this point independent of any grand, metaphysical questions concerning personal survival, immortality, or identity. There are of course reasonable doubts about whether we would ever "survive" such a change. In many if not most interesting senses – those to which various philosophers have turned to pin the notion of personal identity – it is clear that we *wouldn't* survive zombification. Our bodies have begun to decay, our memories have all but vanished, and our emotions and desires have (I would hope!) changed beyond recognition. Zombies have so little self concern that we might reasonably doubt that they have a self at all. But even if, technically speaking, we wouldn't survive zombification, there's something that remains of us that does—namely our remains. Still, we wouldn't wish such a fate on our remains.

Fitting Noel Carroll's definition of the classic horror monster, it's part of the core concept to be loathsome, fetid, disgusting, and repellant. Utterly devoid of any physical or social grace, zombies are plodding and not at all plotting. Their desires—their hunger—cannot be satisfied, not even temporarily. And while vampires salaciously savor their victims, zombies unceremoniously gobble them down with no hint of aesthetic appreciation. Their tormented, inarticulate moaning conveys how much they *suffer* their bodily limitations. In short, *nothing* about them is supposed to evoke envy, awe, or admiration. That's what makes our amplified paradox of horror all the more urgent.

There's even something wrong with their dogged tenacity and resilience. By design, they are the losers, the bottom-feeders, of the undead pantheon. While a zombie horde might eventually overcome or supplant us, we wouldn't be inclined to say that they've achieved *mastery* over us. Instead, humanity's downfall can usually be attributed to our own shortcomings. Individually, zombies can't outwit or overpower us. Since their strength lies in overwhelming numbers, the zombie fraternity cannot afford to be as selective as that of the more individualistic vampire. So if the vampire is the undead emblem of the aristocracy, then the lowly zombie is the undead representative for the vast majority of us unwashed commoners. It is so apt that Glenn prefers to call them "geeks."

Once again, we're left with our initial puzzle. While we might reasonably fantasize about becoming a vampire, fantasies about zombification are much harder to explain. The "ick factor" that's so central to the concept of a zombie just seems to get in the way. Becoming a zombie is much more clearly a fate worse than death. Although it might be "cool" in some as yet unexplained sense to want to play a role as a zombie, zombies themselves are most definitely not cool. We wouldn't want to be one—not *really*. And so our question remains: why in the world would anyone like me ever find it so fun to portray their own zombie counterpart?

Revenge of the Nerds?

So where do we turn to in order to resolve our amplified paradox of horror? I think that we can gain some mileage toward an answer by thinking about the core concept of what it is to be a zombie. I've emphasized the zombie's "ick factor": in order to accentuate the horror of a zombie apocalypse, authors and directors will ham-handedly seek to make zombies as disgusting and repulsive as possible. Kirkman is no exception on this score, and that is no criticism. *The Walking Dead* offers us just what we'd expect of a good zombie apocalypse.

However, there's actually one respect in which that very same "ick factor" can actually bring zombies closer to us. Unlike vampires, you don't have to make a beautiful corpse in order to be a compelling zombie. Quite the contrary! If walkers are what Glenn calls the "geeks" of the undead pantheon, at least they've become somewhat lovable in their loserdom. They are the underdogs that now get to enjoy their day in the sun, the nerds that finally get the upper hand over the popular crowd that bullies and oppresses them. That can explain in part why we might find something in them with which to identify—even though we're not "supposed" to.

Observe how endearing it is the way they stumble around with their vacant expressions and inarticulate moaning, and how they tangle themselves in and trip all over their entrails, and foolishly get stuck in stairwells or swimming pools. Ironically enough, these same endearing features help to bring out their universal humanity. Zombies might be wretched, pathetic, utterly ungraceful and laughably inept. Even so, I suspect many of us harbor, deep down in our souls, doubts of being awkward, pathetic losers as well. So when we look at zombies, we just might see our own insecurities reflected right back at us—as through a magnifying glass. Zombies might suffer their bodily limitations, but don't we all? We too sometimes stumble about, and have trouble finding the exits out of stairwells—not to mention that we're often much less articulate than we'd like to be. Portraying a zombie just allows us to acknowledge and give voice to many of our basic human limitations and insecurities.

Moreover, in their ineptness, zombies are also funny in their own way. As attested by the wave of zombie comedies coincident to *The Walking Dead's* debut on AMC (*Shaun of the Dead* and *Zombieland*, to name two of the more obvious examples), zombies have now broken out of the horror genre into the realm of slapstick. At this point, their antics have become every bit as comical to us as they are horrifying. We have to laugh at something in *The Walking Dead*, and the plight of the central cast is too dire to serve that purpose. Ironically, the comic relief manifests itself instead in the antics of the monsters. Consequently, even though one would never want to become anything like a real zombie, it nevertheless might be fun to portray one temporarily—*if only to clown around*.

Despite their repellant appearance and appalling demeanor, zombies have also become the clowns of the undead pantheon. Clowns are famously creepy as well! So any desire we might have to act out as a zombie might well be of a piece with a very human desire to spend some time just fooling around without having to be taken so seriously. Desiring a stagger-on role is a delicious and thoroughly acceptable opportunity to look foolish, nerdy, and ridiculous, but that's as subversive as it gets. Indeed, if I am at all on the mark here, it is a welcome chance to laugh at our own ineptness.

Zombies are very much like nerds, clowns, fools, and perhaps even my creaky old metaphysics professor—creepy, yes; but awkward in an endearing way. *The Walking Dead* is most definitely not a comedy, but that doesn't prevent it from having some comical aspects. I suspect that something like this association of zombies with clowns plays a role in the recent wave amongst "serious" makers of zombie-horror of packing their zombies with extra agility, speed, or punch. "Fast zombies" are more terrifying, but not nearly as funny. And I for one wouldn't be so keen to play one on TV. After all, AMC bills it as a "stagger-on role," not a jumping, climbing, and sprinting one! That, more than anything else, tells me that the appeal of the AMC promotion stems not out of any desire to *be horrifying*, but rather out of a wish to be more generally endearing and playful. We're simply hoping to participate in a good lark. Herein lies much of our solution to the amplified paradox of horror. The solution lies in not taking zombies so seriously. It's all in fun, an embracing celebration of our own universal nerdiness. The chance to get in touch with one's own inner zombie is equally a chance to become more comfortable with our insecurities.

I find it admirable that *The Walking Dead* bucks the trend toward fast zombies. Such resistance only serves to make them more accessible to our inner nerds and clowns and lends to their universal appeal. We can all be zombies, not just the beautiful people! Kirkman doesn't cast his walkers as symbols for some particular evil. For if we insist upon seeing zombies as the insidious fifth-column of some identifiable social threat, then we'll be inclined to saddle them with unflattering moral characteristics inherited from that which they represent. And that only serves to excavate an unacceptable moral gulf between us.

How, for instance, can we resist seeing Nazi zombies as inherently evil, or question the morals of zombie strippers? But it's not their zombie aspect that's responsible for such negative assessments. Presumably, they were bad before the change, and their zombification serves only to amplify their depravity. As *The Walking Dead* so vividly shows, zombies are no more evil and corrupt than their human forebears. To counter the temptation to think that they are, I'd ask you to consider how you would regard zombies if instead you were told that they represented an elderly population threatening to overwhelm our health-care system. After all, in their ceaseless wandering and bewildered expressions, they bear a striking resemblance to Alzheimer's patients. From that angle, zombies are much more likely to spark our sympathies; aging is common to us all, not just strippers or Nazis.

If *The Walking Dead* had succumbed to the temptation to accentuate an evilness in its dead, then I submit that we would not find the AMC promotion nearly so appealing. At least I wouldn't. That would inject the series with an unwelcome "preachiness." But by letting the zombies just be zombies, the series succeeds in our being able to see us in them, and thereby foster our desires for those coveted stagger-on roles.

7
What's Yours Still Isn't Mine

JASON WALKER

The idea that anyone might desire a zombie apocalypse, secretly or otherwise, sounds absurd, though James Davidson at the popular *Cracked* website managed to come up with five reasons why this might be true. The fourth reason is, "Free Stuff, Without All That Damned Work." Although most people, Davidson concedes, would greet such a world with horror, zombie enthusiasts reach a different conclusion:

> . . . when society collapses under all the zombie dead weight, it's all over. But not over like a nuclear holocaust, where all the warehouses and grocery stores lay in ruins. No, all the stuff is perfectly intact. All manner of stores and malls and mansions will be ripe for the picking. In a world where only a tiny fraction of the population remains, there'd have to be enough food and clothes in the supply chain to feed you and your friends for the rest of your zombie-killing lives. For free. Which means you don't have to spend all day grinding away in front of a keyboard just to keep food in the fridge. All that is swept aside. Killing zombies is your job now. And you won't be getting any damned memos about a dress code. (James Davidson, "5 Reasons You Secretly Want a Zombie Apocalypse." *Cracked.com*, September 29th, 2009)

In zombie stories the survivors inevitably resort to looting, whether the looted goods are necessities like food and weapons or non-essential luxury goods like jewelry. The assumption seems to be that such looting is perfectly justified in such a world; after all, even if money was no object, it isn't as if store clerks are still around to accept payment.

So, is it as simple as free food, clothes, and mermaid necklaces for everyone? Just because there is no government to enforce them, does that mean that *people* have lost their property rights? Does this mean that in Zombieland, I can take your Twinkie stockpile, especially if I have a gun and you don't? Though he wasn't exactly thinking about a world swarming with mobs of flesh-eating ghouls, John Locke saw that there was a question about how people came to claim property without a king designating who owned what. Locke reasoned that people have a basic set of rights, or moral claims, that was revolutionary for his time (life, liberty, and property), which exist even if nobody enforces them. Without government, we might lose *procedural* rights like trial by a jury of our peers, but even in a world dominated by zombies, we keep the rights to life, liberty, and property. These rights establish moral and logistical parameters, allowing us to distinguish between scavenging from abandoned big box stores on one hand, and looting the supplies of fellow survivors on the other.

Of course, this isn't the only theory about what happens in a world without government. An earlier philosopher, Thomas Hobbes, held that morally speaking, pretty much anything goes without government, which is why he argued that even tyrannical government deserves support. Without government shotguns, government, rather than moral rights, make right. Which approach makes more sense in the world of *The Walking Dead*?

It's Only Right and Natural

Locke and Hobbes agree that there are two basic kinds of social environments. In a *civil society*, a single government holds a monopoly on the use of force within its borders. This state, or sovereign, exclusively enforces the rules of justice, punishing offenders, and provides a structure for the adjudication of disputes between its citizens. It is the world that most people take for granted.

The other circumstance is called the *state of nature*. The state of nature is what we have when there is no common government. It is the state humankind existed in before civilization. Locke emphasizes that this state of nature is a real condition, not merely the kind of hypothetical that only philosophers worry about. Real examples he points to include governments themselves (having no sovereign authority common between them) and citizens of different countries in unclaimed territory. In short, the state of nature is the condition in which persons share no one common authority or sovereign. While the "state of nature" is not precisely interchangeable with "anarchy," for the purposes of exploring the world of a zombie apocalypse, it will be close enough. What unites social contract theorists is the notion that the state derives its legitimacy and authority as a *contract* of sorts, even if only metaphorically understood as such. The "contract" is the agreement between the people of a given territory to leave the state of nature and create government to alleviate the problems associated with the state of nature.

In *The Walking Dead*, as in most zombie apocalypse scenarios, civil society collapses, as zombie hordes overwhelm military and police forces, and the few remaining humans are left to their own devices to survive in world where they are outnumbered by zombies. The world of the zombie apocalypse, in short, is a state of nature, with two additional features.

First, typically the state of nature is in effect *global*, not merely limited to an unoccupied frontier or the territory of a "failed state." In *The Walking Dead*, there are small pockets of order such as the Governor's stronghold of Woodbury and the Alexandria Free Zone, but the state of nature is generally assumed to have swept the globe, as all credible governments seem to have vanished.

Second, there are the zombies themselves, who pose a unique threat to survival. The sheer numbers of zombies make them a greater danger in the aggregate than the odd highwayman, severely undermining any attempt to rebuild society as it existed before the outbreak. But that danger, as real as it is for the survivors, may obscure a greater threat, one equally in play in Hobbes and Locke as in Kirkman's *The Walking Dead*: other human survivors. The zombies are at least predictable as forces of nature; they don't have the intelligence or ability to plan strategically as an organized force as seen in some zombie literature, like *Land of the Dead*.

Although Hobbes and Locke agree on the essential idea that the creation of civil society is the preferred solution to the problems of the state of nature, they differ on the nature of one's moral status and rights in the state of nature. To see how profound the difference is, let us consider how the predicament of Rick Grimes and his fellow survivors appears depending on whether it is viewed through either a Hobbesian or a Lockean lens.

To say the *Hobbesian* social contract theory takes a dim view of the state of nature is to put things mildly. In that state, human life is, in Hobbes's most famous phrase, "solitary, poor, nasty, brutish, and short" (*Leviathan*, I, 13, 9). Under this description, individuals are in a war of "all against all." Although all are perfectly free and equal (even the physically strongest person, Hobbes reminds us, must sleep sometime), neither morality nor rights exist until the state of nature is brought to an end with the emergence of a Sovereign, a "leviathan" powerful enough to keep the people in a state of "awe" over his power. Without a credible Sovereign willing to enforce them, talk of rights is mere words. Even morality itself suffers the same fate without a Sovereign to determine its content and enforce it by the credible threat of violence.

For Hobbes, the possibility of such a wretched state of affairs highlights how vital government is to human flourishing, and how important it is avoid war and rebellion, even against tyrannical regimes, for even the worst tyranny offers protections superior to the state of nature. As wretched as we might find the Governor's regime in *The Walking Dead*, for example, it would be hard to blame people for choosing to live under his rule in Woodbury rather than face life against the zombies alone. Of course, Hobbes emphasizes the danger of other people rather than forces of nature like zombies, but the Hobbesian world, like that of many zombie apocalypses, often leaves individuals with the same choice between freedom and protection from the lawless hordes. For Hobbes, as unenviable as the choice might be, the only rational preference is for the latter.

Moreover, the Hobbesian view may also be referred to as the *positivist* view, so called because rights are held to be mere artificial constructs posited by government fiat. There are no rights outside of a state's recognition and protection of them, which for Hobbes is the chief reason why anything that could threaten to return people to a state of nature must be avoided at all costs. But this means that in a state of nature no rights exist in and there is literally no such thing as an immoral act. All's fair in love and the war of all against all that is the state of nature.

Why? As a materialist, Hobbes demands that principles such as moral laws have some hard, physical basis. A Sovereign's enforcement of standards of morality through the law provides just such a mechanism. Take away the Sovereign, and the enforcement he offers, and you take away the mechanism that gives morality and rights talk meaning. Good and bad, right and wrong, and so forth become mere words. Your ownership of anything, up to your own life, only extends as far as it is defended by force of arms.

On the other hand, *Lockean* social contract theory begins with a state of nature in which rights are very much in play. Indeed, it is the desire to seek more vigorous, fair and orderly settlements of those already-existing rights that leads to the social contract that provides the legitimate basis of government for Locke. As with Hobbes, the state of nature, for Locke, is defined in terms of the absolute freedom it offers to all persons. It also offers perfect equality, at least in terms of moral status. However, Locke explicitly distinguishes this absolute liberty from *license*. Just as we have freedom in our own person and property, so too do all others. Among the rights we have in the state of nature is the right to punish those who violate our rights. Such violators put themselves in a state of war against us, entitling us to act in self-defense or to punish them. This means that we don't just have the right to deter burglars and thieves by force of arms; we are morally entitled to be judge, jury and executioner against any who threaten our rights to life, liberty, and property.

Sensibly enough, Locke fears that if people retain the right of punishment and serve as judges in their own cases, simple misunderstandings and minor disputes could degenerate into bloodthirsty struggles for vengeance. The "inconveniences" of the state of nature thus lead people to formulate a social contract, and thereby create civil society. In exchange for individuals giving up the right to punish, the state is empowered with legitimacy to settle disputes and provide more reliable protections than individuals can provide on their own. But if a state proves incompetent in its assigned task, or worse, become a greater threat to life, liberty, and property than the state of nature that motivated its very creation, the people retain a right of revolution to abolish their government and substitute a new one that can better fulfill its purpose.

Why is there no right of revolution for Hobbes, assuming the Sovereign has proven dangerous or inept? In his theory, the social contract is created amongst the people themselves, and is binding for them, but the Sovereign is not himself a party to the contract. Thus, he cannot be accountable for any failures to abide by its conditions: neither he nor the state he governs ever agreed to its terms, and there exists no superior enforcing authority to supervise any such contract even if the sovereign had offered one. Put another way, the Hobbesian social contract *creates* the Sovereign; it is not a contract *with* him, any more than a mortgage agreement is with a piece of property. Hobbes would argue that there is no need for a right of rebellion, as fears of tyranny are misplaced. The Hobbesian Sovereign has no incentive to act tyrannically, unless, that is, his rule is threatened. And even if a Sovereign acts badly, and terrorizes his citizens with no cause, such terror is always preferable to the unpredictable terror of the state of nature.

Take the case of Woodbury. The Governor is hardly a model Sovereign. But Hobbes would counsel would-be rebels in Woodbury to consider that the Governor's rule at least establishes authority that makes interactions between his subjects peaceful, and his authority allows for sufficient organization and planning to keep the walkers at bay. Defying his authority and mounting a revolution introduces chaos and unpredictability, something Hobbes had some personal experience with during the English Civil War. Hobbes's advice wouldn't apply to Rick Grimes and Michonne, for the Governor has already established a state of war against them. They are under no obligation to submit to his rule once that happens, because they remain in a state of war whether he stays in power or a rebellion ensues.

Whatever the strengths of the Hobbesian approach, it is the Lockean perspective that has a special resonance for Americans, given that it was Lockean political theory, not the Hobbesian, that influenced the American Founding. Nonetheless, Hobbes retains considerable influence as well. His *Leviathan* is regarded by many as the greatest work of political philosophy composed in English, and even his many detractors will credit Hobbes as the first true political scientist. And the state of nature, whether in its Hobbesian or Lockean guise, continues to provide fertile ground for literature, as we will see in the case of *The Walking Dead*.

Property Rights in the State of Nature

Why does Locke believe rights of any kind exist in the state of nature? It begins with property.

> Though the earth, and all inferior creatures, be common to all men, *yet every man has a property in his own person: this no body has any right to but himself.* The labour of his body, and the work of his hands, we may say, are properly his. Whatsoever then he removes out of the state that nature hath provided, and left it in, he hath mixed his labour with, and joined to it something that is his own, and thereby makes it his property. (*Second Treatise on Government*, V, §27, emphasis mine)

As Locke understands the concept of property, he means something broader than the mere ownership of stuff. Lockean property begins with the individual's own body, with property rights in oneself providing the basis for personal autonomy. From here, Locke has an argument for how property in this sense can extend outward into things in the world, even in a state of nature. For Locke, protection of individuals' life, liberty, and property provides the purpose of government and thus precedes government itself.

The Necklace

Someone might argue that because Grimes and his group do not become thieves, *The Walking Dead* implicitly assumes that, at least for the living, property rights still exist. For example, Grimes and his group might have been able to steal the farm from Hershel and his family, but when asked to leave in the comic series, they peacefully comply. (Though threatened at times in the TV series, Hershel never evicted Grimes and his group in that version of the story.) But it is not convincing to infer that characters in a story accept that some action is not an action one should do, simply because they don't perform that action.

Instead, consider a case that, at first glance, suggests that *The Walking Dead*'s state of nature justifies a cavalier attitude about property rights. In "Guts," Grimes allows Andrea to steal a necklace from a department store in which his group has sought refuge from walkers.

GRIMES: See something you like?

ANDREA: Not me, but I know someone who would.... My sister. She's still such a kid in some ways. Unicorns, dragons ... She's into all that stuff. But mermaids... They rule. She loves mermaids.

GRIMES: Why not take it?

ANDREA: There's a cop staring at me. Would it be considered looting?

GRIMES: I don't think those rules apply anymore. Do you?

The first question to ask is whether what Andrea, and by omission, Grimes, did was wrong. On one side of the ledger, we have a straightforward case of theft. Andrea did not manufacture the necklace, nor did she bargain with its owner for a mutually-agreed exchange of values. She simply helped herself to it; whether it was as a gift for her sister or herself is immaterial.

The owner of the department store had no say in the matter. The fact that he wasn't there generally doesn't matter. If a shop owner closes her shop for two weeks, two months, or longer, it does not imply that anyone who wishes may pilfer the shop's goods. Looting, even during emergencies like Hurricane Katrina, is still a prosecutable offense. And Andrea can hardly claim that seizing this necklace was a justifiable response to an emergency situation. At least Glenn could make a case that he simply needed any car to facilitate a distraction and escape from Atlanta; the fact that he happened to locate a sports car for that end, one that he enjoyed driving at high velocity, was secondary.

On the other hand, given the circumstances, the situation is considerably worse than a mere riot or a hurricane with a reasonable likelihood of the owner's survival and return; it is *apocalyptic*. It is highly unlikely that either the store's owner or his heirs are alive by time Andrea and Grimes arrive there, nor that they will take inventory and consider themselves the victims of a theft.

We can probably assume that if the owner is among the ranks of the undead, he or she has no rights, and certainly no property rights. Once a zombie, a person's higher brain functions are forever destroyed. He or she is incapable of joining a social contract of any sort, cannot plan for the future, and cannot carry out any productive work. Property rights would make no more sense for a zombie than for an animal.

Hence, Grimes responds to Andrea's query about looting with, "I don't think those rules apply anymore." As if to emphasize the point, just after these words are exchanged, the large mob of walkers breaks through the store's first glass barrier, making the recovery of any of the store's goods that much less plausible. Even if the shop owner survived, it's unlikely that he values the jewelry, and money itself is by then is meaningless as a medium of exchange. Andrea can plausibly claim that she had justifiable reason to believe that neither the owner nor his or her heirs would be alive, much less that they would care one way or the other about the fate of a necklace.

The assumption guiding the writers of the show, as with most writers of zombie apocalypse literature, is that Andrea did nothing wrong. If John Locke, the defender of the robust property rights view sketched above, is right, then this intuition may be perfectly justifiable.

Locke places a limit on what you may make your own property by mixing your labor with it. You have to leave over for other people "enough, and as good" of the resource in question. I may not mix my labor with all the world's supply of water, for example, and thereby claim ownership of all of it, for it would not leave "enough, and as good" a supply of water for other people. If all jewelry shops around the world were abandoned, and Andrea attempted to claim all the world's necklaces for herself, this could conceivably apply. But she takes only a single necklace, from a stock that would be soon practically unavailable to anyone else.

There is also the restriction that you may not appropriate more than you can use. You can't make something your own property merely to let it spoil:

> It will perhaps be objected to this, that if gathering the acorns, or other fruits of the earth, &c. makes a right to them, then any one may ingross as much as he will. To which I answer, Not so. The same law of nature, that does by this means give us property, does also bound that property too. God has given us all things richly, *1 Tim. vi. 12* is the voice of reason confirmed by inspiration. But how far has he given it us? To enjoy. As much as any one can make use of to any advantage of life before it spoils, so much he may by his labour fix a property in: whatever is beyond this, is more than his share, and belongs to others. Nothing was made by God for man to spoil or destroy. (*Second Treatise*, V, §31)

There are some important differences between the example Locke has in mind and Andrea's necklace. Locke's discussion contemplates natural goods, especially perishable goods or land, where such goods would spoil if left to the man or woman who cultivated them beyond his or her ability to make use of them. The advantage of precious metals as mediums of exchange, and why they foster the evolution of an economy beyond simple barter, is precisely that they are not subject to spoilage, thus making it advantageous for a person to produce surplus goods beyond what he or she can immediately consume or trade. A necklace, like money, cannot be expected to literally spoil.

However Locke's point still holds. With Atlanta overrun by walker hordes, there's very little hope for the survival of the necklace's owner or heirs to ever be in a position to reclaim the store's merchandise for use, and with the demise of money as a medium of exchange, Andrea can rightfully claim that a state of nature resumed with the rise of the zombie apocalypse. The necklace would not literally spoil as perishable food might, but it would go forever "wasted" and unused in a city that "belongs to the dead now."

This conclusion might seem at first to vindicate Hobbes's view of property: no civil society, no property rights, no morality. But for Locke, there are still rights to be respected, and rules to be followed, in the State of Nature. Grimes suggests only that the *old* rules don't apply, not that there are no rules.

Consider Guillermo's faux-gang defending an Atlanta nursing home in "Vatos." Grimes and his crew discover the gang is all bark, no bite, and reclaims his stockpile of weapons without a fight. By the end of the episode, Guillermo no longer has a hostage or enough force to compel Grimes to surrender any of his weapons, but Grimes voluntarily chooses to share just "less than half" of the weapons with the group. Other members of Grimes's group do not agree with his decision, but the point remains that Grimes's generosity is hardly the expected outcome in a Hobbesian war of all against all. Grimes and his group do not prey upon living people or steal from them. This benevolent policy only works if we're living in a Lockean, rather than a Hobbesian, state of nature.

A counter-example could be the prison Grimes and his crew locate near Woodbury. Dexter himself refers to it as *his* prison, with the revolt he led merely being about expelling trespassing interlopers. However, the prison is probably not property in Locke's sense, because the four surviving prisoners found there had been trapped in the cafeteria. They were not mixing their labor with the property, and thereby *using* it, in the sense that Hershel's farm was being used, or as the prison would come to be made useful as a shelter and community, after the arrival of Grimes's group.

House Squatting

In the first episode of the television series, as well as the first issue of *The Walking Dead* comic, we encounter Morgan and his son Duane. Morgan and Duane are holed up in the house next door to the Grimes family home. Both versions highlight the awkwardness with which Morgan feels he must justify to Grimes, as a representative of the law, his decision to occupy Grimes's neighbor's home. It turns out that Morgan needn't have worried:

> GRIMES: I'm not going to arrest you, if that's what you mean. Most of the houses on my street had been looted. You seemed to be fixing the place up. The Thompsons will probably thank you when they get back. As long as you don't put up a fight over the place.
>
> MORGAN: It's not like we're stealing the place. Your neighborhood just seemed safer. We don't figure that we're hurting anybody by staying there . . . And in my book that makes it okay.
>
> GRIMES: You don't have to justify anything to me. You're keeping your son safe. I'm worried sick about mine. I understand. (Issue #1)

There's no indication here that Morgan intends to keep the Thompsons' home should they return. Morgan suggests a "no harm, no foul" attitude with his "don't figure that we're hurting anybody by staying here" remark. And Grimes observes that if anything, Morgan and Duane are doing a favor for the Thompsons by squatting there, since their presence will protect the home from looters and walkers alike. Improving the property, if only by maintaining it, increases the stock of property beyond what it would have been had it been left to degenerate.

Just as Locke's "spoilage proviso" limits property rights to active use, forbidding property rights in that which would go to waste, it also emphasizes the role of property rights in *increasing* the stock of goods made available to humankind. By occupying the home, Morgan and Duane actively prevented the "spoilage" of the house to looters, walkers, and the elements, keeping more resources available than would otherwise be the case. So while property rights still hold, even in the state of nature, they do not yield absurd outcomes that endanger life and the very property meant to be protected in the first place.

Self-Ownership and the Right to Punish

So far, we've looked at how the "good guys," the hero-protagonists of Rick Grimes and his group, functioned by an implicit Lockean understanding of property. But property isn't merely about ownership of *stuff* in the world; that kind of property is an outgrowth of the more basic ownership that each person has in themselves: their own bodies, minds, and labor.

The Walking Dead also shows us characters who treat the zombie apocalypse as a fully-realized Hobbesian state of nature, who no more respect property as stuff or property in one's own person.

Consider the group of cannibalistic hunters led by Chris, encountered by Grimes while en route to Washington. There is perhaps no better contrast between the Lockean and Hobbesian implications of a state of nature than between Grimes and Chris. What is striking here is just how far Chris and his group have taken the Hobbesian war of all against all to heart. Consider these examples from his long-winded diatribes:

> CHRIS: [to Dale] There's an order to how things work now, and it's unfortunate for some ... the way things work.... But my friends and I didn't create this situation, we're just living with it. Just like you. We play the hand we're dealt. We don't want to hurt you. We didn't want to pull you away from your group—scare you like this.... These aren't things we want to do—They're things we have to do. So I promise you ... None of this is personal ... But at the end of the day, no matter how much we may detest this ugly business ... A man's gotta eat. (Issue #63)

> **CHRIS:** [to Grimes] Food is scarce. . . . If we weren't doing this, we'd starve to death. I hate to say it, but it's me or you . . . and whenever that's the situation—it's very easy to choose me. No offense. (Issue #65)

Grimes even asks Chris if they could be persuaded to reconsider:

> **GRIMES:** Just came to ask you this. Any amount of talking going to get you to back off? Will you stop coming after my people?
>
> **CHRIS:** In all honesty? Probably not.

With this second exchange, Locke would probably find vindication for the idea that predation, even in the state of nature, is necessarily a war against nature's law and against reason (*Second Treatise*, II, §8). Chris makes it explicit, upon direct questioning, that he and his group are beyond the persuasive force of reason. (Though if he had read Hobbes, he could assert that without a Sovereign to keep everyone in a state of awe, there was already a state of war of all against all, and thus there was nothing immoral in claiming ownership of other people.) Grimes, fortunately, has the upper hand over Chris and his group, and Chris finds his "it's me or you" confession to be the proverbial petard upon which he is hoisted.

It's not an accident that Chris attempts to convince Dale that he and his group are "just like you." Chris needs to convince himself that the world he inhabits is a war of all against all, where he can believe his actions are justifiable as the kind of thing (he thinks) Dale would have done in his shoes. To be sure, neither Hobbes nor any self-described Hobbesian *advocate* the path taken by Chris; nor would Chris's group's descent into savagery refute Hobbesianism by its ugly example. The Hobbesian state of nature, as a concept, is intended to provide a reason to avoid at all costs the collapse of even the most oppressive of governments.

Two ironies are suggested by Chris's example. First, Chris and his group have adopted the very "way of life" of the zombies themselves. They coped with the zombie apocalypse by blurring the distinction between human and zombie. Second, a powerful leviathan is no guarantee of safety from such savagery, as people have resorted to Chris's group's tactics under the most oppressive governments of the twentieth century. Cannibalism has been documented in the mass starvations of Maoist China, North Korea, and Soviet Russia, particularly in the Ukraine and amongst Gulag prisoners. In the case of the Ukrainian *holodomor*, cannibalism became so rampant that local officials distributed propaganda posters admonishing parents that "To eat your own children is a barbarian act."

As a foundation for rights, self-ownership was hardly any more secure in the hands of the Governor than from Chris's band of savages. The Governor, after all, was the head of a state, with all the accoutrements implied, down to an army at his command. Chris's band of savages wasn't "just like" Grimes and his group; if anything, Chris had far more in common with the Governor. Neither respected the self-ownership of other persons, viewing them as mere means to be exploited for their own ends. The only significant difference was scale: the Governor headed a much larger, better organized gang.

This is the point of Locke's divergence from Hobbes on social contract theory. When the state's behavior is as injurious toward life, liberty, and property as the ravages of the state of nature itself, then the state has violated the terms of the contract, and any continued rule is by violence alone rather than by any sense of moral legitimacy. Why else would a rational person consent to government if her plight were no different than if she stayed in the state of nature?

The fate dealt to Chris and his group illustrate the role that the right to punish plays in a Lockean state of nature. The absence of a state, for Locke, means that the right to punish still belongs to all persons. Having openly declared a state of war against the law of nature and reason, Chris and his group opened themselves to a punishment that would offer none of the protections the accused enjoy in a civil society.

Grimes and his group, as well as other "good" guys in *The Walking Dead*, follow an implicit morality grounded in self-ownership. Although they scavenge from abandoned properties for food and other goods, they never prey upon other survivors for their property, even where it may be expedient. Others who believe their might makes right, like the Governor and Chris's group, meet terrible ends. The Governor, for example, is mutilated and left for dead by Michonne in retaliation for her treatment at his hands, and ultimately meets his death at the hands of one of his own soldiers when she uncovers his deception. Had either the Governor or Chris left other survivors alone, neither would have met their respective fates. Even in the state of nature of *The Walking Dead*, violations of self-ownership prove self-destructive.

Hobbes insists that there are no rights without a mechanism of enforcement. While Locke disputes that such a mechanism is necessary to validate the principle of self-ownership or other property rights, the fates of Chris and the Governor illustrate a mechanism Hobbes overlooks: the right to punish. Predation in the state of nature carries its own terrible risks. Such behavior in civil society at least offers procedural protections for the accused. But in a state of nature, potential victims retain the right to punish. While less certain, it will be far less merciful. The chance that one's victims could retaliate in a brutal fashion may serve to deter many from predation, providing a validation of sorts for the rights to life, liberty, and property by Hobbes's own standard.

If there is a lesson that would-be violators of self-ownership may take from all of this, it's that they are safer in the hands of the Leviathan than in the single hand of Rick Grimes, and safest of all when they respect the rights of others.

8
Women in a Zombie Apocalypse

ASHLEY BARKMAN

Being eaten alive by the decomposing, limbs-missing, entrails-hanging undead is the last on anyone's list of preferred ways to kick the bucket. The method is painful, the company unpleasant and any glimmering hope of a glorious afterlife is significantly reduced; a bullet to the head is the merciful exit.

With such an unsavory death so ubiquitous and imminent in a zombie apocalypse, survival depends on those who volunteer to scavenge for food, water, shelter, medicine, and weaponry, along with protection from those outsiders who are not quite undead, yet have reduced themselves to their basest desires (murdering to steal property, practicing cannibalism, or raping the captured). What keeps most of the survivors who maintain some sort of moral compass enduring is the chance that there is a scientific cure to defeat this "disease" or that there is a community of people dwelling behind secured walls somewhere accessible, looming in the distance.

The Walking Dead maintains this motif as is customary of the zombie genre. And it encounters a dilemma abhorred in a post-Enlightenment and postmodern world: Is feminism relevant? Are men and women equal? Should they share in the same duties?

Feminists believe in equal opportunity for women along with gender equality that encompasses the social, economic, and political realms. The evolving face of feminism has also come to include the notion that sex and gender are mere social constructions. It is hard to deny that masculinity and femininity exist on a continuum: some men are more or less masculine than others, while some women are more or less feminine than others. *The Walking Dead* gives us Eugene who is not as masculine as Rick or Glenn, or Michonne, who is not as feminine as Amy or Lori (who both coincidentally die).

In opposition to some feminist notions, recent research has shown that men and women are different in design beyond their sexual organs. Evidence has shown that newborn boys and girls differ in their ability to hear sounds, that their brain develops in different regions at different stages, and that their visual system is arranged differently, which all translates into how they differ in the way they play and learn, how they express feelings, and their general nature: girls tend to be more emotional and collaborative than boys, while boys tend to be more competitive.[1] Likewise, Albert Bandura's Bobo Doll experiment from the early 1960s showed that boys are innately more aggressive than girls. Bandura conducted two experiments to study behavioral patterns associated with aggression. He hoped to prove that social learning theory could explain aggression as a learned behavior: observation leads to imitation. Seventy-two children, 36 girls and 36 boys, between the ages of 3 and 6 were exposed to an aggressive adult model who would hit an inflatable Bobo doll. Of those exposed to this aggression, the boys exhibited twice as many aggressive instances as the girls.

These biological differences partially explain the initial struggle between Rick and Shane and also the absence of female leaders—no woman asserts this role (nor desires to fill this role) in either the television series or the graphic novels.

Contrary to those feminists who maintain that gender is a "social construction" or that masculine and feminine are mere choices people make or are forced to make, I will take a different view—a more scientific view—in analyzing The Walking Dead. My approach is based on five assumptions.

First, men and women are not just biologically different (male and female), but also spiritually different: differences between masculine and feminine exist at conception.

Second, we can know this to be true naturally. For instance, men are generally stronger than women—a distinct gender difference. This isn't to say that there aren't men who are weaker

---

[1] Leonard Sax, *Why Gender Matters: What Parents and Teachers Need to Know about the Emerging Science of Sex Differences* (2005).

than women, but when discussing masculinity and femininity, we recognize that most often the masculine is physically stronger than the feminine.

Third, in this area—as in the case of other basic truths (such as $1 + 1 = 2$)—what is natural is also what we should act in accordance with, as the Stoics would say, or according to heaven as Confucius would say; it is moral to be natural and immoral not to be.

Fourth, masculinity has qualities that lend itself to leadership, whereas femininity lends itself to being led. Leaders necessarily need followers, and followers necessarily need leaders. This makes leaders powerless without their followers, and the followers ineffective without their leader. Without Rick, the survivors couldn't survive. Without the survivors, Rick wouldn't get very far.

Fifth, this is a general preference, not an absolute one. There will sometimes be exceptions. If two politicians were equally competent in knowledge, power, and experience, but one was a man and the other a woman, then because of this general requirement, we should always prefer the man. If, however, the woman is far superior to the man, then we need to think carefully about how to weigh all the relevant factors and values. There is room for disagreement here. On the whole, it is right that Rick remains the leader even though someone like Michonne is a better fighter and perhaps at times wiser. On the other hand, Ed or the Governor are instances of men who are masculine, but because they are deeply immoral, they should never lead; in such cases, it'd be easy to agree that a woman— one who has leadership qualities—should lead.

Laundering Feminism: Women and Domestic Duties

In *The Walking Dead* post-apocalyptic world, the roles of men and women are clearly demarcated by a feminist's nightmare: men "hunt" while women "gather"—traditional gender roles are almost organically claimed. Men assert roles of leadership, while the women remain behind fulfilling domestic chores—doing the laundry and watching the kids. In the TV series, Jacqui expresses her bitter frustration toward this seeming social regression, especially as Ed sits around smoking a cigarette supposedly on watch, and Shane goofs off with Carl in the groundwater trying to "catch frogs" in a rock quarry:

> **Jacqui:** Could someone explain to me how all the women ended up doing all the Hattie McDaniel Work?
>
> **Amy:** The world ended. Didn't you get the memo?
>
> **Carol:** It's just the way it is. ("Tell It to the Frogs")

While the other women seem complacent, Jacqui questions "the division of labor." Clearly this is not an attack on the four men who are on a rescue mission into walker-infested Atlanta, but rather on the two men who are not actively fulfilling their assigned duties as stoically as the Papal Swiss Guards.

The injustice here is apparent: women do work for which they receive little to no gratitude while men are given roles of leadership and authority just because they are men even if they are not taking their roles seriously.

Jacqui's annoyance is exacerbated while she, Andrea, Amy, and Carol scrub clothes on a washboard and hang laundry to dry and they muse about life-enhancing technology they miss, from Maytags to vibrators—technology which is often associated with liberated women. Ed overhears laughter and in a threateningly male-chauvinist manner orders the women to focus on their work: "This ain't no comedy club here." This context elicits greater sympathy for Jacqui's complaint.

However, when a similar conversation ensues in the graphic novel, the context elicits little sympathy. As Donna, Carol and Lori go off to do the laundry, Donna—a character already established as opinionated and judgmental—complains, "I just don't understand why we're the ones doing the laundry while they go off and hunt. When things get back to normal, I wonder if we'll still be allowed to vote" (*The Walking Dead*, Issue #3). In response, Lori appeals to practicality: "This isn't about women's rights. It's being about realistic and doing what needs to be done." Lori also points out that those who know how to use a gun are the ones doing the hunting, which is clearly a reasonable requirement.

Donna's frustration seems uncalled for, childish in its exaggeration. She implies that hunting is important, while doing the laundry is demeaning—but Lori is aware of the value of both. Laundry may not be dangerous or heroic, but "the possibility of clean smelling clothes" would be "a welcome change at this point." People need more than the bare essentials to maintain morale and some degree of optimism in a bleak apocalyptic world. Laundry may not save lives, but it does help distinguish the living from the dead, and it enhances one's sense of well-being, much like the luxuries people enjoy in a civilized world—a clean towel, a cup of coffee in the morning, a novel we just can't put down, music which lifts our spirits or echoes our sorrows: things we take for granted, but whose absence we would notice because humans are defined by more than food and shelter.

Both the feminism that defines certain duties as unimportant and demeaning for women (whether it be taking care of children or doing the laundry—ironically, the solution is often getting other *women* in a lower income bracket to do it instead) and the feminism that would rather fulfill quotas and have women wielding guns alongside men regardless of their ability to shoot, for the sake of absolute equality—just to make some women *feel* better—would quickly lead to a less efficient and less effective community which would in turn reduce not only quality of life, but chances of survival as well.

So, while Jacqui expresses appropriate annoyance at Ed and Shane, Donna's complaint is unmerited. Without her intending it to be, her comment is ironic since returning to the banality of daily routine in a pre-apocalyptic world is likely the wish of all who endure. To go beyond guarded and secured zones of seeming safety for whatever purpose—to rescue a friend, to scavenge for food or medicine or weaponry—may be thrilling, but in truth it is an undesirable situation to be in, especially if the odds are against your survival and death is guaranteed to be gory.

The men "go hunting" because it is necessary for survival, not because they derive some sort of thrill by risking their lives; one might be able to argue this is the case for *human* warfare (though even that is unlikely), but not in a zombie-riddled world where the existence of God, or the soul, or the promise of a glorious or a peaceful afterlife needs re-examination, a world where there is absolutely no certainty of anything, not even a tomorrow. In this situation, doing the laundry seems to be the privileged work: doing work which has minimal risk and being protected by individuals who are willing to risk their lives for the welfare of the community.

Girls in an All Boys' Club?

In both the TV series and graphic novels, Rick emerges as the leader with minimal opposition. On the TV show, four men—Rick, Glenn, T-Dog, and Daryl—attempt a rescue mission for Merle while the four women do laundry at the quarry, "protected" by Ed and Shane. In another community of survivors, Guillermo is portrayed as a leader, flanked by several other Hispanic men who defend their community of the weak and elderly.

Likewise, in *The Walking Dead* issue #24, the survivors form a committee to make decisions and four men are selected. Rick asks, "No women?" but it is revealed that the women agreed to this all-male leadership. Later, we learn of another community of survivors, Woodbury, which is also led by a man, Phillip, better known as the Governor. Women are not given positions of leadership in *The Walking Dead* universe. In the midst of chaos, leadership takes place almost organically: for better (Rick) or worse (Phillip), some people have what it takes, while others don't.

On the biological level, women generally have the disadvantage not only in their lack of testosterone-driven aggression, and overall physical strength and size, but in the vulnerability that comes with being female. A woman using her strength to brutally rape a man is unheard of, if it is even possible. But the temptation of a man to rape a woman is a popular motif in any zombie tale.

Furthermore, a woman has to deal with her ability to get pregnant—a reality which can limit a woman's chance at survival. These factors of the female sex do not exempt women from being good leaders, but in the chaotic state of a zombie apocalypse, where survival is only of the fittest, the necessary qualities of a leader comes to entail masculine traits that are generally lacking in their female counterpart. This is not to say that aggression or physical strength is the sole means by which one can become a leader, but it is a desirable trait when used appropriately. If the world hadn't come to an end, we have the luxury to give everyone a more equitable shot at leadership.

Similarly, if society hadn't met its demise, we might be more picky about the food we eat, and the water we drink. But, Rick and his peers don't have these luxuries.

There are moments where the established leadership is challenged, and the resolution involves grappling and punching. It is rare for women to instinctively transition into this mode of fighting, and to successfully hold down a man of equal or greater size with her bare hands seems improbable. On some occasions, men communicate and assert authority in different ways than women. Rick's leadership in the community is first established when he overtakes Merle by knocking him over the head with a pipe, handcuffing him to another pipe and calming him down before others get hurt. Rick calmly and clearly, with authority that comes from being a sheriff, states that racial conflicts and social problems do not exist anymore now that humans need to overcome walkers ("Guts").

A bigoted man like Merle is more likely to heed the authority of a physically strong man over a woman—and in situations like these, a woman would require extra time to establish her authority. But there is little time. In "Tell It to the Frogs," Rick explains to Daryl what happened to his brother Merle, Daryl attacks Rick, but Rick is able to shove him off. The authority of an individual who can be physically beaten in such a situation would quickly be challenged in the eyes of the audience. It would take time, and perhaps extremely clever strategizing to recover from that.

While Rick establishes himself as a leader in Atlanta, Shane maintains his authority on the campground. When Ed and Andrea's argument escalates into Carol being slapped by Ed, three women try to stop Ed, but to no avail. It is clear that Ed has no self-control and will likely hurt the other women as well. Fortunately, Shane intervenes and stops the violent Ed with physical force ("Tell it to the Frogs"). Similarly, when Jim becomes delirious and starts frightening the others by digging holes by their campsite, calm reason does not deter him from stopping and so Shane tackles him to the ground to stop him ("Vatos").

Research has shown that boys respond to physical forms of punishment (such as spanking—obviously spanking that is controlled and not excessive) in a positive manner, whereas girls do not (Sax, *Why Gender Matters*).

In a world where physical violence is limited or has been conquered, women may make successful leaders, but in *The Walking Dead*, where survival necessitates retaliatory or pre-emptive violence, women are less fitted for the role of leadership. It's highly unusual for women to assert their authority through physical strength or violence, especially directly administered. Gender is beyond social construction as can be observed in *The Walking Dead*: women and men are different in how they solve problems and assert authority.

Exceptional Women

There are exceptions to the rule. In both the TV series and the graphic novels, women are not excluded from dangerous missions—Andrea and Jacqui are scavenging alongside the men when they meet Rick, and in the graphic novels, two women are given abilities that would generally be ascribed to singular men: Andrea is the best sharpshooter and Michonne can wield a sword like no other. Women can fight, too.

Women not being cut out to be leaders in this zombie apocalypse in no way limits them from heroic feats or intentions or from bearing leader-like attributes of initiative and willingness to sacrifice themselves for the greater good. In a conversation with Shane and Dale, Lori insists that other survivors need to know what has become of Atlanta and is willing to risk her life if someone would give her a vehicle so she can "put signs up on 85 and warn people away from the city" ("Wildfire").

Lori seems to want to fulfill a moral obligation to society at large. She knows something that the wary traveler might not know and has an ethical duty to share that information. She does not want to commit the sin of omission. But, the general consensus seems to be that this is not a reasonable quest; everybody has moral obligations to his society, but at the risk of Lori's life (she already has duties as a wife and mother), the loss of a vehicle for the group, possible exposure of the group to walkers—what's at stake is far too great for the group to agree to her request.

With some of these factors in mind, Shane refuses, telling her they do not have the time, even though she is insistent. We've seen that Rick, for example, will take on extreme measures to fulfill a task he sees as important (like going back for Merle and the guns)—he does what his mind is set on. But, though Lori views her position as important, she takes no other measures than verbal insistence. She is moral, but she doesn't take forceful action like Rick who can't be stopped with words. However, Lori's character reveals that women are not without a voice or inner strength in *The Walking Dead*. For when the situation requires it, the women use shovels to fight the walkers alongside the two men, Shane and Dale, who have guns (*The Walking Dead*, issue #3).

Examples of women who use their physical skills to fight alongside the men are best illustrated in Andrea and Michonne. In the graphic novels, Andrea is often shown wielding a gun, and as the best sharpshooter, she is vital to the group's survival. She consistently fights alongside the men and there is no hesitance or question about her ability to perform. She knows she is skilled, and willingly applies her skill as a sharpshooter to protect as is required of her. She knows this is her primary duty and does it without arrogance or sense of entitlement. And furthermore, regardless of gender, Rick's goal near the beginning of the story is to ascertain guns for all the individuals in his camp because he realizes the gravity of their situation, and the need for everyone to fend for him or herself should the time come.

And lastly, Michonne is a mysteriously extraordinary woman overcoming tremendously difficult circumstances. She is a skilled swordsman who has survived on her own before she joins Rick's group. With her boyfriend and his best friend, who have both become walkers, shackled and chained, she pulls them along her journey to The Prison to deter the other walkers. Her spirit is never broken, even at the hands of Phillip who chains her up and repeatedly brutalizes and rapes her for the location of The Prison. She even defeats all the participants in Phillip's gladiatorial fights, and later has her vengeance on Phillip.

Michonne's story remains mysterious, her physical abilities above that of the men. She has the strength, but is mostly portrayed as a quiet loner type. However, her presence in the story reveals that a woman is not limited to doing domestic chores. If a woman has the ability to partake in physical battles with walkers and criminals, she is not exempt from fighting alongside the men. In the Alexandria Safe-Zone, she is assigned duties of maintaining order equal to that of Rick. And she is shown to go out of her way to protect Rick, out of deep respect. Rick unquestionably remains the leader of the survivors, but this does no disservice to the role of women in *The Walking Dead*. This doesn't mean he always makes the right decisions—he is human after all.

The Feminist Apocalypse

In our world, equal opportunity for men and women in most vocations is just. However, *The Walking Dead* attempts to portray real people under extraordinary circumstances. In a zombie apocalypse, it is most appropriate that leadership remain in the hands of good men. Feminism, which argues that gender is a social construction and thus women should be given the same roles and duties as men is not only unrealistic, but also ineffective and inefficient. Everybody cannot have the same role and expect a community to function. All the various roles become important parts of one body with the common goal of survival and sanity.

These considerations should trump feminism. Feminism should not thrust leadership positions upon people who do not have the ability to optimally fulfill such roles. The zombie apocalypse opens our eyes to what feminists misconceive as a "gruesome" reality: men and women are not only different, they are not equals, and being equals is not the be-all and end-all of life—getting away from the flesh-eating undead, preferably with the ones you love, is. Political correctness shouldn't rear its haughty head in life-or-death situations.

I'll take the telekinetically inclined superhero Alice Abernathy as my protectress in an Umbrella Corporation—ruled world, but in the much more plausible zombie apocalypse of Kirkman's creation, give me Rick Grimes.

9
Dead ~~Man's~~ Party

DANEE PYE AND PETER PADRAIC O'SULLIVAN

Popular culture has trained us for the zombie apocalypse: Forget the iPod; forget the laptop; bring food, water and as many guns as you can find. But in the event of a zombie emergency, nobody ever tells you to leave the cultural baggage behind. An apocalyptic event like the one in *The Walking Dead* is the perfect opportunity for a fresh start, particularly if you weren't on the top of social ladder to begin with. Better yet, it's a chance to destroy the ladder completely—a chance for true equality.

The walkers get it (although you probably shouldn't ask them to expound on it). The only remnants from their old lives are the clothes on their backs, and even those will only last so long. In the land of the living, however, the survivors can't seem to break the shackles of their previous roles, and within the universe of *The Walking Dead*, men lead and women follow. In the television series these tendencies differ slightly from the comic books, but taken in combination the show and the comics demonstrate that gender is a social construct, that it can be constructed differently, and that in clinging to outmoded ideas of gender roles the survivors increase the likelihood of their falling prey to the ravenous walkers.

Zombies in Drag

In discussing how *The Walking Dead* deals with gender it's important to understand the difference between the terms "sex" and "gender," and in general, zombies are a pretty great example of this distinction. The walkers are genderless. The only potential gender distinctions are the clothes they were wearing when they died, and (presumably) their genitalia. Zombies do have the trappings of biological sex, but they don't exhibit masculine or feminine behaviors that would distinguish male zombies from female zombies. Within their own "culture" they do not differ in terms of behavior, leadership, social roles, or even strength. In other words, they may be externally male or female, but they don't act masculine or feminine. Because they reproduce asexually, they have no need to identify each other by either sexual or gender roles—they only need to distinguish themselves from human beings. And even in this role, they don't perform differently; they all just want to eat your face regardless of their (or your) sex.

Because they are differently sexed, but have no clear gender roles, the "geeks," as Glenn calls them, demonstrate philosopher Judith Butler's claim that gender is *performative*; it is something one *does*—not something one *is*. While the very first scene of the show seems to contradict this distinction, it in fact sets up the social dissonance inherent in the new zombie order. The series begins with a dazed Rick, encountering what appears to be a lost little girl. He calls out to her repeatedly and when she finally turns around she is (of course) actually a walker. This creates a troubling moment where we, along with Rick, cannot decide if he should kill her. Is she a monster? A little girl? Both?

According to Butler, this "troubling" is a result of our constructions coming "undone." Butler often uses drag queens as examples of "undoing" or "troubling" gender, because they create a problem with our everyday understanding of gender. Zombies, like drag queens, "trouble gender." They make us do a mental double-take because of the contrast between perceived biological sex and their gender performances. But, even little girl "geeks" won't hold onto any of these cultural relics for long, primarily because these concepts have little to do with eating brains. As time goes by the walkers' clothing will tatter and fall away; their flesh will rot (assuming that bacteria still trump zombies as the top of the food chain); and any residual traces of gender and sex will vanish completely.

Cultural Baggage Flies Free

The survivors also carry cultural reminders with them, but theirs are both more obvious and social constructions that (unlike decaying flesh) can be revived. In "Days Gone Bye," we find that society as we know it has ceased to exist, but by the second episode, "Guts," it is clear that as the Atlanta camp attempts to rebuild, old gender assumptions have started to creep in. In this same episode Amy says, "The world ended, didn't you get the memo?" but obviously this isn't quite the case. It's not as if the characters are working from a clean slate, with no memory of their former selves. They all bring cultural baggage along with them. This encumbrance leaves them not only weighted by these assumptions, but also partially blind to their nascent freedom from them. When you're being chased by zombies, it should go without saying that weighted down and blind are not your best options.

All of the characters operated within a patriarchal society prior to the outbreak, so it's no surprise that they begin to recreate patriarchal norms as they rebuild new societies. As former cops, Rick and Shane reclaim roles of authority. As Carol scrubs laundry on an old washboard she complains that it "ain't half as good as my old Maytag back home." (Isn't it nice to see product placement is going to survive the apocalypse?) It may seem as though the roles are innate, but it is equally possible that they are just so used to thinking of themselves this way that they cannot conceive of other possibilities. In other words, they just revert to old habits. Furthermore, given the psychic trauma these characters have suffered, a certain amount of conservatism is both expected and maybe even necessary for coping with a new, unwanted social order. When faced with uncertainty and events beyond their control, human beings find comfort in the familiar.

According to Butler, we do this on a cultural level too. Our tendency is to think of gender as fixed and binary. This mistake can be explained by the related concepts of the *primitive clan* and *the incest taboo*. Think of a primitive clan of people. Assuming that they would want to avoid incest, there would be a need to procreate with the members of another clan. However, to keep the initial clan intact, only the women would be exchanged. In such a clan, identity is produced through a continuous male blood-line created by the exchange of women. The women then become the protected commodity, while the men become the protectors. Through procreation these roles are reproduced, as the child identifies with either the mother (protected) or the father (protector) and assumes the corresponding cultural identity as masculine or feminine.

Shane's group, living in the woods, is about as primitive as a clan can get in terms of social constructs. The men attempt to protect their women, and kinships form. The clearest example of this is when Shane steps in to replace Rick as both father to Carl and mate to Lori. Similarly, Dale forms a bond with Amy and Andrea. In the comics Dale and Andrea's relationship is explicitly sexual, whereas in the show his role is ambiguously paternal, but in either case a protector/protected bond is formed. Because the women in the clan are viewed as needing male protection, the gender roles privilege the men. They are the hunters, doctors, and leaders, while the women do the laundry, nurse the sick, and care for the children. And, these roles are reinforced through repeated performances.

In "Tell It to the Frogs" there is a scene in which Lori is cutting Carl's hair (which is in itself a way of maintaining gender differences). While she cuts, Shane talks to Carl about being manly and offers to teach him to catch frogs. Carl, who is unsure about this, looks to Lori, who responds, "I'm a girl, you talk to him." This is a perfect example of how young children are encouraged to perform either like a man or like a woman. They often recognize who they "ought" to act like, but even when they don't they are given subtle (and sometimes not so subtle) clues about whom they should identify with. In this case, Lori makes it clear that Shane is a more "appropriate" role model for Carl than she is. After all, where else is Carl supposed to learn about cooties?

These learned roles are also reinforced through negative consequences for stepping outside of socially accepted roles. For instance, when Andrea tells Ed that if he has complaints about the laundry he can do it himself, he tells her, "Ain't my job." He also calls her an "uppity smart-mouth bitch" and warns her, that just because she has a college education doesn't mean he can't knock her on her ass. As he reminds her, "You don't tell me what. I tell you what." However, even the men are constrained by previous social norms, and when Ed takes his misogyny too far, he is put in his place by Shane, whose intervention merely serves to reinforce the protector/protected binary.

Making a New Start

Throughout the series, even within Shane's extremely patriarchal group-structure, there are clues that gender is learned, and can be learned differently, and these clues are the series's saving graces. The primitive clan and kinship provide the basis for our cultural fantasy of gender as biologically given, and *The Walking Dead* includes clear examples of the repetition of this fantasy. However, there are also counter-examples throughout the series that point to the ways in which gender roles can be constructed differently. In "Tell It to the Frogs" Andrea and Amy go fishing and discuss how their father taught them the practice. They come back with plenty of fish in hand, and Morales praises them by saying, "Ladies, because of you my children will eat tonight!" In this case, the women are performing the traditionally masculine role of hunting and providing food. This scene, combined with the knowledge that their father taught them to fish, is a subtle nod to the notion that activities like hunting and fishing are learned activities that can be taught to both boys and girls. Impressed by their catch, Carl asks the women to teach him how to fish, another suggestion that gender identifications are not ingrained. That Carl lacks the preponderance of gender baggage that most of the adults have makes this question, at least to him, all the more natural (and perhaps he'll never get to the cooties stage of thinking).

"Vatos" provides multiple examples of how cultural roles, including gender norms, can be learned differently. In this episode, Glenn is taken hostage by what appears to be a group of Latino gangsters. As Rick and Guillermo, who runs the "vato" camp, negotiate Glenn's return, Guillermo asks, "Who's that dude to you anyway? You don't look related?" Rick responds, "He's one of our group. More or less." Here Rick alludes to the fact that new clans and kinships are forming, and they are not necessarily based on anything from the pre-apocalyptic world.

Guillermo's group is also an interesting case of the creation of new cultural norms. Although at first appearance, he seems to be a ruthless dictator and the epitome of machismo, the actual structure of his camp is much more complex. It's true that Guillermo is calling the shots, but the group's main priority is to protect and care for the elderly patients who were left to die. Because of this, there is a deep reverence for the elderly, regardless of gender, and even Guillermo submits to the requests of one of the elderly women when she interrupts his standoff with Rick. This demonstrates a more complicated performance of gender roles than first appearance would suggest. In fact, these "vatos" resist all forms of stereotyping, despite their outer appearances. The term *vato* is itself Spanish slang meaning man or dude, and can imply an almost hyper-masculinity, yet Guillermo, pre-apocalypse, was a custodian, and Felipe, a nurse, a once traditional feminine role. While there's a certain amount of gender-role reinforcement with their protector statuses, these two play much deeper roles as both caretakers and caregivers. There is almost a sense, after the revelation of their true roles, that they're both vaguely uncomfortable with the hyper-masculine, or vato persona they have had to adopt. But sometimes you have to adopt and adapt as the world's falling apart.

Another pivotal moment is when the Atlanta camp is attacked by a group of walkers. Many of the men (and guns) were in the city on a mission to retrieve Merle, so the camp was particularly vulnerable. Because they lack the weapons needed to defend themselves, there are many casualties. The most notable loss is Amy. Knowing time is short, the men are eager to do what's necessary to keep her from becoming a walker (read: shoot her in the head). Andrea, on the other hand, won't let anyone near her dead sister. As the group begins to get more and more anxious, Shane tells them he'll "handle it" (again: shoot her in the head) but when he approaches the women Andrea puts her gun to his head and warns, "I know how the safety works." Here she alludes to an earlier episode where Rick taught her how to take the safety off a gun her father gave her.

A Freudian might say that her father passed on the phallus to her, and she didn't instinctively know how to use it, but Rick's (the man's) instruction alleviated that shortcoming. Of course, sometimes a gun is just a gun, but any way you want to look at it this contradicts the group's tacit assumption that the men are innately better equipped to handle the guns; in some ways the two exchanges belie the fact that guns are tools, human made, and that once upon a time Rick and Shane have probably both been trained in their proper use. In one brief moment, Andrea shows that not only can women learn to use guns, but the guns are where the true power lies.

Old Habits Die Hard

Because guns represent power, it's disappointing but not surprising that in the first episode of Season Two, "What Lies Ahead," the men take Andrea's gun away from her. In the previous episode, Andrea decides to stay in the CDC and die in the explosion, but Dale won't leave without her. At the last moment, she agrees to leave but only in order to save Dale. Dale assumes she'll be grateful that he convinced her to leave, but later she says, "What did you expect, I'd have some epiphany? Some life-affirming catharsis?"

Since she's deemed unstable, Dale and Shane agree that she should not possess a firearm. Although the men decide to take the gun in order to protect her from herself, their actions can be read as gendered. There aren't any checks on the mental stability of the men in the group, and considering his violent temper, they should be equally concerned about Daryl walking around with a crossbow. One might argue that the reason the men take Andrea's gun but do not take Daryl's crossbow has to do with sexual dimorphism, or the idea that men are naturally stronger than women. This can also be seen as a justification for men being natural protectors and women needing their protection. While it may true that generic men as a population are stronger than generic women as a population, this does not mean that a man is automatically stronger than a woman (for instance, we're willing to bet that Andrea could kick Glenn's butt in a fight). Still, the group seems to operate under this assumption. Andrea has no problem taking down a walker, but it doesn't seem to occur to her to use physical means to get her gun back. So, perhaps the reason they take her weapon but don't take Darryl's is due to an underlying assumption that men are always naturally more powerful than the women. Even if the assumption isn't always true, social conditioning reinforces this notion, and blind adherence to this conditioning has unfortunate consequences for both sexes.

In fighting a genderless enemy, old habits put the entire group at risk. The walkers are basically humans stripped away of the social contract. They are devoid of ego and super-ego, and even of hatred and fear. Consequently, they're worried much more about dining on brains and much less about what women can or can't do. Because the geeks don't discriminate, the living women are at just as great a risk as the men, and without guns, the risk is even greater. We see this in "What Lies Ahead" when Andrea is alone in the RV, cleaning her gun, and she can't get it back together in time to use it on a walker. Fortunately Dale comes to her rescue by dropping a screwdriver down through the vent. Without his help she would have surely died. But, it isn't only the women who are harmed by outdated gender assumptions. In the comic, Andrea not only recognizes the power of guns, but also masters them to become the best shot in the group. She is a zombie-age Annie Oakley, who surpasses her male cohorts. By depriving her of a weapon, the group deprives itself of one of its best defenses.

Checking the Baggage

The Walking Dead does contain moments which contradict a natural theory of gender and, therefore, could be seen as containing a pro-feminist message by inviting viewers to question our assumptions about gender. As pragmatist philosopher Richard Rorty puts it, "assumptions become visible as assumptions only if we can make the contradictories of those assumptions sound plausible," and insofar as feminists would like to create new societal norms by making what was once perceived as natural seem unnatural, *The Walking Dead* may help change perceptions for the better. Unfortunately, the televised version only hints at such a message.

Although *The Walking Dead* series raises interesting questions about the constructed nature of gender roles as we know them, the show does little to confront traditional conceptions. The comic is better at this, but there are already several major divergences of character and plot between the television series and the comic. As Season Two begins, it seems that the survivors will cling to what they know.

If they're going to make it, they need to view the event as a chance to make a new start, and they have to let go of old habits. So far, the show gives us little hope that they will do so. Too often, the characters (and the writers) defer to unimaginative performances of gender and, even with their mindless consumption, the zombies almost come across as more enlightened when it comes to gender relations.

On the survivor's side, the lack of movement toward a new understanding of gender, even one that is crucial to their continued survival, is itself understandable, if not entirely forgivable. They are again trapped in the comfortable Snuggie of familiar roles and familiar assumptions, even when the premises for those assumptions prove to be wholly false and a bit itchy. What the survivors and the writers fail to grasp is that when it comes to the zombies, "They are us." For all of their unthinking ravenousness, zombies are a reflection in a clouded mirror of humanity, a rich metaphor for very human conditions.

Because these zombies represent the ultimate other (and what do we fear in the other more than those things we deny in ourselves?), "There can be no more divisions among the living" (George A. Romero, *Dawn of the Dead*). Through the introduction of this extreme other, the rest of humanity should be unified, and in some ways they are. In the penultimate episode of Season One, "Wildfire," the group must decide how to deal with the dead, which includes both walkers and human bodies. As Darryl and Morales drag a body toward the fire, Glenn stops them, yelling, "We don't burn our people! We bury them." By moving all significant division to that between the living and the dead, the walkers spotlight the rather arbitrary and artificial nature of the divisions that the living create amongst themselves. However, if success requires a unified humanity, it calls for the erasure of all human divisions. This holds especially for gender divisions. The walkers don't have time for such divisions; they're after living flesh. The survivors have a choice to make: to retreat into patriarchal power structures and ensure their continued destruction, or embrace this opportunity to shed themselves of the cultural baggage and the dangerous *isms* of yesteryear. While this seems like a simple choice, it is actually one that requires quite a bit of social deprogramming.

If we accept the premise that zombies are a metaphor for the human condition, a foggy, brain-eating mirror in which we see ourselves (and occasionally check for skin blemishes), then how the survivors respond to a world of zombies should be an even clearer reflection of both how we see ourselves and how we wish to be. The survivors, for the most part, embrace the patriarchal assumptions of their pre-apocalypse lives, not because of any qualities inherent in such a system, not because of any qualities inherent in the different sexes, but because a rebooting of the world neither reboots the people left in the world, nor reboots the audience. The world was hit by the blue screen of death, but the users saved all of their bad data first. As they are, the survivors cling as tightly to their assumptions as they do to their guns; as an audience, we hope against hope that the survivors begin to shed the fetters of patriarchy, which have thus far proven to be more detriment than boon.

The survivors' inability to re-imagine gender has dangerous consequences, and this failure of imagination could ultimately be their downfall. If they truly want to make a new start, they should bring food, water, and guns, but leave their cultural baggage behind. This baggage merely slows them down when the shambling horde scratches at their heels. Human beings are adaptable, and the survivors may, indeed, learn to relinquish the more destructive of their impulses. As an audience, we certainly hope so. A (living) leg up would not be amiss for the survivors: Max Brooks, perhaps it's time to consult with Judith Butler and release a new edition of *The Zombie Survival Guide*.

Miles Behind

10
Better Off Undead

RACHEL ROBISON-GREENE

In the first episode of AMC's *The Walking Dead*, police officer Rick Grimes enters an idyllic Victorian farm home in Georgia. A wicked stench leads him to the living room where a man and his wife lie dead on their recliners, their brains splattered all across the room. All available evidence points to murder-suicide. Sprawled on the wall across from their decomposing bodies are the words "GOD FORGIVE US." This disturbing image is one of many in the first episode of the series alone that points to the desperation of those left behind—the living that must almost inevitably serve as food for the undead during the zombie apocalypse.

I know that I for one (and I am sure that many others who watch the show are in the same boat) find myself wondering what I would do under similar circumstances. All of the available options are terrifying. I know that my chances of surviving would be pretty slim. But it isn't even the thought of a walker gnawing on my skull that unsettles me the most. It's what comes next. Some things are worse than death. Being a walker really screws with a person's value system. One minute, you're a person with goals and projects you take to be important. You have people that you love. You have TV shows that you never miss. One bite later, it's all over. You no longer care about growing the best garden on the block or about getting that big promotion at work. You would sooner dine on your five-year-old's leg than teach him how to ride a bike. All you care about is consuming human flesh. And even that isn't fundamentally valuable to you. You just feel an irresistible urge to do it.

Not all futures are desirable. There are some ways in which we view ourselves now, some projects that we take to be so important, some causes that we commit ourselves to so passionately that we would sooner die than give them up. And most of us would rather die than live a life where nothing is fundamentally valuable at all, right?

Apocalypse Now

Albert Camus claims that there is "only one truly philosophical question and that is suicide." Camus is interested in what our reaction should be to a life without fundamental meaning. Zombie life seems like a perfect model for this kind of existence. Zombies' lives are tedious. They spend all day every day pursuing the same goal. And it will never end. As long as they (almost) live, zombies are doomed to an eternity filled with the pursuit of flesh to eat.

As meaningless as this life may seem, it is not really the zombie's life that provides the best model for what Camus is concerned with. Zombies are actually really a lot more like digger wasps. Consider a set of experiments conducted by researchers. Digger wasps look for vacant holes in which to hide their eggs. Before they bring the eggs into the hole, they first check to see if the original owner or any other dangerous customer inhabits it. They crawl inside. While they are checking out the situation, scientists move the eggs the digger wasp left behind over just a bit. If the wasp comes out and her eggs are not right where she left them, she will start the whole process all over again and will continue for as long at the scientists choose to be malicious.

The wasp's situation is tedious and lacks meaning, much like the zombie's. But these kinds of lives are not of particular interest to Camus because these creatures lack the capacity that, were they to have it, would make their existence particularly agonizing. These creatures lack the capacity for conscious self-reflection. As Camus says, "Consciousness poisons the experience."

A gloomy fact about self-reflective creatures is that they are capable of recognizing what Camus call "absurdity." Camus defines absurdity as "the confrontation between the longings of humans and an indifferent universe." In *The Walking Dead* universe, the characters whose lives are truly absurd—who are capable of recognizing that their lives lack fundamental meaning or value—are the living human survivors. They are conscious of the fact that the universe defies the expectations that they have of it. They desire to see their lost loved ones again. Morgan Jones and his son Duane, whom Rick befriends in the first episode and issue of the series, want Jenny, the wife and mother that they knew, back. They long to live as a family as they did before. Andrea and Amy want to go fishing with their father again, or to celebrate birthdays the way they once did. Everyone would just want the dead to stop walking. But the universe does not comply. Jenny is a walker and isn't coming back. Andrea and Amy may never get to Florida to see if their father's still alive, let alone fish with him again. And, as we find out in "Wildfire," Amy won't be celebrating any more birthdays.

Camus describes a similar sort of doomsday situation in his novel *The Plague*. Much like in *The Walking Dead*, a group of citizens are thrown without warning into a horrific situation that no one could have predicted. The citizens in the town of Oran are suddenly struck by the plague and their lives change entirely. People begin to die, but officials are hesitant to believe local doctors who suspect an outbreak of plague. At first, the response to the outbreak is optimistic, even hopeful, authorities and citizens believe it will end as quickly as it began.

Like the characters in The Walking Dead, the citizens of Oran believe that there must be someone out there who will save them, that their loved ones, their families, will certainly survive the outbreak because something like this just couldn't happen to *them*. And, also like the survivors in *The Walking Dead*, they are ultimately proven wrong. In *The Plague* a serum arrives, but it is not nearly enough to treat everyone, and ultimately, it doesn't even work on this strain of plague. The city's gates are locked. No one can come in or go out. The only means of communication is telegram. Citizens are isolated and alone, left to fend for themselves.

Much like zombification, the plague is dehumanizing. People are forced to treat their loved ones as sources of possible contagion. Andrea is forced to do the same thing when she must shoot her walker sister. She must come to terms with the fact that the person she sees is no longer the sister she loved, but someone she must kill in order to save the others.

While Andrea waits to see Amy's eyes open for the last time, the other members of the community are off chopping up the remains of the walker attackers. These creatures were recently human beings as well, but the last bit of sympathy for them died with the last person to remember them the way they used to be.

Burials in Oran are strictly supervised. Eventually, bodies are cremated or dumped into mass graves. The death rate is too fast to keep up with. This kind of body disposal is also dehumanizing, as if each individual person is not worthy of respect and remembrance. As if each death is insignificant. *The Walking Dead* brings this point home powerfully in the scene early in the series when Rick Grimes goes out behind the hospital and encounters rows and rows of bodies. These bodies once belonged to people's mothers, fathers, friends, and neighbors. Now all they are to anyone are rotting walker corpses. The situation is absurd because the indifferent universe doesn't care who these people were.

Apocalypse-type situations are perfect tools for bringing the absurd into focus. These extreme cases make us think about our existence in a new way. They force us to consider how powerless we are in the face of the (perhaps bizarre) forces of the universe. No one knows what caused the plague. The citizens of Oran desire to at least understand what is destroying their community. The world is not obliging. Anyone can fall victim to the plague, it does not care about our demands for justice. Camus illustrates this with a particularly chilling death scene. A small boy, one of the children of an important city official starts to show the symptoms and the main characters watch his condition quickly worsen. This death exemplifies the indifference of the universe. Camus describe the death:

> In the small face, rigid as a mask of grayish clay, slowly the lips parted and from them rose a large, incessant scream, hardly varying with his respiration, and filling the ward with a fierce, indignant protest, so little childish that it seemed like a collective voice issuing from all the sufferers there. (Albert Camus, *The Plague*)

The Walking Dead uses a similar mechanism to illustrate this point. In the first scene of the TV series, Rick carefully walks through a lot filled with abandoned cars. From the back, we see a young blonde girl who looks to be around six or seven years old. She bends down to retrieve a tattered teddy bear from the ground. Rick calls out to her and, in typical horror-movie style, she turns around to reveal herself as a walker, blood dripping from her fetid jaw. No one is immune, not even a cute little girl.

Though these cases are excellent tools for bringing the absurd into focus, Camus is not concerned with zombies, nor is he really concerned about the plague. These tools are meant to highlight something about *our* day-to-day lives— zombie-ridden or not, *our lives are absurd*. We make demands on the universe that it simply doesn't (and can't) care about. We want justice out of the world. We want the guilty punished. We want the innocent to be spared suffering. But that isn't the way the world works.

We work hard on our projects. We want to be respected, or perhaps even just remembered fondly. If we're lucky, someone might remember our name in two hundred years' time. But conscious creatures will only live on this planet for so long and ultimately there will be no one left to remember. Though we strive to feel significant, at the end of the day we aren't.

Most of us don't want to die. We don't want our loved ones to die. Personally, the very idea terrifies me. Every time it pops up, I try to push it to the back of my mind as fast as possible. But no matter how much we may want to live forever with our loved ones, the universe is not accommodating.

This is why Camus thinks that the only real philosophical question is suicide. Once we recognize that our live are absurd, do we really have any other choice? Really, what is there to live for if life is ultimately meaningless and we are all insignificant?

There are three possible responses available to us. The first two are what we might call escapist strategies. The first is to go ahead and commit suicide. This is the approach that Jacqui and CDC researcher Dr. Edwin Jenner take. When the CDC is about to self-destruct and they are forced to make a decision between living and dying in an absurd world, they choose death. This is a legitimate option. But Camus doesn't think it's our only option.

Another escapist strategy is to simply pretend that life is not absurd. This might involve a response much like mine when I think of my own death or the death of my loved ones—

simply push it to the back of your mind. The problem with this response is that it is inauthentic. It involves self-deception. If you are all right with that, fine, but if not, Camus has another suggestion for you.

Another escapist strategy, according to Camus, is the appeal to religion. Religion helps us to discount the source of absurdity as genuine. We are not insignificant—we're part of some greater plan created by God, how much more significant can you get? Moreover, we're not really going to die, at least, not in the depressing way. When earthly life is over, if we live right, we have another life to look forward to in heaven. We do not have to despair over the injustices in the world; God will make them all right in heaven. The guilty will be punished and the innocent who suffered will be rewarded. Again, if this response works for you, more power to you. But many writer on this issue, Camus included, find this response to be inauthentic as well. Camus calls it philosophical suicide.

The futility of escapist strategies is well illustrated by these apocalyptic metaphors. Consider the citizens of Oran. For them, there is no escape. Camus says:

> Always a moment came when we had to face the fact that no trains were coming in. And then we realized that the separation was destined to continue, we had no choice but to come to terms with the days ahead. In short, we returned to our prison-house, we had nothing left us but the past, and even if some were tempted to live in the future, they had speedily to abandon the idea anyhow, as soon as could be, once they felt the wounds that the imagination inflicts on those who yield themselves to it.

Similarly, the survivors in *The Walking Dead* can't escape their situation. They can't close their eyes and pretend that walkers aren't taking over. They must respond to the absurdity of their situation head-on.

Holding Out for a Hero

Camus offers a solution that preserves authenticity. He suggests that we become what he calls "absurd heroes." His primary model for the absurd hero is the character Sisyphus from Greek mythology. Sisyphus is damned by the Gods to push a boulder to the top of a high mountain, only to have it roll back down again. Once it does, he must start over and he must do this for eternity. This task is, on its face, tedious and meaningless. By dooming Sisyphus to this fate, they are dooming him to an eternity of absurdity. But Sisyphus rebels. He becomes an absurd hero by making his response to absurdity his own. A person can only become an absurd hero if they live in full recognition of the absurd. The response that Sisyphus has when he watches the rock roll back down the hill is crucial. Camus says:

> It is during this return, that pause, that Sisyphus interests me. A face that toils so close to stones is already stone itself! I see that man going back down with a heavy yet measured step toward the torment of which he will never know the end. That hour like a breathing-space which returns as surely as his suffering, that is the hour of his consciousness. At each of those moments when he leaves the heights and gradually sinks toward the lairs of the gods, he is superior to his fate. He is stronger than his rock. (*The Myth of Sisyphus*)

There are many ways that we can interpret Sisyphus's response. The first is that he learns to love his rock and his task. He memorizes each groove in the rock, each bump in the road. He devotes himself fully to his responsibility, no matter how mundane. Similarly, we can interpret Sisyphus as taking each success as a victory that he celebrates each time he gets to the top of the hill.

However, in order to be absurd heroes, we don't have to be content with our plight. One reaction is as good as another, so long as we make that reaction our own. Another way of interpreting Sisyphus's response is that he is shaking his fist at the gods. He isn't going to let their punishment break him and he will never stop being angry with them, and there is no fate that can't be triumphed by scorn says Camus. Because Sisyphus battles absurdity head on, it doesn't matter what form his response takes. He is authentic.

Camus also presents us with several examples of absurd heroes in *The Plague*. For example, Dr. Bernard Rieux is a doctor who spends the duration of the story attempting to fight the plague. He makes the decision to do so even though he recognizes that this is a fight he may never win. Jean Tarrou is a friend of Rieux who helps fight the Plague and meticulously records the events that transpire, though perhaps none may survive to read what he has written. The most entertaining example of an absurd hero in *The Plague* has to be Joseph Grand, a municipal clerk who aspires to write a book, though he never gets past the first sentence. He aspires to make that one sentence perfect (though this is unlikely to happen, given that he is not a very talented writer.)

The Walking Dead provides us with examples of absurd heroes who are as powerful as any that Camus provides. The living survivors are unquestionably abandoned in a world that is absurd. Not only are they faced with the future of meaninglessness presented by the likelihood of turning into walkers themselves, but all of the things that were previously valuable to them are now worthless. Take the scene where Rick and Andrea are in the jewelry section of an abandoned department store. Andrea glances longingly at a necklace with a mermaid on it that he is sure that her sister would love to receive for her upcoming birthday. Sheriff deputy Rick Grimes advises her to take it. After all, does it really matter anymore? The very person who would have been responsible for enforcing the law is now advising someone to break it.

By making their response to the absurdity of their situation their own, the characters in *The Walking Dead* are absurd heroes. Like Dr. Rieux in the face of the plague, Rick continues to look for solutions to the problem—for some ray of hope. Even though he faces impossible odds, he continues to believe that his family is still alive and goes looking for them. He goes to Atlanta and survives several brushes with death there. Though it would seem that redneck Merle is almost certainly dead up on the roof, Rick insists on going back for him. When Jim is bitten by a walker and needs immediate medical attention, Rick convinces the others to go and seek help at the CDC rather than stay at camp and wait to die. Despite the desperation and meaninglessness of this situation, Rick insists on retaining his moral compass, though he likely finds his value scheme much changed.

Shane also finds that his value scheme has changed. The first scene in the series gives the impression that he's sort of a misogynistic jerk. The very first thing we hear him do is make generalizations about women and how they can never remember to turn off the lights. But after the walkers take over and Shane starts a relationship with Lori, he turns into a family man whose main goal is to take care of Lori and Carl. This is his main focus even after Rick comes back and is often angry with Rick for not making the protection of his family more of a priority.

Like Sisyphus and the absurd heroes from *The Plague*, many of the characters embrace some sort of task that gives their lives some value for them. These goals are quite varied. In "Vatos," we meet another group of survivors whose main consideration is to take care of the elderly who were left behind at a nursing home. Not all responses to the absurdity are as warm hearted toward others. We get the distinct impression that Merle has a shoot first ask questions later philosophy and is primarily considered with self- preservation. For Camus, this response to absurdity is okay as well, so long as you fully embrace it in full view of the absurd.

Like the citizens of Oran in Camus's *The Plague*, the survivors of the zombie apocalypse are all experiencing absurdity together, and so are we. One positive thing about living absurd lives then, is that it contributes to the sense of solidarity we feel because we all experience it together.

Dale is one character who comes to value this sense of solidarity. This explains why he gets so angry with Andrea. Her grief about the death of her sister causes her to consider staying at the CDC to wait for the imminent explosion. He tells her, "If you are staying I stay too. He's right; we know what is waiting for us out there. I don't want to face it alone. You don't get to do that, come into somebody's life, make them care, and then just check out. I'm staying. The matter is settled" ("TS-19"). This is enough to get Andrea to leave the facility too. All they have is one another.

Isn't It Ironic?

You might find yourself dissatisfied with Camus's solution. One reason for this reaction is that it really seems like anything goes. So long as we make our response our own, we can commit ourselves to any project we choose, even one that may seem to justify bad actions.

You might also think that Camus is wrong about the source of absurdity. This is the approach that Thomas Nagel takes. He claims that it cannot be our insignificance that makes life absurd. After all, were we to live forever, our lives would be infinitely absurd. It cannot be our size in relation to the universe; our lives would be just as absurd if we were larger. Instead, Nagel focuses on the fact that we're the kinds of creatures that are capable of taking two different kinds of perspectives: the objective perspective and the subjective perspective. From the subjective perspective, our goals and projects seem valuable. But from the objective perspective, it may not be possible to find any fundamental meaning or value for the things that we care about.

His solution is that we accept that we live ironic lives. The fact that we can take these two different perspectives may be the source of some agony for us, but it is also what makes us really interesting creatures.

You might not find this response to absurdity satisfying either. But there is something to both Nagel and Camus' accounts—something that makes us cheer for Rick Grimes and other characters like him. During Season Two, I found myself audibly cheering Daryl on as he struggled to survive after falling off his horse onto his own arrow, encountering ravenous zombies at the bottom of the hill and, like Sisyphus, fighting as hard he could to get to the top of the hill where no fundamental meaning was in store for him. Similarly, I felt for Rick at the end of "Pretty Much Dead Already" when Shane broke open the door to Hershel's barn and zombies came pouring out. Others in the party were willing to shoot people whom they didn't know in life. Why not? They're just zombies. But only Rick had the courage in this situation to shoot Sophia—a child they all knew and loved and had spent so much time searching for. Rick does not give up his basic sense of the value of humanity, even in a world where the value of human life is undermined. Daryl does not give up his will to live, even in a world in which life might not be worth living.

We feel for these characters because of the strength of their subjective commitments. Becoming an absurd hero, finding some subjective meaning in the world does not create objective meaning where there was none before. Perhaps intuitively though, the absurd heroes' fight, even if it is not pleasurable, is admirable and even noble. On some level, we may respect characters like Rick Grimes because he provides us with a model for living noble lives in our own indifferent universe.

11
Realistically, Nice Guys Finish Last

Si Sheppard

Zombies are big business right now. The undead are rising up everywhere, on screen, in print, and online. They are used as metaphors to explore everything from issues of class and race to the dynamics of pandemic contagion. Even the Center for Disease Control has a recommended plan of action outlined in response to a zombie apocalypse.[1]

But what can zombies tell us about what we really need to know: how to get by after the total collapse of modern post-industrial civilization?

All that remains of humanity in the post-apocalyptic environment depicted in Robert Kirkman's *The Walking Dead* is small bands of isolated survivors. In this environment the priorities for these proto-communities are:

- Phase 1. **Short Term: Survival**—strategies for resolving the immediate threat of the outbreak: *run, hide, or fight*

- Phase 2. **Medium Term: Establishment**—strategies for meeting the ongoing basic needs of the community: *farming, logistics, manufacturing*

- Phase 3. **Long Term: Diplomacy**—strategies for negotiating interaction with other communities: *alliance, détente, conquest*

---

[1] <http://emergency.cdc.gov/socialmedia/zombies_blog.asp>.

As soon as possible—certainly no later than the transition from Phase 1 to Phase 2—each community will have to arrive at a consensus on a constitutional order that will serve as the basis for its decision making and allocation of individual responsibility.

Some bands of survivors in *The Walking Dead*, deliberately or otherwise, never get past Phase 1. The rural cannibals and the urban scavengers retain a nomadic existence over the course of the series. But three permanent settlements emerge out of the post-apocalyptic chaos. They are the Alexandria Safe Zone in the suburbs of Washington, DC, led by Douglas Monroe; the town of Woodbury, Georgia, led by Philip Blake (a.k.a. the Governor); and the nearby West Central Prison, led by Rick Grimes.

All three leaders share one common trait; in order to secure their leadership status they each had to assert their authority by force. Monroe exiles his rival, Alexander Davidson; Rick gets into a fatal confrontation with his erstwhile partner, Shane; while the Governor dismembers *anyone* who might even potentially challenge his authority. Otherwise, each man takes his community on a very different trajectory, from the communitarian model in Alexandria to the totalitarianism of Woodbury to the anarchy in West Central Prison.

The least viable of these models, according to the political philosophy called Realism, is the third. The close proximity of Woodbury and West Central Prison forced those communities to make a quick transition from Phase 2 to Phase 3. In playing that game Rick is at an immediate disadvantage, because whatever ethical superiority he maintains over the Governor counts for nothing in their confrontation. It's power, not morality, which rules relations between states. Power comes from loyalty, and to inspire loyalty, in the words of that great Renaissance Realist, Niccolò Machiavelli, it's better for the Prince to be feared than to be loved, if he cannot be both. The Governor understands this. Rick doesn't.

But isn't the Governor, by any standard of measurement, a sick, twisted individual? Yes, undoubtedly. But so what? To the Realist, the worst autocrat is superior to the best anarchy. The first Emperor of China, Qin Shi Huang, was a megalomaniac who butchered his rivals, burned books, buried scholars alive, and drafted the common people into his great road, canal and wall-building projects where they died in droves. But he forcibly ended the Warring States Period, two-and-a-half centuries of anarchy, and his legacy was the model of a unitary Chinese state that endures today, two-and-a-quarter millennia beyond his own death and that of his dynasty.

For Want of a Conch Shell

According to Realists, states are formed to move individuals out of anarchy. Individuals surrender their autonomy in exchange for security.[2] The term "failed state" is applied to sovereign entities like Somalia that have ceased to function in terms of providing their side of this bargain. But it should also be applied to those proto-states that sought to achieve sovereign status but did not succeed in doing so—because they either disintegrated internally or were snuffed out by external forces—and completely ceased to exist.

Anyone who has read *Lord of the Flies* knows how this plays out. And from the historic examples of Pitcairn Island and Clipperton Island, where the societies founded by mutineers and outcasts degenerated into an orgy of rape, murder, and madness, we can predict what happens to self-contained little worlds where there is no government and no law.[3]

The post-apocalyptic environment is perfect for mapping this process of internal disintegration. Realism "is perfectly comfortable in the zombie universe," Daniel W. Drezner points out.[4] In the original *Night of the Living Dead*, despite the common external threat posed by the zombies, the seven people trapped in the farm house utterly fail to achieve any solidarity. Two separate sovereign entities (the basement and the first floor) quickly emerge, ruled by separate individuals (Harry and Ben) whose constant squabbling over resources, access to information, and strategy culminates in a fatal confrontation even while the other survivors are being picked off one-by-one all around them.

---

[2] For a useful introduction to the theory by one of its great theorists, see Hans J. Morgenthau, *Politics Among Nations: The Struggle for Power and Peace* (1978) pp. 4–15, <www.mtholyoke.edu/acad/intrel/morg6.htm>.

[3] Trevor Lummis, *Life and Death in Eden: Pitcairn Island and the* Bounty *Mutineers* (1999).

[4] Daniel W. Drezner, *Theories of International Politics and Zombies* (2011), p. 36.

The persistence of this dynamic has been a recurring theme throughout *The Walking Dead* series. The central figure of this ongoing saga, who ultimately fails to lead the people he assumes responsibility for not only out of danger but out of anarchy, is small-town Kentucky police officer Rick Grimes, who awakens from a coma to find the world he knew entirely swept away by the zombie pandemic.

Rick is eventually reunited with his wife, Lori, and young son, Carl. They have been shepherded to safety by his erstwhile partner, Shane Walsh, who has assembled a small community of survivors on the outskirts of Atlanta. As Rick later reminisces, Shane "was the leader of our group at first. Not that we took the time to make those distinctions. But he was the one everyone looked to for answers" (*The Walking Dead*, Issue #76).

Shane occupies a position of assumed leadership because he is an authority figure, a representative of a system of law and order (the fact that system no longer works if anything only deepens the respect for it among the survivors who, having lost everything else from their world, cling to its vestiges even more tightly). The problem is, the foundation of his leadership is little different from that of a prehistoric clan or tribal chieftain. It is based solely on respect; if that respect is undermined, there is no provision for the peaceful transition to an alternative. Rick's arrival immediately threatens Shane's authority because the two officers have equal claim to the qualifications required of a leader in their current circumstances.

Shane and Rick become increasingly confrontational over the best course of action for the group. Rick wants to move to a more secure location, while Shane is convinced that staying put and waiting for the restoration of order is the better option. Underlying these practical considerations is a deeper tension. Shane is infatuated with Lori, and Rick's survival has forced Lori to transfer her affection from Shane back to her husband. To what extent their disagreement over policy is really a manifestation of their intensifying personal animosities is unclear. Does Shane refuse to move the camp, even after it is swarmed by walkers, because he genuinely believes remaining in place is a good idea? Or is his bloody-minded obstinacy the product of his personal animosity towards Rick? Conversely, is Rick being completely honest when he later asserts that Shane's assumed leadership didn't "really matter to me until he started making decisions that weren't good for the group." Was it the interests of the group that were his primary concern, or his personal claim on his wife?

With no conflict resolution mechanism available, and the rest of the group totally excluded from the decision-making process, the confrontation between rival alpha-males Rick and Shane rapidly escalates to the point where Shane draws his sidearm on Rick, only to be gunned down by Rick's son, Carl.

Rick now assumes leadership of the group as it struggles to make the transition from Phase 1 to Phase 2. But his authority remains derived from his personal qualifications; he makes no effort to definitively break with the past by establishing a new constitutional order. So the community remains splintered and extremely vulnerable to individualistic and anti-social initiatives. It fails at every level and ultimately implodes.

Rick leads the group in search of a secure location in which to settle down. After numerous misadventures, they arrive at West Central Prison, Georgia. This fortified structure is ideal for meeting the immediate need of providing a secure perimeter against walker infestation. However, typically, the moment the external threat recedes, the group begins to atomize internally. The community (if it can be called that) drifts into a state of pure anarchy. There's no executive veto, no separation of powers, no checks and balances, no government whatsoever. There is no legal code and no mechanisms for enforcing collective decision making, negotiating differences, or conflict resolution.

In other words, West Central Prison fails to achieve even the most rudimentary standards of state formation according to Realist political theory. The bottom line was boiled down by Max Weber; once you strip away all the rhetoric about manifest destiny and a city on a hill, at the end of the day, "a state is a human community that (successfully) claims the monopoly of the legitimate use of physical force within a given territory." Or, as Charles Tilly put it, "If protection rackets represent organized crime at its smoothest," then states—quintessential protection rackets with the added veneer of legitimacy—"qualify as our largest examples of organized crime."[5]

---

[5] Charles Tilly, "War Making and State Making as Organized Crime," in Peter B. Evans, Dietrich Rueschemeyer, and Theda Skocpol, eds., *Bringing the State Back In* (1985), p. 169.

Anarchy in Georgia

There are plenty of criminals, but little organization, in West Central Prison. After Chris and Julie engage in a botched murder-suicide pact, Tyreese murders his daughters' killer and later freely admits to Rick, "I enjoyed it. . . . I turned into an animal on him—I mutilated him over and over—I ripped him apart and watched him come back for more" (Issue #23). Rick lets it go; there are no repercussions, setting a precedent for vigilantism as the means for resolving inter-personal conflicts. This is a significant marker in the failure of state formation. By refusing to enforce any penalty or sanction, Rick loses this opportunity to impose a formal, uniform code of justice. This surrender of the monopoly of the legitimate use of physical force is an invitation to anarchy. Rick is a now a lawman in an environment where there is no law, and without law, there can be no order.

A second critical flaw coded within the social order of West Central Prison is the total failure to establish a formal hierarchy of command and control beyond the assumed leadership of Rick Grimes. Rick never has, and never aspires to, anything more than a first-among-equals, one-of-the-boys style of authority. This has catastrophic implications whenever Rick is not personally in a position to assume responsibility for the resolution of a specific crisis impacting the group. For example, without declaring his intentions or destination, Rick spontaneously leaves the prison in order to exorcise his demons by eliminating the reanimated corpse of his partner-cum-nemesis Shane. In his absence, the community immediately degenerates into complete anarchy. Tyreese launches a suicidal attack on an entire gymnasium full of the undead; two little girls, Rachel and Susie, are murdered by one of the remaining prison inmates, Thomas; and another inmate, Dexter, is accused of the crime and locked up.

The disintegrating bonds of trust within the community are highlighted in Dexter's bitter remarks to fellow inmate Andrew: "These fucks ain't our friends. They ain't fucking normal. They crazies. . . . What they been through, out in the world—it's tore 'em up. They broken. Now they killing each other an' blamin' us" (Issue #16). With no institutional means of seeking redress, for Dexter there is "Only one way out of this." That way is by force.

Thomas is apprehended after he attempts to murder Andrea. Having returned from his personal mission in the midst of this crisis, Rick savagely beats Thomas and condemns him to be executed on the basis of the doctrine "you kill, you die" (Issue #17). The terms he uses to justify this unilateral assumption of both law enforcement and judicial power speak to the basis of his leadership: "I'm a cop – I've been trained to make decisions like this. I'm the only one here in a position of authority. I'm making the choice that's best for all of us. That's what you all look up to me for. That's why everyone comes to me for advice and guidance. I'm in charge."

In reality, Rick isn't in charge of anything outside of his line of sight. Patricia attempts to set Thomas free. After Thomas turns on her, Maggie guns him down. Patricia subsequently sides with Dexter and Andrew as they seize control and order the outsiders to leave at gunpoint.

This insurrection is aborted when, during a walker attack, Rick takes the chance to gun down Dexter. Andrew flees, right into the carnivorous embrace of the walkers. Rick again justifies his unilateral exercise of lethal force in terms of social responsibility: "I saw an opportunity during the walker attack and I took it.... Dexter had threatened to kick us all out of this prison. Send us back on the road. I couldn't let that happen. I wouldn't" (Issue #23).

Rick asserts that he is acting out of obligation. "I've been asked to shoulder the responsibilities of everyone here—and I've taken it upon myself to keep everyone safe." But he is aware of the increasing distance between the source of his authority (his status as the physical manifestation of law and order) and his actual exercise of power. He is determined to keep the fact of his actions from the very people he claims to be acting on behalf of: "I knew everybody would think it was a stray bullet and I let everyone assume that's what had happened." The alternative would be his looking like "a total hypocrite in front of everyone. It wouldn't be long until people started asking questions after that. I would lose my effectiveness as a leader. And again—that would be bad for the group" (Issue #23). Rationalizing murder in terms of the group interest is the slippery-slope to anarchy, not society; it would have been Shane's justification had he succeeded in assassinating Rick.

In the absence of any binding force now that the walkers are (it is assumed) securely outside the perimeter, the group struggles to maintain even a semblance of equilibrium. The failure to properly sweep the prison for walkers leads to the death of Allen, leaving two orphaned children. Another refugee, Michonne, is offered shelter inside the prison; she steals Tyreese from Carol, who subsequently commits suicide, leaving behind another orphan. In another of Rick's absences, the walkers storm an inadequately secured exit; the facility is temporarily overrun and Otis is killed.

Empire-Building among the Undead

Depressed by the persistent instability, Dale suggests to Andrea they leave the prison. His argument has a deeper imperative: "The death toll certainly hasn't slowed down. We're secure here—but for how long? This place has got to be a target.... What happens when someone more organized wants it?" (Issue #18). Andrea accepts the reality of this concern: "What happens when another group shows up—a bigger group. What if they come and don't want to share? What then?" (Issue #30). This is the conundrum Dale later sums up as: "Find a place strong enough and you have to worry about other people wanting it. Get a place that's not desired by other people—and it's not strong enough" (Issue #54). These misgivings are about what's called 'second anarchy'. Having evolved out of first, or individual, anarchy, societies interact in second anarchy, the competitive rivalry of states in international relations.

The problem is that the West Central Prison community never fully made an effective transition out of first anarchy. This is never more apparent than when Rick takes Glenn and Michonne to track down a helicopter, the first indication of potentially organized human survival outside their perimeter.

When this expedition encounters the downed helicopter, Rick presses on in search of survivors. His impromptu decision leads the trio right into the heart of the apparently flourishing town of Woodbury—and into the lair of its malevolent dictator, the self-proclaimed Governor.

After mutilating Rick, the Governor savagely abuses Michonne as part of his attempt to discover the location of Rick's enclave. His intention is identical to that of empire-builders throughout history; expansion at the expense of resource-rich potential rivals.

Because Realism measures the viability of states in terms of cohesion, not morality, to Realists, the Governor's leadership is superior to Rick's at every level. Woodbury is not only larger but much more cohesive than West Central Prison. The Governor has established a perimeter, has enforced internal security, and maintains a bread-and-circuses style of patronage that satisfies the primary and secondary needs of his community.

In expounding on the unfortunate fate of survivors from the helicopter crash, the Governor justifies the bloody arena entertainments he stages as part of his strategy for retaining popular support and, hence, a secure base of political power: "They were holed up at some news station in Atlanta—Channel Nine or Whatever. . . . There were about twenty of them. . . . They turned on each other—ran out of food—something—started killing each other. . . . There's a lesson there. You gotta keep people occupied or they'll turn on you. Reading and fucking will only keep people busy for so long. Eventually there's gotta be something else" (Issue #28).

The success of this strategy is explained by Woodbury's medical practitioner, Dr. Stevens, who admits that his own disaffection places him firmly in the minority:

> "We started out as a small group soon after all this started. We found this town pretty early on. The National Guard station, the narrow alleys—we decided we could defend this place. So we staked our claim. Started out, he was tough but he got the job done. [The Governor] emerged as the leader of our group very quickly. He did what had to be done, what needed to be done to keep people safe. . . . I hate the son of a bitch but I can't do anything. Whatever else he does . . . he keeps these people safe. That's enough for most people. As long as there's a wall between them and the biters they're not too concerned with who's with them on their side of the wall" (Issue #29).

With the connivance of one of the Governor's loyalists, Rick is allowed to "escape," the intention being for Woodbury to track the fugitives back to their settlement. Rick foils that trick, but a state of open war now exists between the two communities.

The preferred response under Realist theory would be for West Central Prison to balance against the superior power of

Woodbury by building a coalition against it. Unfortunately, the two states are operating in a complete diplomatic vacuum; so far as both sides know, they are the only remnants of civilization still in existence, islands in an ocean of undead who only recognize warm flesh, not potential alliance partners.

Facing this reality, Rick warns: "It could be weeks, it could be months, but they'll eventually find us. We just need to make sure that when they do get here . . . we're ready for them" (Issue #36).

War, or the threat of war, can be a major asset for state formation. One of the great Realists, Otto von Bismarck, understood this. By engineering a series of carefully calculated, sequentially escalating wars (against Denmark, then Austria-Hungary, then France) in the mid-nineteenth century, Bismarck brought together the rival principalities of Germany and forged them into the mightiest state in Europe, the Second Reich.

Unfortunately, under Rick's "leadership," West Central Prison does practically nothing to effectively mobilize for the anticipated struggle. Aside from an expedition to a local National Guard post in search of munitions (which leads to a confrontation with a Woodbury patrol at a nearby Walmart), there is no attempt to monitor progress at the rival site, by scouting, infiltration, or any other means. There's no attempt to even the odds by proactively whittling down Woodbury's numerical and material advantage through sniping or sabotage. There's no attempt to sow insurrection or encourage the disaffected to defect. The sudden assault by a massive Woodbury task force therefore achieves complete surprise.

In this crisis, the fundamental weakness of the prison leadership structure becomes tragically apparent. When Michonne volunteers to slip outside the perimeter to adopt a more proactive defensive posture, Rick vehemently rejects this proposal: "No, dammit! No. You leave here—go on the other side of those fences—and you die! Frankly, we need you too much now. We have to decide right now that we're going to work together—or we're all dead" (Issue #44).

Rick's orders are explicit. Unfortunately, they are only effective when he is able to enforce them. There are no formal or informal mechanisms to uphold his decisions and ensure continuity of his policies when he is incapacitated by a gunshot in the first Woodbury assault. Rick has no deputy, vice president, political party, supreme court, or priesthood able to stop Michonne and Tyreese setting out on exactly the kind of force recon mission he had explicitly vetoed. As a direct consequence, Tyreese is killed and Michonne forced to flee. The defenses of the prison are further depleted when Dale evacuates in the RV, taking three other adults (including Andrea, the community's ace sharpshooter) and three children with him.

Although the battle hangs in the balance, during the final attack the prison garrison is stretched too thin and overrun. Axel, Patricia, Hershel, Billy, and Alice are killed, while Rick can only watch as his wife, Lori, and infant daughter, Judith, are gunned down. Rick escapes with Carl. It is small consolation that the Governor has little time to savor his triumph; in the devastation wrought by the attack, the prison is overrun by walkers, and the Woodbury invasion force is apparently wiped out.

Second Chances, Lessons Learned?

On the run again, Rick later reconnects with the other evacuees, integrates more survivors into the group, and is invited to join the Alexandria Safe Zone community on the outskirts of Washington, DC. Rick isn't impressed by the social organization of his new home; "I don't trust these people not to ruin this place," he grumbles; "If they ever try to make us leave we'll just take this place from them and make it *ours*" (Issue #71). Rick immediately assumes authority he has not been allocated and has not earned, based, once more, on his own self-perceived qualifications; "I'm the one who does what needs to be done—no matter what," he tells Monroe; "You need me. I make the hard decisions. I do whatever it takes to keep the people around me alive. If you think you can survive without me you're wrong" (Issue #75).

Once again, however, Rick is promising more than he can deliver. His ham-fisted efforts to keep the domestic peace end tragically. A breach in the community's defenses leads to its being almost overrun by a walker incursion, during which Rick chooses the wrong option (flight, not fight) that gets more people, including Monroe, killed, and leaves Carl mutilated.

Throughout the series Rick consistently manifested the *personal* qualities of post-morality necessary for leadership in a post-apocalyptic environment. If we accept that society is moral, then decisions in a post-apocalyptic environment must be driven by post-moral criteria. In a discussion with his wife, Rick confesses that "I'd kill every single one of the people here if I thought it'd keep you safe. I know these people—I care for these people—but I know I'm capable of making that sacrifice." He retains enough integrity to ponder the moral implications of this attitude: "Does that make me evil? I mean . . . isn't that evil?" But, given the circumstances, he is forced to accept that it is only a manifestation of an inescapable reality (Issue #36).

Rick's ultimate flaw is his inability to translate those qualities into the *institutional* basis for his leadership. In the final analysis, who is Rick? What does he stand for? What's his long-term vision? Where is he leading his people? Is he going to write a constitution? Is he going to establish a dynasty? Is he going to proselytize a new faith? He was never going to do any of these things because, ultimately, his priorities never extended beyond day-to-day survival. He never attempted to make something of his inchoate little community that would enable it to outlast him.

Sitting at Carl's bedside in the aftermath of the Safe Zone walker incursion, Rick appears to have, finally, come to a closer understanding of his key flaws as a leader. The undead are "a manageable threat," he recognizes. The problem is, and always has been, people, specifically, his failure to mobilize the human material at his disposal effectively. "Our people need to be better trained—better equipped to deal with anything that could happen—we'll need to invest in training and preparedness," he vows; "We'll turn ourselves into an army that can protect us" (Issue #84). Rick is now, at last, a Realist.

With Monroe gone, Rick has been granted a second chance to lead a community out of anarchy. At least now he knows what *not* to do. Bitter experience has taught him a harsh lesson in the realities of power. Rick's moral center throughout the series has been his bond with his son, Carl. Given the circumstances, no one could begrudge him this. Rick was never a bad father; he was just a bad founding father.

12
The Optimism of *The Walking Dead*

BRANDON KEMPNER

Imagine your typical zombie nightmare, just like the one in Robert Kirkman's *The Walking Dead*. You've got a ragged group of survivors, terrified, dirty, starving. Everything they know is gone; their world has been shattered. All that's left is a brutal, bitter, and terrifying struggle for survival. Zombies are everywhere, the living dead, broken caricatures of human beings. They claw at the windows, lusting for human flesh. To survive, those left behind must do horrible things. Conventional notions of "good" and "evil," of "right" and "wrong" mean nothing. Life has no purpose beyond mere existence. The survivors become the very walking dead that they fear so much.

This zombie nightmare gives us an optimistic picture of the human condition.

Huh?

That's right. Kirkman's *The Walking Dead* presents a profoundly humanistic and therefore optimistic landscape. While the surface of Kirkman's zombiepocalypse is bleak, there's a surprisingly optimistic philosophical core to the narrative, one that celebrates the freedom and responsibility of human choice. This freedom transforms Kirkman's main character, Rick Grimes, into a truly humanistic hero.

The philosophy of existentialism, as developed by the French thinker Jean-Paul Sartre argues that humans are alone in the universe, without God or Truth. As a result, they're forced to make all their own choices. Sartre sees that this freedom as both a great privilege and a great burden. It would be easier if our moral choices were already made for us, but would we then be truly free? This freedom to choose is, for Sartre, the highest form of humanism, because only through existential choices are humans truly responsible for their own lives.

Sartre's essay, *Existentialism Is a Humanism*, shows us how to interpret *The Walking Dead* as an existentialist story, and, as such, a humanist one. While this may seem like a strange way of looking at zombies, this seemingly perverse interpretation of *The Walking Dead* allows us to dig into the complexities of Kirkman's terrifying world.

Truth or No Truth?

Existentialism is a mid-twentieth-century philosophy that stands traditional thinking on its head. Existentialism junks the whole idea of a pre-made meaning to life, and instead argues that human life means only what humans make of it—no more, no less.

Since the values and the meaning of the old, pre-zombie world have been destroyed, Kirkman's characters are free to make their own choices. Some of the people in Kirkman's world embrace this freedom; others refuse it. The second story arc, *Miles Behind Us*, gives us an early example of this kind dilemma. Rick and the survivors discover a farm, where Hershel is clinging to his abstract and outdated concepts of God and family. Despite all evidence to the contrary, Hershel believes that the undead will be restored to their former selves. Hershel is even keeping the zombified body of his undead son locked in the barn. His refusal to let go of his son's body reflects his refusal to let go of his old values. In typical *Walking Dead* fashion, Hershel's plan goes horribly wrong; the zombie son gets out and kills several survivors (*The Walking Dead*, Issue #11). By refusing to give up his old understanding of the world, Hershel brings death upon his community.

This is one of the core lessons of *The Walking Dead*: sticking to pre-made ideas will get you killed. As philosophers, we refer to these fixed concepts as existing *a priori* (Latin for existing before), since they allegedly exist beyond and outside of any individual human experience. Almost all traditional models of philosophy rely on *a priori* concepts, whether they be religious, logical, or even biological. We even use this kind of essentialist thinking in everyday life when we refer to something like "human nature," which exists above and outside any individual human existence.

Existentialism is like the bad kid in the philosophers' playground: it rejects all *a priori* values, and, with them, any grander meaning to human life. Instead, existentialism argues that no meaning comes before human existence, and that there isn't any God, purpose, pattern, or form that exists before the individual. For the existentialists, there are no transcendent truths to be found, no ultimate meaning hidden out there. There's just existence in the world, nothing more. Human beings are stranded alone in the universe, with nothingness all around them.

While this may sound frightening—a life without any greater meaning—the existentialists argued that this emptiness gave humans absolute freedom. Since there is no God or Truth, each of us is totally free to make our own meaning in the world. Existentialists like Sartre claim that this state of total freedom is better than anything else. Without any stable values, man (and woman! think about Michonne or Andrea) can finally choose his or her own values; these humans are completely responsible for their own beings, and, as such, totally free.

Michonne, the one-time lawyer and now a sword-wielding survivor extraordinaire, is a great example of someone who has completely rejected her past life and values. Of all the characters Kirkman has introduced, Michonne is one of the most capable, using her sword to slice and dice her way to continued existence. That sword, which has become synonymous with her character, represents Michonne's existential independence. While other characters are foolishly clinging to guns—as Rick points out in *The Best Defense*, they aren't making any more bullets (Issue #26)—Michonne has adopted the weapon best suited for killing walkers: silent, deadly, efficient. All traces of Michonne's past life are gone—she never acts like a lawyer in the series (a good thing, by the way)—and she has completely adapted to the new post-zombie world. In Kirkman's world, she's rewarded with continued survival; she continues existing where other, less adaptable characters perish.

Sartre, King of the Existentialists

Existentialism comes in a variety of flavors, all focusing on the concept of human freedom in an absurd universe. Some, like

Christian existentialist Søren Kierkegaard, argue that we can use this total freedom to embrace God and make a "leap of faith" into religious certitude. Friedrich Nietzsche and Martin Heidegger are often quoted as forerunners of existentialism, and even novelists like Fyodor Dostoevsky and Albert Camus are extolled as being existentialist thinkers. Nonetheless, Jean-Paul Sartre is the king of the existentialists, and his version of atheistic existentialism remains the best known argument for absolute human freedom in a Godless universe.

Sartre laid down the core philosophy of existentialism in his massive work *Being and Nothingness*. It's an absolute brick of a volume, weighing in at some eight hundred pages. Fortunately for us, Sartre also tried to sell existentialism to the masses. In his blessedly short *Existentialism Is a Humanism*, Sartre gives us a nice, concise guide to the high points of his philosophy, without all the tiny print of *Being and Nothingness*.

In *Existentialism Is a Humanism*, Sartre tries to defend his philosophy from numerous detractors. As you can imagine, a lot of people found Sartre a total downer. If there's no "goal" or "purpose" to living, why live at all? To battle these charges of pessimism, Sartre focused on his official existential motto: "Existence precedes essence!" With that radical slogan, Sartre rejects any notion that there is an *a priori* meaning to life. Life (existence) begins, and then we make meaning (essence) of it.

While Sartre's argument can get very technical, most of it boils down to this: there is nothing absolute in the universe. There is no God, and because there's no God, there can be no God-given Truth. The only thing we can be sure of is that we exist. If we didn't, there wouldn't be much point to anything, would there? So, instead of beginning with some pre-ordained purpose, we begin with existence. With existence comes choice and freedom. Human beings have absolute freedom because there is nothing to stop us from being free.

Sartre argues that each human has to make his or her own identity, and that he or she does not come into the world fully made. Each human creates himself or herself by choosing his or her own moral code, and humans have no alternative other than to choose their own moral code. Compared to older philosophical systems, this may seem incredibly depressing. You can't be "right" or "wrong" because "right" and "wrong" don't exist. There's nothing fixed and stable to follow. Each of us is alone in the universe, confronted with absolute and total freedom. Or, as Sartre elegantly puts it in his novel *Nausea,* "There is nothing, nothing, absolutely no reason for existing." Since there's no absolute reason for existing, all we can do is create meaning out of our meaningless lives.

In zombie terms, this means that each human has to come up with their own way of dealing with the zombie apocalypse. There is no "right" or "wrong" way to exist in Kirkman's world, because "right" and "wrong" have been done away with. This doesn't mean that nothing is at stake, though, because there is one constant left: existing. Surviving. If Kirkman's survivors want to keep living, they will have to create their own meanings.

Depressed yet?

Still, Sartre argues that existentialism is really the highest form of humanism because it places human freedom first. Sartre defines humanism as "a theory that takes man as an end and as the supreme value." According to Sartre, other philosophical systems—whether religious, Marxist, abstract, Platonic—tend to put God first, or logic first, or materialism first, and humans come out a distant second (or worse). As such, Sartre argues that existentialism is the only philosophical system that gives man any actual dignity, because all other systems make human beings into things. Existentialism is a humanism because it values human choice above all else.

So how do we apply that to zombies?

Existentialism and Zombies

So, existentialism takes humanity and strands it alone in the world, with no fixed values, guideposts, or maps to guide it. Each individual human has to make their own choices on how to behave and act, and through this freedom they achieve their own meaning.

A zombie story takes humanity, strands it alone in a zombie world, with no government, security, or authority to guide it. Each individual survivor has to make their own choices about how they'll act and behave in this new world, and only through this freedom can they survive.

In a zombie world like that of *The Walking Dead,* our various characters are confronted with the fact of their total and absolute freedom. With society destroyed, there is no authority to enforce *a priori* moral codes. Instead of relying on society, or police, or religion to provide values, the survivors have to create their own. They can behave in any fashion they choose. They have nothing but their freedom and their existence.

The Walking Dead presents its characters with innumerable existential moments, where they can either choose to adapt to their new world—to choose freedom—or fail to do so. When characters in *The Walking Dead* refuse to adapt, they retreat to the patterns and forms of their old lives. Sartre would divide these zombie survivors into two basic categories. Those that rise to the challenge of accepting nothingness and freedom would be labeled "authentic"; those that cling to their *a priori* delusions would be branded "inauthentic." Authentic individuals embrace freedom for themselves and all humanity. Inauthentic individuals deny that this freedom exists, and, as such, seek to limit the freedom of others.

We see this clash—between individuals embracing their "existence" in a zombie world and those insisting that their pre-zombie "essence" will return—time and time again in *The Walking Dead*. Some characters quickly establish themselves as existentialists: Rick (although he wavers at first), Dale, Glenn, Michonne. Others refuse to accept the new world, and insist that the old world will (and must) return: Shane, Hershel, Douglas (the leader of the Alexandria Safe-Zone).

This tension, even more so than the danger from walkers, is what defines *The Walking Dead*. In most of the story arcs of *The Walking Dead*, we get a conflict between these two types of characters, usually in the form of the existentialist Rick confronting an essentialist thinker such as Shane. Now that we've got the basic theory down, let's see how Kirkman delivers existentialist drama in action.

Rick's Zombie Rebirth: A New World

While the first season of the television show closely follows many of the events of *Days Gone Bye,* there is one critical difference: the *Days Gone Bye* comic arc ends with Shane attempting to kill Rick. When Rick arrives at the camp outside Atlanta, we learn that Shane has done more than keep Rick's family safe. He's insinuated himself as the new "Rick," even going so far as to sleep with Rick's wife. On the most basic level, he's trying to steal Rick's "essence." Or, in other words, Shane is the true zombie, a mindless drone, a man without a life. He's conformed to the blueprint of Rick's identity instead of being his own man; he's adopted an *a priori* mode of being rather than accepting his existential reality.

But before we tear Shane apart, let's get to Rick.

Rick begins the series alone, gasping awake in a hospital bed. The hospital setting is important, as it represents Rick's rebirth into a new world. Rick has been thrust into an absurd, existentialist situation: his old ways of understanding the world no longer work. Any *a priori* knowledge he had of the world is now completely irrelevant. In fact, his relying on old knowledge almost gets him killed. As he stumbles to his feet, weak as an infant, Rick meets his first walkers. Still thinking he's in his old world, Rick tries communicating with them, asking, "Can't you understand?!" and "What the hell was all that?" The walkers, of course, try to eat him.

Like an existentialist, Rick has to develop and create a new method of being human; he can no longer rely on past patterns or instructions. Rick's rebirth into a zombie world mirrors the birth Sartre sees for every human: we first exist in the world, and only after existing can we define ourselves. We start out as nothing, and only through an act of will do we develop into anything meaningful. This is exactly Rick's situation: he materializes in the zombie world, encounters the walkers, and only afterwards does he develop a method of dealing with them.

However, at this point in the series, Rick is not a true existential hero. In fact, he starts as almost the exact opposite. Instead of accepting the changed world he finds himself in, Rick sets out to restore his previous identity. First thing, he goes to the sheriff's office and puts back on his cop uniform.

Confronted with a zombie apocalypse, this is what most of us might do. We'd cling to the past, and hope that the government would save us, or that we would still be the people we were in our old (and now meaningless) lives. The end result: we'd be eaten by walkers. We'd be helpless to deal with our new situation. This is how Rick begins in *The Walking Dead*. If we run this through Sartre, we can see that the newly reborn Rick is falling into the old trap of "Essence precedes existence." Rick still believes that his former identity—as a police officer—is still his "essence."

A little exchange early in the television episode "Days Gone Bye" illustrates this problem. When a fellow survivor asks Rick, "So you're a cop, huh?" Rick answers "Yep." But cops, of course, don't exist anymore in this world. The absurdity of Rick in his police uniform underscores the existential nature of *The Walking Dead*. What is he going to do, arrest the walkers? Tell them that they have the right to remain silent? That any groaning will be used against them in a court of law? Throw them in jail?

Instead of embracing his freedom, Rick is trying to run from it. He's moving backwards instead of forwards. Since freedom is difficult, according to Sartre, many humans try to give up that freedom to a variety of "stable" institutions, whether the government, religion, or well-established clichés of human behavior like "cop" or "father." They choose the lie of the familiar over the freedom of the new.

The Walking Dead shows us the danger of these comforting patterns. Every time Rick tries to rely on his former life, his former idea of what he was, Rick almost gets killed. When he jettisons his past essence and instead accepts his current existence, he thrives. Take Rick's disastrous trip into Atlanta; he's believed the government's promise of safety and rescue. Of course, everyone who listened to this promise has wound up dead, as Glenn explains: "The government tried to herd everyone into the cities so we'd be easier to protect. All that did was put all the food in one place . . . It took a week for just about everyone in the city to be killed" (Issue #2).

This is one the main lessons of *The Walking Dead*: sticking to your old life and your old identity will get you killed. This is a hard won lesson, though, and as Rick arrives in the survivor camp, he's only beginning to understand it. Rick is fast becoming an existentialist, realizing he must let his past life go— those *Days Gone Bye*, if you will. Once he makes it to camp, he quickly runs into Shane, who is trying his hardest to get back to those bygone days.

Shane versus Rick

If the Rick of *Days Gone Bye* is a budding existentialist, Shane is firmly stuck in the past. Like Rick, he's still wearing his cop uniform; unlike Rick, he refuses to believe that things have changed. Shane is adamant that the government will rescue them, that their lives will go back to being normal. Despite the enormous walker population, Shane wants everyone to stay near Atlanta: "Are you crazy?! What happens when the government starts cleaning this mess up? They'll have to start with the cities . . . They'll find us faster if we stay here!"

The conflict between Rick and Shane quickly develops into an existential crisis. Will the survivors cling to their old systems and old identities, or will they become a new kind of human being, free to make their own choices beyond the bounds of government and their old identities? Serious as that conflict is, Kirkman gives it even more juice by showing how Shane is attempting to live Rick's former life. Shane wants to be the perfect husband, father, cop, and protector. Since he can't be those things himself, he has to steal them from Rick. As Rick is trying to change into a new sort of person, Shane is literally trying to turn into Rick. One is trying to embrace new patterns of living, and the other is running back to the old.

Other characters in *Days Gone Bye* are struggling with the same issue. In one scene, Rick decides everyone in camp needs to be armed—even his eight-year-old son Carl. Rick's wife objects, saying that Carl is too young—but what does too young mean any more? Everything they've known about their past world needs to be thrown away, and they need to start again. Rick wins the argument, and Carl gets his gun (Issue #5).

One convenient thing about Kirkman's world is that these issues are always quickly resolved. Shane's point of view is proved wrong when walkers attack the camp, killing several of the survivors. Shane's method of living equals death. Kirkman has raised the stakes; in existentialist philosophy, not living an authentic life results in nausea, depression, and alienation. In Kirkman's zombie fantasia, it results in death—or, even worse, zombification. Being a walker is the ultimate existential nightmare, since walkers are without freedom, without will, without individuality, and simply condemned to an eternally meaningless existence.

Even Carl gets a few shots off with his gun, proving that Rick was right to arm him.

Faced with this direct evidence, you'd think Shane would relent. Instead, he becomes increasingly shrill and dangerous, insisting that his way is still the right way, and that it's the *only way*. In the climactic confrontation of *Days Gone Bye*, Shane and Rick are out in the woods. Shane finally snaps. He curses at Rick, screaming "I've got nothing, Rick!! No friends! No family!! No respect!! No fucking life!! This fucking world! This fucking god-forsaken world of shit! There's nothing for me here Rick!! Nothing!" (Issue #6).

Shane is talking almost like an existentialist. He's recognized that the world is full of "nothing," that it's "god-forsaken," that there is no absolute meaning. If you cross out the swear words, you could almost fit that speech into *Existentialism Is a Humanism*. However, instead of embracing the emptiness, Shane rejects it. He can't stand the nothingness and freedom; he has to become Rick, to take his place, to be someone by stealing Rick's identity.

The humans are worse than the walkers.

It looks like the end for Rick.

But then Carl appears out of the woods and shoots Shane.

Why does Kirkman have the kid do it? Can't we keep someone—or something—in his god-forsaken world innocent?

Rick's Killer Kid

In what is one of the defining moments of the series, we have an eight year old child gunning down a grown man. *The Walking Dead* takes us on an important existential journey with that gunshot. Any illusions we might have that these zombie survivors will return to society, and the values and conformity civilization represents, are blasted away when Carl pulls that trigger. This is an entirely new world, where children are now killers.

Did Carl do the right thing?

Remember, if we've moved to an existentialist viewpoint, there is no "right" or "wrong" thing, because there are no absolute values by which to judge right and wrong. Carl has made a choice, to kill Shane and save his father. By embracing that choice, and the freedom to make that choice, Carl has becomes an existentialist.

In our society, we tend to think children need to be innocent, protected, and sheltered. At the least, we'd object to the "trauma" Carl has suffered, to the way he'll be changed as a result of his actions. Of course, though, our concepts of "child" and "innocent" don't mean anything in Kirkman's zombie world. If Carl is going to survive, he's going to have to choose to survive; the walkers don't care if he's "innocent" or a "child." They'll kill him just the same.

When Carl pulls that trigger, he's made a choice to act. He's not hiding behind an idea; he's not waiting for his father or mother to save him. Like Rick, he takes action to save himself in a harsh world. There's a freedom in what Carl does, a profound choice, one that tramples on some cherished ideas of the innocence of children.

Most writers might try to shield us from the harshness of this zombie reality. They'd keep Carl a child, protected and safe. But in Kirkman's world, there's no safety, only freedom. It goes farther than this, of course. Fathers are supposed to protect children, but Kirkman has reversed the traditional (*a priori*) family roles: the child is protecting the father. Rick is a new kind of father, and Carl is a new kind of son; they've moved beyond those "Days Gone Bye" into a new and freer existence. They'll have to recreate their relationship based on the zombie world they live in, not on classic ideas of how fathers and sons should behave.

Couldn't Kirkman have given us a nicer existential world? Sartre says no, and that anyone who is a true existentialist is likely to find reality disturbing. Since existentialists claim that God will not help us, and that humans are left to make meaning for themselves, this places enormous responsibility on the individual. Instead of being part of a pre-made order, human beings are alone in an indifferent universe. The final panel of *Days Gone Bye*, which shows Rick hugging Carl in an idyllic wood and Shane's bloody corpse sprawled next to them, underscores the aloneness of these characters. Amidst the peaceful woods, death lies at their feet. Nothing will save them but themselves; they have no greater truths or meaning to rely on.

They are alone in the universe. Carl has become like his father, an existentialist. His mother cannot protect him from the violence of the universe, nor can his father. The only thing he has, that anyone has, is freedom.

Forced to Finally Start Living

Once you have the basic idea of existentialism in place, it's easy to find all sorts of other existential moments in Kirkman's series. Take the character of Dale. An elderly man who has just lost his wife, he takes in two young women and eventually starts a romantic relationship with Andrea, who happens to be some forty year his junior. Various members of the camp disapprove, but Dale doesn't care. He chooses his own path. While the relationship may be "inappropriate" by the standards of our current society, that society no longer exists. Why should Dale be confined by it? Why can't he make the choices that will make him the happiest?

Time and time again, the same sort of conflict arises: a survivor or group of survivors will try to re-establish old world values, and then those values dramatically and horribly fall apart. The characters that survive are the ones who have left their past selves the farthest behind. Usually, the plot goes something like this: the survivors discover something that will allow them to recover their previous lives (a farm, a prison, a seeming peaceful community). They struggle to return to what they deem "normality"; that fails utterly, and the characters most involved in holding on to the past end up dying. Rinse, lather, repeat.

We've only begun to explore the existential content of Kirkman's universe. As Kirkman begins to develop longer story arcs, the vision grows more complex. Later volumes of *The Walking Dead* address the possibility—or impossibility—of an actual existentialist community. This is the one of the common objections to existentialism. If everyone has absolute freedom, how can people get along together? What can hold a society together?

A couple things stand out from this perspective. First, people don't get along very well together in Kirkman's universe, and it seems like whenever communities arise, they very quickly fall apart. Even Rick's relationship with Carl is strained as the series goes on, as Carl begins to behave more and more independently. If we leap forward to *Fear the Hunters*, we can see how truly independent and radical Carl becomes. In this story arc, Carl kills Ben, another child traveling with the survivors. Ben has been showing more and more signs of being dangerously psychotic: killing and torturing animals, and eventually killing his twin brother Billy because he thinks Billy will come back to life (Issue #61). When the adults of the group cannot kill him—he's only a child after all—Carl takes on the duty himself, sneaking out and killing Ben. Carl is acting to protect his community, and is making a choice independent of conventional morality. Kirkman indeed holds nothing sacred, as this brutal sequence—children killing children to protect the group—takes us far outside of any conventional notion of right and wrong.

Carl is also mirroring choices he's seen Rick make: Rick has acted at several times to kill people to protect the group. If a choice is morally right for Rick, the same choice must be morally right for Carl. Sartre addresses this issue extensively in *Being and Nothingness*, arguing that "Being for Others" is an essential aspect of existentialism. One thing Sartre insists upon is that no one human is more exceptional than another, and that, thus, when an individual makes a choice, he makes that choice for all humanity. An existentialist can't say something like, "This choice is fine for me, but not fine for you." We see this kind of "choosing for all humanity" when Rick refuses to tell Carl he was wrong for shooting Shane. Kirkman certainly plays with the ideas of hypocrisy and exceptionalism with later figures like the Governor, and even with Rick's reluctance to set himself up as a true "leader" of the survivors.

The Sternness of Optimism

On the surface, existentialism—or *The Walking Dead*—may seem deeply pessimistic. These works abandon man alone in the universe, and humanity is "condemned to freedom." While this freedom may seem overwhelming at first, Sartre reminds us that freedom is the deepest form of "stern" optimism.

Kirkman's zombie universe is not pessimistic, but rather sternly optimistic. As Sartre puts it, existentialism is a humanism because humans matter, and only humans can make choices. The characters of *The Walking Dead* are equally forced to make their own choices. They can't rely on past modes of living, and have to accept their freedom in order to survive. Their absolute freedom puts humanity first, ahead of God, or Truth, or any other abstract concept. To put it differently, we could simply quote the tagline on the back of each paperback volume of *The Walking Dead*: "In a world ruled by the dead, we are forced to finally start living."

Thus, *The Walking Dead is* a humanism because it is an existentialism.

So, next time someone accuses you of reading comics when you're reading *The Walking Dead,* you can claim that, in fact, you're reading a story about the highest and most humanistic form of freedom, an existential journey of incomparable optimism.

13
The Horror of Humanity

JULIA ROUND

Zombies are everywhere—but it seems we're no longer afraid of them. While Edward Cullen is crying over his latest school report, Woody Harrelson is kicking ass in *Zombieland*, young people around the world are taking part in zombie walks, and writers like Max Brooks have created a whole world war history based on the zombie threat. Although the living dead continue to decay, their stories have definitely evolved, and in these tales man is often the new zombie and the real horror.

Early zombies in movies were freak supernatural figures, created in exotic lands through magic and necromancy, and pitted against virtuous humans. But today's zombies may not even be dead, as technology and viruses are often responsible for a murderous 'infection' (*28 Days Later, The Signal, Pontypool*)—taking the genre closer to science fiction than supernatural horror. In addition to this redefinition, many stories now seem to emphasize human rather than supernatural evil. Rather than being the central threat, zombies are slowly being excised from their own stories and replaced with a critique of humanity that is no longer restricted to isolated and individualized characters (such as *White Zombie's* Murder Legendre). The social commentary on racism that underlies George Romero's *Night of the Living Dead*, the deliberate infection of the humans in *Resident Evil*, and the attempted gang rape in *28 Days Later* are based on an immorality that makes human characters the real villains of these films.

This sort of morally ambiguous portrayal of humanity is emphasized and explored most clearly in *The Walking Dead*.

For what happens to personal morality in a world where zombies can attack at any time and resources are scarce? Is it alright to steal from our fellow humans to save ourselves? Is it possible to hold onto our humanity when we're forced to act inhumanely—for example mutilating the bodies of our friends and loved ones to prevent them from returning from the grave, or having to decide who should live or die for the greater good? In such a world, can we ever be more than just 'the walking dead'?

A Cold (un)Dead World

Today's zombie stories seem to have 'braaaaains' added, and to understand why they have evolved in this way we need to examine how we understand ourselves—and nothing accomplishes that better than existentialist philosophy. For existentialists there is no independent, pre-existing human soul—our humanity is determined by choices and actions. This philosophy relies on the idea that *existence* precedes *essence*: each human being creates his or her own values and so determines a meaning for his or her life. The world around us just *is*—there's no inherent right or wrong—and we project our own meaning onto it. Projected meaning is fragile and its breakdown confronts us with the total meaninglessness of our world, which can be devastating. But just because the world does not have values in itself, this doesn't mean that there are no values. We all have our own ethics—but must realize that these are personal and changeable. We cannot excuse ourselves with reference to society's morals—we choose to follow systems like these. So ultimately, all our choices are our personal responsibility.

In *The Walking Dead*, Rick takes existential control of his life by assigning himself a series of tasks (to find his family; to protect his wife and children; to keep his group alive) that give him a method for understanding the world and negotiating his way through it. When he fails at his self-imposed missions (for example after the attack on the prison by the Governor) he goes literally crazy and becomes physically ill—even sounding like a walker ("Gruhugggh") as he reaches out for Carl, who thinks he has reanimated (Issue #50). He's not the only one who does this and throughout both the comic book and TV series characters find different things to live for; Andrea and

Dale are a good example of this. Both put their purpose for continued existence in each other: in the television series Andrea decides not to commit suicide because of Dale's decision to die with her and their relationship follows a similar path in the comic. Other characters, such as Glenn and Maggie, also find meaning in each other for a time: "You make this life, even *this* life, worth living, Glenn. I love you" (*The Walking Dead*, Issue #60).

Accepting that our world and its events are random and without moral purpose or meaning is distressing—we want this planet to be a warm and welcoming place; not a cold, uncaring one. What better way to illustrate the world's absurdity than a world populated with zombies (it doesn't get much colder!) and filled with cruel and random events? In *The Walking Dead*, Rick's fairy tale reunion with his family and 'miraculous' baby daughter end tragically and pointlessly. The AMC series contains its own nod to absurdity when it reveals that Dr. Jenner is little more than a lab assistant and his genius wife (who could maybe have found a cure) was the one who died. The meaninglessness of her death while her average husband survives is obvious.

Like the dead themselves, the landscape and appearance of *The Walking Dead* also emphasize emptiness and stillness. In the comic, after an initial (and traditional) zombie encounter in the hospital cafeteria, Rick is shown wheeling a bike down a deserted road, stopping only to weep. A nine-panel grid of Tony Moore's repeated drawings of the empty, silent space takes up a full page, emphasizing the isolation (Issue #1). The AMC series takes the same approach—surprisingly few walker attacks happen in the first season, and some of the most impressive visuals are the wide-angled shots of Rick's solitary journey to the city, which replicate the comic ("Days Gone Bye").

At the end of the first episode, a close-up shot shows walkers swarming over the tank that Rick is trapped in, messily gutting and eating his horse. But then a slow camera pullback leaves us with an extended birds-eye view of the city that makes even these frantic, violent creatures seem remote: framed by distance and deserted skyscrapers. This is a truly absurd world—distant, indifferent, and silent—emphasized firstly by Rick's tinnitus (after he fires his gun inside the tank), then the silence of the tank interior, and finally by the slow rhythm of the non-diegetic music ("Space Junk," Wang Chung) that plays before the credits.

Existentialism says that our cold and unfeeling world just *is*; much like the zombies themselves, who simply exist. To live in this place we must accept ourselves for who we are and find our own reasons for living. Acknowledging that we each have the absolute freedom to do precisely whatever we want, whenever we want, can be just as terrifying as this realization. There are moments when we all want to excuse ourselves from making difficult decisions but (in contrast to nihilism) thinkers like Albert Camus say that we must persist against the absurdity of the world and that if we do we will *create* value and meaning.

But there is a downside to having such complete freedom to find one's own meaning in life. This is angst, a feeling of intense anxiety and fear that comes from the realization that we have unlimited freedom to do as we wish: for example the thought that we could deliberately crash our car at speed while driving, punch a baby in the face, or throw ourselves off a cliff. Angst comes from a lack of control that relates to having freedom without limits. The feeling is impossible to remove as there is no tangible source that inspires it, and those characters who commit suicide in *The Walking Dead* demonstrate its effects. In the television series Jim chooses to be left behind to die alone after he is bitten ("Wildfire"); then Jacqui chooses to die at the CMC plant ("TS-19"). Carol's suicide attempts in the comic serve a similar purpose (Issues #22, #41). These characters are exerting the only control they believe possible over their lives.

Living with Yourself (and with the Living Dead)

Rather than killing himself, Rick takes control of his life by trying to follow his own moral code—his self-imposed missions are attempts to do what is 'right' or 'good' according to his personal philosophy. His purpose is ultimately acknowledged by characters such as Michonne: "... you didn't just do what was 'right', you did what *you* thought was right.... And what *you* thought was right ended up being right. You saved that girl's life" (Issue #56). But he also shows that notions of 'right' are flexible and changeable: Rick has gone from law-enforcer—"I can't think of a better way to '*protect and serve*' under the circumstances" (Issue #1), to a law-maker—"You *kill?* You *die*. It's as simple as *that*." (Issue #17), to a murderer—". . . kinda throws the whole '*you kill, you die*' thing out the window, huh?" (Issue #19). He shot Dexter in the back of the head during a battle while his guard was down (Issue #19), slaughtered the would-be rapists of his son with a knife and his bare hands (Issue #57), brutally killed and mutilated unarmed men (Issue #66), and has even considered infanticide (Issue #61). He's able to change his morals to suit his understanding of his circumstances and his world, allowing him to live authentically: "There's no guidelines for behavior in this situation—everything is *unknown*" (Issue #41).

Existentialism means acknowledging that everyone's value system is personal and alterable in this way. We choose to behave in the way that we do, and so there is an independent relationship between freedom and responsibility. The goal is authenticity: you should act as yourself, not as you think 'people in general' should act, or how society suggests, or how your genes dictate. But existential freedom does not take place in an abstract, theoretical space where everything is possible and universal laws can be agreed. It is restricted by people's choices and by the world they exist in. In his famous "We are the walking dead!" speech (issue #24), Rick recognizes this as he says "Things have *changed*. The *world* has changed. And we're going to have to change *with* it."

Kierkegaard uses the story of Abraham and Isaac to show how universal ethics cannot tell us how an individual should act in any particular situation. In the Bible, Abraham agrees to kill his son, despite knowing that this is wrong ("Thou shalt not kill"), because he concludes that, if God asked him to do it, it cannot be wrong. He privileges his religious beliefs over his ethical beliefs. Rick follows a similar process when he revisits his earlier statement "You *kill?* You *die*," and admits "That was probably the most naive thing I've *ever* said." As he explains: "I killed Dexter to protect us *all*. He was threatening to kick us out of this place, our *sanctuary*. He was going to force us out into the *wild*. How humane would things have been out *there?!* How many people did we *lose* on the way *here?*" (Issue #24). Existentially speaking, Rick makes a decision to kill Dexter based on his own authentic morality—he weighs the cost of taking a single life as less than the consequences if Dexter had forced his group to leave their new home.

Sergeant Abraham Ford's story also criticizes notions of universal ethics. This Abraham brutally killed the friends and neighbors who raped his wife and daughter, but was rejected by his family after they saw this violence: "They left because they were terrified to be around me." When Rick hears what happened to Abraham's family he says "You did what you had to—" but Abraham interrupts "No. I did what I *wanted* to do." He acknowledges that he *chose* to act this way, and that he and Rick "can't go back to being dear old Dad" (Issue #58). Their actions have changed their perspectives; and so Abraham is obviously angry when he finds out that Dr. Eugene Porter, whom he has been protecting, isn't really the government scientist he claims to be. While Eugene whimpers "I did what I had to do," denying that he had a choice, Abraham reassesses his actions: "I led a bunch of people to their deaths for that guy" (Issue #67). He's forced to confront projected meaning but this leaves him feeling out of control, and he begs his friend Rosita not to let him kill again (Issue #56)—showing that he too feels the lack of control associated with existential angst.

Although he feels that he's lost himself, Abraham's decisions acknowledge projected meaning as they're based on a morality that depends on the situation, rather than a set of inflexible rules. The goal of existential philosophy is to enable each individual to live an authentic life: that is, a life that is true to himself or herself rather than one dictated by convention or dogma. Rick's speech in issue Issue #24 epitomizes this argument, as he says: "You can sit around *trying* to follow every retarded little *rule* we *ever* invented to make us feel like we *weren't* animals—*and you can die!*" Like his demand to "stop fooling yourselves" this is a call to stop behaving with 'bad faith'— Sartre's term for when we deny our freedom to choose and therefore behave inauthentically, for example by pretending not to realize we have choices open to us ('I had to do it'). Abraham's confession that he killed people because he *"wanted* to" is key here.

Existentialist thought always allows for choice—even prisoners have a choice as to whether to follow the rules imposed on them, flout these, negotiate, rebel, or simply opt out. Hiding behind society's rules or pretending that there are no options

('I had to') are not allowable solutions. Rick is the first to acknowledge that he can—and must—make difficult choices in order to exist authentically in the world of *The Walking Dead*. Throughout the comic he calls attention to his actions and judges himself by them. As he tells Abraham after he kills another (human) attacker: "I've done things—this isn't the first thing to chip away at my soul until I wonder if I'm still human" (Issue #57). Rick knows he's free to choose how to behave, even though his actions affect how he views himself, and how others view him: "If Carl knew about the things that I—" (Issue #58). He wants his friends to arrive at the same conclusion and admit that their actions have made them into new people: "The *second* we put a bullet in the head of one of these undead monsters—the *moment* one of us drove a hammer into one of their faces—or cut a head off. We became what we *are!*"

Hierarchy or Horde?

Rick tells his group that they need to accept the fact that they are (and will be) walkers—they just haven't died yet. Marxist thought (in particular the work of Theodor Adorno) critiques existentialism for being mystifying and designed to create a power structure within an advanced, industrial society. The acknowledgement that the world just 'is' and the ability to either create or deny personal and social morality means that those who view their rights as more important than others' can justify any efforts to achieve their personal goals. The Governor's town of Woodbury is a good example of this, as he has created a hierarchical system to allow him to continue to live in luxury. His people are denied their ability to make authentic choices while being told that they have the right to do as they wish; the Governor tells them Rick and his friends killed Dr. Stevens and shows them Caesar Martinez's zombified head to manipulate them into attacking the prison (Issue #43). Woodbury is an inauthentic society, in many ways more reminiscent of pre-zombie priorities: "People get restless without entertainment" (Issue #27).

Rick's group, on the other hand, has changed its leaders to suit its requirements at various points and Rick himself separates his own search for meaning and his self-imposed moral framework from the hierarchical position of being leader: "You don't want me to be the leader? *Fine.* I don't *care.* I'm *happy* to be without the pressure.... I will do *whatever* I have to do to keep us safe" (Issue #24). His leadership is existential in nature (as much as any can be) as opposed to the Governor's authority, which is all about repressing individuals' freedoms for his own benefit, so he can become more powerful and rule over a larger population. The very idea of a leader goes completely against existentialism in some ways, since by leading and therefore limiting the choices of those below, leaders deny the opportunity to be authentic. However, Rick's leadership tries to maximize the individual freedoms of those he lead: nobody is obliged to stay with the group, and many of the characters go their own ways at various points (they also come back). As Dale says, "Being the "leader" of our little group ... even when we didn't want you to be ... it was never about bossing people around. It was never about control" (Issue #66). The goal of Rick's leadership and his speech is to bring his group to the same conclusions he has reached, so that they can decide how to live an authentic existence too.

But leadership (like a walker) eats away at Rick. Thinking about the things he has had to do, Rick says "It haunts me" (Issue #66), and coming to terms with his new identity is certainly difficult in *The Walking Dead*. Existential identity relies on freedom (to choose how to behave, and therefore who to be) in order to construct your own self-image. However, existentialism also warns against being trapped by this image, or by our history, just as it warns against being trapped by society's rules. Blindly allowing either to dictate our behavior will result in an inauthentic existence. This is where the concept of facticity becomes important.

Facticity says that our past, while part of us, is not the only thing that makes us ourselves. The value ascribed to it is within a person's control. So our past actions are not unavoidably part of who we are today; we can choose how much power to afford our behavioral patterns. To deny our personal history leads to an inauthentic existence; but to claim that our past unavoidably traps us in the same behaviors and particular ways of being is also inauthentic.

The exchange with Tyreese towards the end of Rick's speech in Issue #24 puts forward this idea clearly. Whereas Tyreese and the group want to try and re-establish "life—as it *was* ...

We don't *want* to become *savages.*" Rick alone is able to see that they are clinging too much to their past visions of themselves. He responds: "We *already are* savages . . . The *second* we put a bullet in the head of one of these undead monsters—the *moment* one of us drove a hammer into one of their faces—or cut a head off. We became what we *are!*" It is this argument that brings Rick to the point of his speech, which is to convince his group that they are already engaged in a new existence.

"Other" Zombies

Another key idea in existentialism is the notion of the Other. This idea is felt when we're confronted with the understanding that there are other, conflicting beings in this world which affects how we view ourselves and the world around us. The Other jerks us out of our singular, personal viewpoint, and allows us to re-imagine ourselves or see ourselves through another's eyes.

The concept of the Other is often used by the media to demonize those of a different race or with a different point of view to ourselves, by assigning them characteristics and traits that are completely opposed to the ones we hold. In war, for example, our side has 'freedom fighters' (a concept based on morality and idealism); whereas the opposing side has 'terrorists' (based on disinformation and scare tactics). Logically, the Other in *The Walking Dead* (and its contemporaries) should be the walkers—but instead the humans are defined through opposition with each other. They're the 'bad guys'—after all, the walkers have no autonomy or freedom to choose (they're an existentialist's worst nightmare!) while the humans make decisions to attack, torture, and steal from each other. As Abraham says, "Hundreds of those flesh-eating fucks out there—never thought I'd locked up my family with something worse" (Issue #58).

The Walking Dead rejects the easy option of placing 'good' humans against 'bad' walkers and instead presents the 'zombie Other' in existential terms: outside the conditions of our existence. Rick's speech summarizes this idea:

> You people don't know what we are. We're *surrounded* by the *dead.* We're *among* them—and when we finally give up *we become them!*

> We're living on *borrowed time* here.... You think we hide behind walls to protect us from *the walking dead!* Don't you *get it?* WE *ARE* THE WALKING DEAD! (Issue #24)

He thinks that his group are not living authentic lives anymore; they won't admit that their circumstances have changed and still think that 'society' will come and rescue them from anarchy. They need to stop being zombies themselves, and be authentic, if they want to survive. In this way 'the walking dead' becomes a phrase that acknowledges the existential nature of our lives. If we're not living authentically then we might as well be zombies—unchoosing, uncaring, and unfeeling—because we're all certain to die eventually and existence (not essence) is therefore all that matters.

This sits in stark contrast to traditional zombie narratives where zombie-related death is the primary danger—whether by 'zombification' or simply being eaten alive by brain-munching monsters. In *The Walking Dead* the primary threat comes instead from other people and a lack of resources. Other contemporary zombie texts contain a similar interpretation: Max Brooks's *World War Z* focuses on the breakdown of civilization; the protagonists of *28 Days Later* are under as much threat from the other survivors they encounter as from the slavering 'infected'; and a supercomputer becomes the main threat in the *Resident Evil* franchise. In Stephen King's *Cell* the narrator feels very little upon seeing his zombified former wife, shoving her roughly aside to help his companions and the horror of becoming a zombie seems absent from many contemporary narratives. Zombified humans (such as Michonne's companions, the Governor's daughter and Morgan's son Duane) become pets—outside humanity, unable to choose or maintain any kind of authentic existence. The AMC series amends this important detail, for example by having Morgan's wife return to the home she used to live in, again and again ("Days Gone Bye"). This definitely implies an element of residual humanity—perhaps giving the show a more traditional zombie 'feel'—but it also highlights that repeating actions by rote does not make for an authentic 'life'.

The story of *The Walking Dead* is about the ongoing survival of its protagonists, rather than the dreadfulness of zombification. Walkers are redefined as simply one more threat, often secondary to the dangers of the natural world (starving, exposure, human violence and so forth). This is not to say that Rick is not haunted by dreams of his zombified wife (Issue #55) or that the deaths of his companions are not emotional, but the focus in both instances is different from the tradition. Rick's nightmares are motivated by guilt and some characters in fact commit 'suicide by walker' (such as Carol in Issue #41). It has become just one more way to die.

Evolution after Death

So, has the zombie genre lost its bite? It's certainly not just about the zombies any more. Whereas the first zombie texts treated the creature as exotic, modern movies and books instead normalize these figures, and fantasy has been replaced by realism. One way this is done is by redefining zombieism as a disease. The 'zombies' of *28 Days Later* and *28 Weeks Later* are living people infected with a disease named 'rage' and their precursor *Resident Evil* offers a similar interpretation in both the computer game and movie. Later texts such as *Cell*, or horror movies *The Signal* and *Pontypool* also depict the zombie threat as one of mass *infection*; all invoking a fear of technology as the 'virus' is transmitted via cell phones, television, and radio. The AMC series offers a similar discovery in "TS-19," showing clearly that zombification comes from a virus of sorts, and the comic reveals that *all* the dead reanimate regardless of whether they are bitten (Issue #14), suggesting widespread general infection, rather than contamination from a bite (Issue #15).

Zombies are obviously linked strongly to the dominant fears of their era. A fear of the Other is expressed through racial and sexual exoticization and animalism in films such as *White Zombie* and *I Walked with a Zombie*; along with a Luddite impetus that attacks industrial and post-industrial society in *Metropolis*.

George Romero's *Living Dead* films are the most famous examples of this type of commentary on contemporary racial and political themes; particularly *Dawn of the Dead* whose shopping mall setting has famously been interpreted as a critique of mass consumerism. Reading contemporary texts as a similar commentary (on technological overload in today's society) therefore seems logical.

Zombies have gone from magic to virus, and their stories have become more authentic as they become more grounded in reality. *The Walking Dead* reflects these trends, with its emphasis on survival rather than cure, and a post-apocalyptic setting that could have been caused by any non-specific catastrophe. Unlike Romero's zombies, Kirkman's are depoliticized: emptied of metaphorical or symbolic significance. They become a negation—they're certainly an aspect of this brave new world, but not its defining feature. Instead, the dominant elements of Kirkman's world are emptiness and stillness. This shift and Rick's speech both seem easiest to understand using existential philosophy. The removal of zombies as the primary threat in their own stories, and the new focus on human conflict can both be explained from an existential viewpoint. Personal freedom is a heavy responsibility (particularly in a world with no laws or enforcers) that must be arrived at through choice in order to live authentically and create our personal identity. More importantly, if there's no such thing as a separate, pre-existing human soul then *this cannot be lost*.

Existentialism's denial of an essential soul (other than as constructed through one's actions) means that in an existential society the zombie no longer poses the threat to identity that it once did. In this way, *The Walking Dead* also represents the next phase in a developing narrative of zombies. Early themes (possession, slavery) that gave way to twentieth-century concerns (consumerism, technology) have now been replaced by a 'post-zombieism' that, although it claims to sustain the presence of these creatures, actually diminishes their role within their own narratives in order to better illustrate the existential plight of humanity: the real walking dead.

14
Monsters of Modernity

STEPHEN BRETT GREELEY

There is no humanity in the eyes of the dead that walk. In their gaze is neither recognition, nor understanding, nor pity. From the living dead, all that we hold in common with our fellows has been removed; the thoughts and emotions that define the human person are *not*. Though the dead have flesh and bones, they are utterly unlike us. For once the living spirit is removed, our flesh is emptied, and we see its true limits. Our bodies, once so familiar, become unrecognizable monsters.

From George Romero's startling masterpiece *The Night of the Living Dead*, to the breakout success of the American Movie Channel's series *The Walking Dead*, we have found popular culture beset by the cemetery horde. Why do we seem to be so afraid of losing our humanity, a fear perfectly embodied in the image of the zombie?

Losing the Human

The horror of the undead in film and fiction is of a distinct kind. Unlike other terrors that stalk the landscape of popular culture, werewolves, sharks, and psychopaths, zombies are death incarnate. In their desecrated visages we see our fate, for there is no more stark reminder of our mortality than human remains. In the zombie tale, those remains are in motion, imbued with unholy life by mysterious forces, and coming after us.

While images of death are frightening for obvious reasons, the fact that a zombie was once a person speaks to a loss of our very nature. But what does it mean to lose one's humanity? And is this something modern humans, in particular, fear?

For Aristotle, the human capacity to do good implies that doing the best one can do is our highest aim. This applies to your overall nature as well as specific tasks: if you're a lyre-player, then you must be the best lyre-player you can be. Looking at it this way, the walking dead can no more live up to human potential than can a rat. But we never had much expectation of rat. In this way, the ancient idea of "the fall" is quite poignant: the greater the potential, the greater is its loss.

Thomas Aquinas, who was heavily influenced by Aristotle, would probably say that pursuing a life of contemplation is our highest goal. What is highest or best can be debated, though few would say that being good and being thoughtful are undesirable traits, and we certainly know that zombies are neither. As humans stripped of their potential, they are the worst kind of depraved killer. They are *un*human because they have lost their essential nature. What remains can only be monstrous.

The creators of *The Walking Dead* seem to understand this sense of loss. Three times in the first season, Sheriff Rick Grimes practically eulogizes the person who once was: a crawling corpse of a woman, a former deputy, and a twice-dead man whose gore is about to be used to camouflage Grimes' scent to the walkers. Each time, his words are delivered with a poignancy unexpected.

To the crawling corpse he leans perilously close, telling her, "I'm sorry this happened to you," before administering the *coup de grâce* ("Days Gone Bye"). To his deputy, he remarks on some of the man's shortcomings in life but acknowledges he didn't deserve *this*. And the last time, he finds the man's driver's license, learning he is an organ donor (a sign of the man's concern for others, as well as a gruesome omen), and bemoans the loss of his humanity. Others might simply have seen just another dead body.

In my experience, such sympathy for the undead in zombie films is unprecedented, and it speaks loudly to the essential worth of the human being. Here we're faced with two related but distinct fears: the fear of death, and the fear of losing our very nature.

A History of Death

Death is simply frightening to the living; perhaps no more explanation may be needed for the persistence of this image in contemporary culture. And yet, considering that attitudes about a great many things can change over time, we'll see that humans haven't always been as afraid of death as we are now.

French researcher Philippe Aries, in *The Hour of Our Death*, notes that human beings before The Enlightenment showed no evidence of what he called "death anxiety." Oh, people did fear death, but not to the degree that seems prevalent today. Aries concluded that at least three changes account for this massive irony, for one would think that in a world arguably much safer, we would fear death less. But that is among one of his reasons: our technology *has* created a safer world, making death more of a mystery as we are exposed to it less frequently. And *despite* the incredible advances of technology, death remains a certainty.

Other changes include the moving of society from town to city, where rather than being surrounded by friends and loved ones at the hour of your death, there is now a better chance to die alone amidst the maddening crowds. In the city, we also no longer see the churchyards through which most would pass on their way to service. Cemeteries are now largely kept out of town and out of sight. Connected with this is the removal of religion as providing a sense of comfort, and its replacement for some by science as a central determiner of meaning. But science can really offer no comfort regarding the meaning of death, and what may happen after it.

A Distant Beacon

Many of us moderns might be surprised to learn that at one point in history, science, or its predecessor, philosophy, and religious belief were not so opposed to each other. The relationship between faith and reason, science and religion, is a complex one that Catholic philosophers during the Middle Ages had mostly worked out. The Catholic Church virtually founded the University system, and for even such revolutionaries of science as Galileo and later Newton, God was a given.

Perhaps it is because of the split between faith and reason, which began in its final phase at the end of the Middle Ages, that modern humans sometimes show an unreasoning fear of science. Without being informed or guided by the moral code of religion, science may be seen as led significantly by the search for profit, power, and pleasure. Popular culture, especially movies, gives us suggestive evidence of this fear, as science is often depicted as creating terrors that threaten the world.

In *The Walking Dead*, this implication occurs quite clearly during Dr. Jenner's tirade about all the microscopic horrors kept deep in the vaults of the Centers for Disease Control and Prevention, which would devastate humanity if released. In this scene, it is *almost* confirmed: whatever is raising the dead, the CDC knew about it. In some way, it doesn't matter that the true origin isn't revealed here; it's a kind of guilt by association.

There is, both in the series and in real life, a sense of inevitability about the progress of science that can seem frightening to the layperson, even as its many benefits are enjoyed. Some argue that the technology we rely upon so greatly is becoming too complex for us to understand, creating a sense of detachment and vague unease. On the other hand, it's also possible that the diminishing quality of science education is causing more Americans to be oblivious to, and potentially fearful of, its principles.

While many Enlightenment thinkers regarded scientific progress as a great step forward, especially as it supplanted faith, this was arguably a mistake; not only is it possible to see science and faith as compatible, with no need for the one to replace the other, but science alone can offer no solace in the face of our mortality. All it can do here is struggle to find ways to fend off death, and even its success in this regard, as Aries found, contributes to our fear of death.

Fittingly, in one of the final scenes of "TS-19," Dr. Jenner is at an utter loss to explain the dead coming back to life, and Jacqui offers her own explanation: it is the wrath of God. The scientist begrudgingly acknowledges there may be truth in this. But we don't really think he's convinced, and it wouldn't be surprising if some viewers thought the "God explanation" was just a sign of his hopelessness. Eventually, science will find a cure, we hope, or else we're truly doomed. God cannot help us here.

It turns out, though, that neither can science. At the end of "TS-19," all science can do is offer the survivors a quick death through the Center's self-destruct mechanism. Here the powers of science to cause harm and not hope are starkly realized in the manner of death to be found at the CDC's hand. An emotionless, mechanical female voice gently intones the details of destruction, as the very air will be set on fire by a weapon second in power only to a nuclear blast. Those survivors with the will to continue flee, though it is rather interesting that Jacqui, who suggested the possibility of God's wrath, chooses to stay and be incinerated. Is it that the shred of faith she had left was not strong enough to give her hope? Did she, unwittingly, place too much hope in science? In a culture dominated by sophisticated technology, it would be nearly impossible for her not to have.

And so the heroes, at the end of the first season, head to an uncertain fate. Modern science and technology have failed them, and cities are to be avoided. This other common feature of zombie tales, the devastated city, can shed light on why modern humans may fear the loss of their very nature.

Returning to the Primitive

From the beginning of *The Walking Dead*, it's revealed that at least some humans have fled the cities and dwell now in the forest. This makes sense. Cities have become supermarkets for the dead.

It's appropriate that cities are depicted as such terrors, for here we may see another latent fear in modern humans; while cities offer much, they cost us much as well. And while it's natural for humans to live in communities, modern cities are becoming megalopolises, vast swaths of urbanization that cover the earth. It is estimated that more human beings now live in cities than don't.

In the crowds of cities, it's easy to get the impression that you're a mere number, faceless, unnoticed. A death in a small town is noticed by the entire community; in a city, it is hardly realized at all, unless it is on the evening news, where it is almost a form of entertainment. In previous generations, people lived where they worked, died in their homes, and were laid to rest in the local churchyard, a surviving memory in the minds of their neighbors.

Both zombies and their ruined urban haunts speak to the same fear that modernity renders us inhuman. Many recent thinkers have spoken about the alienation and lack of humanity in modern urban and suburban life. We may know more about celebrities than our neighbors. Our utilities are supplied by unseen hands many miles distant. In the masses of city crowds and the cubicles of towering office buildings, we begin to lose our sense of individuality. This might seem a strange statement, given today's self-obsessed, technology-bound society, except when you consider the way in which people are utterly enmeshed within their electronic connections.

You can see two people sitting together but both texting someone else, while being numbed by an endless stream of music from their earphones. Or you hear of those who walk into traffic and fountains, distracted by their technology into a walking mindlessness chillingly reminiscent of the zombie. Fewer and fewer people, it seems, have the ability to disconnect, to be on their own, to think things through. In C.S. Lewis's *The Screwtape Letters*, the devil Screwtape is furious with his nephew Wormwood when he allows the man he is supposed to tempt "to go for a walk and read a book." That such a simple act should enrage Screwtape reveals its true power, for now the man is thinking deeply, which devils hate. For Lewis, the distracted man is one more easily seduced by bad things, both spiritual and intellectual. The scene is a potent critique of modernity, which is pleasing to devils, for it is full of distractions.

Fearing the dangers already manifest in cities by the eighteenth-century French writer Jean-Jacques Rousseau was largely out of step of with contemporaries who valued reason and scientific progress. To his mind, humans in their natural state were good, or at least neutral, while modern society was corrupting and artificial. Rousseau envisioned the idea of the "noble savage," very much a romantic one, but one that modern people have often found compelling, especially in the 1960s counterculture. In *The Walking Dead*, returning to nature is an imperative for many, and at least some of the survivors seem to prove Rousseau correct.

For the survivors, life in the woods has certainly become a challenge, but their group has also become closely knit, dependent on each other for survival and forging strong emotional ties. They provide for themselves, and know where their needs are to be found. There is some role reversal, with Amy and Andrea providing food by fishing; though with the women washing clothes and Dale serving as lookout, it is clear that traditional roles have also to some extent returned. And in a nod to a bygone, less industrial era, Rick appears as a horseman, if a somewhat inept one, complete with white hat ("Tell It to the Frogs"). That he still wears his sheriff uniform is an interesting counterpoint to Rousseau, as in the midst of chaos he wishes to make clear we still need law and order. But while Rousseau's views were certainly challenged by his peers as a kind of nostalgia, even he recognized that modern humans were probably too used to the conveniences of civilization to be able to function well back in nature. We can see this yearning in the series, too, when the women long for chocolate and vibrators, and know all too well what threats may lurk in the darkness of the forest.

Once the safety net of civilization has been removed, however, people's true natures are revealed. For some, that nature is essentially good. Those who aren't good can be said either to challenge Rousseau's beliefs in the nobility of the savage, or confirm his realization that humans are too used to civilization's benefits to fare well without them. Nonetheless, a telling scene ensues when Rick, T-Dog, and Daryl go to rescue Glenn from the thugs who have abducted him ("Vatos"). Here they encounter Guillermo, a seemingly ruthless warlord who reigns over an industrial ruin. But looks are deceiving, and the truth is glimpsed in Guillermo's use of language not likely to come from a kingpin's lips. Eventually we learn why he and his men are here: they are protecting the abandoned patients of a nearby nursing home. And the kingpin? Back in the world he was the custodian. Apocalypse can bring out the best in us.

Another striking example of this is during the attempted rescue of Merle. After Glenn lays out his plan, demonstrating knowledge of the city's streets and alleys, the others look at him with admiration, and Daryl asks him, "What did you do before this?" Glenn tells them he delivered pizzas. This remarkable little exchange reveals, at one level, that his job made him particularly well-suited for coming up with such a plan. But again we see the deeper implication. Before civilization ended, *all* he did was deliver pizzas; now he is leading a plan to save someone's life. Indeed, Glenn is noted for his daring and his compassion. These powerful traits are not realized in the mundane jobs of a civilized society. Only when the fetters have been released and the walls crushed can the hero arise.

Numerous thinkers of the twentieth century were concerned with the dehumanizing effects of modern, technologized society, and one in particular seems to be given respect in a brief but tantalizing scene in *The Walking Dead*. Ray Bradbury, in *Fahrenheit 451*, drew vivid pictures of the lifelessness to be found in the virtuality of television and other such modern entertainments. In Bradbury's novel, society is hopelessly decayed; in the series, the decadence of civilization is hinted at in the first episode when Rick and the other survivors find themselves cornered in a department store, that ubiquitous symbol of modern American life. It does not seem accidental that when the dead come crashing through the doors, we see a large sign in red hung inside the store that reads, "Bradbury's Storewide Sale." Are we not to see ourselves in the undead's mad rush, pushing others out of the way for great savings? Perhaps we are meant to recall that terrible incident during the 2008 Christmas shopping season, when a horde of mindless shoppers trampled a New York Walmart employee to death. We fight for televisions as if they are the last ribs of the wildebeest.

Slouching Toward Gomorrah

Humans have long had stories of global threats to species and civilizations. Those threats have become real plenty of times. While it is difficult to say for sure whether we fear the "end times" more than our ancestors, there are strong suggestions we do. Regardless, we can certainly say something about the nature of our fears, and in this chapter we have attempted to do just that. There is, however, one last source of these fears left to consider.

Twentieth-century psychoanalyst Erich Fromm noted that four hundred years ago, the literary form known as the utopian novel was invented, and it was essentially hopeful that humanity could find a way to achieve a more idyllic existence. But four hundred years later, people are writing *dystopias*, far more cynical and barely hopeful at all about our future. He asks, "Why?" and so must we.

In the last century, an idea philosophers call "scientific materialism" challenged the notion of an objective truth and morality; if all existence was the result of random collisions of atoms, any such concepts about meaning must exist only in our minds. At worst, this leads to relativism of a profound sort, where one can justify just about anything, including claims about objective truth. This, argue some, can especially be seen in the regimes of Hitler and Stalin, whose beliefs were based on a materialist understanding of human beings, and it was this that allowed them to justify first eugenics, then mass murder.

But scientific materialism has had other troubling implications. It has also undermined the idea of personal responsibility, claiming that our actions and values are really just the result of a brain chemistry over which we have no control. If science is right here, we have no free will and are no more in control of our lives than zombies. The door is shut on morality.

And lastly, we have seen a disturbing trend toward what some call "coercive utopianism," where politicians and social planners devise massive social programs meant to improve society, but not necessarily with society's consent. Rousseau fearfully imagined a future society where people were "forced to be free" and anticipated such eventualities as Lenin's "revolutionary vanguard," a group of elites who would decide what was best for the average person, who was incapable of making wise decisions. We may see versions of this behavior occurring in our own country; in New York City, Mayor Michael Bloomberg traveled to London in 2010 to learn how that city managed to cover every inch of public space with video surveillance. Already there has been an increase in the numbers of these cameras here, though no one has asked the public if this is what they want. We are told it is for our security, and in post-9/11 New York, that seems fine. Either Bloomberg never read *Nineteen Eighty-Four*, or he hasn't made the connection. Orwell's London is the birthplace of "Big Brother," where watching people led to a most insidious method of manipulation.

We moderns seem to have a vague but growing fear that the truth and our fates are controlled by forces beyond our reach, which can no longer be supplicated by prayer, nor understood by a reason based on relativism. Perhaps we Americans are simply beginning to realize that a life of "getting and spending," as the poet Wordsworth once said, is no life at all. The more things we gather, the more we lose ourselves.

Or perhaps working in the seething masses of cities fills us with a dread that we have somehow been reduced. Spending so much of our lives at work leaves little time for being human, as most of us only have one or two days a week set aside for ourselves. The richness of the human person finds few opportunities for expression in our increasingly busy lives, and we suffer as a result. Where is the time for the artist or the hero within us? Where is the time to spend with family and friends over a slow meal and conversation? Where is the time to raise our own children? Must the things that make us fully human be crammed into the corners of our lives?

In the world of *The Walking Dead*, the survivors find that living close to death and shivering in the cold makes them, in some ways, more alive than ever before. Such apocalyptic tales ask whether it is possible for a meaningful life to be found amidst the pursuits of modern life. Though the world's wisdom traditions say that material wealth is not the way to true happiness, *The Walking Dead* suggests we moderns have little knowledge of this wisdom.

The zombie, then, rises from its crypt as us: always hungry, never sated, and having lost all sense of what it means to be human. Or perhaps we rise looking more and more like them, as we get up each morning and shamble off for another day at work, another fast food dinner, another evening spent listless before the television. Fromm once said, "Destruction is the outcome of unlived life." Is it the sense of potential unrealized that troubles us? Or is it a vague awareness of having lost something vital that we never knew we had? It is no wonder our culture produces such violent fantasies as *The Walking Dead*.

Only our culture could make such monsters.[1]

---

[1] I would like to thank Dr. Robert Delfino for his invaluable assistance and inspiration.

The Heart's Desire

15
People for the Ethical Treatment of Zombies (PETZ)

JEFFREY A. HINZMANN AND ROBERT ARP

Is it morally right to kill zombies? Are you violating some ethical principle when you kill your zombie mom? How about when you kill your zombie wife or child? Do zombies have rights or privileges of any kind that must be respected and upheld? Is it morally wrong to use zombies as slave labor? How about using them for entertainment? How about keeping one as a useful pet, like some guard dog?

Robert Kirkman's *The Walking Dead* is one of the richest zombie stories to come along in quite some time. While it adds little to the zombie genre in terms of the basic premise, its open-ended graphic-novel format—later developed into an acclaimed TV series—allows for the exploration of themes that shorter formats like movies can only touch on. One of these themes has to do with the moral status of a zombie, and whether zombies can be morally harmed in some way.

Can Zombies Morally Be Harmed?

"Whether zombies can be *morally harmed* in some way?" What!? They're the friggin' flesh-eating undead, for Christ's sake! Maybe some hippy characters from *The Walking Dead* stories could start an organization like People for the Ethical Treatment of Zombies (PETZ)?

While it may seem strange to grant rights and privileges to the flesh-eating undead who terrorize the human survivors of post-apocalyptic Atlanta, philosophers are weirdos who have wondered about the moral status of all kinds of people and things; enemies in war, serial killers, infants and embryos, animals, plants, and even the Earth itself. Against this backdrop, asking if a zombie can be morally harmed is an interesting opportunity to consider how our concepts of morality operate, and how a zombie's moral status is similar to, and different from, that of an animal.

After all, zombies seem to act like the lowest kinds of savage beasts, and it could be argued that even savage beasts should only be harmed, killed, used, or objectified when there are good reasons for doing so. In the end, we'll see that according to certain kinds of utilitarian moral positions, zombies should probably be placed on some kind of zombie reservation where they can roam free and eat other animals, unmolested by humans. This would definitely satisfy the PETZ people.

A Mindless Killing Machine?

Although there are some good objections to thinking this way, people generally feel that the more consciously aware something is, the more it has rights and privileges and, therefore, the more it should be treated with dignity and respect. So, more mind means more moral status and merits more moral rights associated with that mind (Jeepers, that's a lot of alliteration!).

We don't think we're doing anything immoral when we crush a rock, for example, but we do think that the guy who drags a cat behind his pickup truck and joyrides around town for the fun of it should be castrated. Poaching a gorilla might cause some to think that the poacher should receive the death penalty. And, obviously, many think that murdering a person warrants an "eye for an eye" kind of moral response for the murderer. So, before we can talk about zombie morality, we need to say something about zombie minds. What kind of a mind does a zombie have? More specifically, what kind of as mind does a zombie have in *The Walking Dead* series?

First off, it seems that non-living things—things that are not biological or are in fact human-made—do not have a mind. Planets, chairs, trains, atoms, and tornadoes, for example, don't seem to think about, or feel, anything, and so, are mind*less*.

On the other hand, there seem to be living things that have more or less of a mind. Mice, dogs, and cats would have less of a mind, while monkeys, gorillas, and humans have more of a mind. These aren't arbitrary distinctions. They're based on qualities that we can argue that tornados lack and gorillas have. Mice lack some mental qualities that gorillas have, so they have less of a mind. So what are these qualities?

1. *Perceptual Awareness or Perceptual Mind*—the ability to recognize an object through some sense mechanism, as well as associate a stimulus with some memory, which requires a fairly small brain (or older part of an advanced brain, like the brain stem).

Fishes, lizards, and birds will move toward someone who is about to feed them because they seem to recognize or remember, that it's feeding time.

2. *Basic Reasoning or Reasoning Mind*—the ability to perform a basic inference like "this is an animal that will eat me; therefore, I must get out of here," as well as the ability to solve a simple problem like using a stick to get at food just out of reach, which requires a bigger brain capable of storing more memories.

Cats, dogs, aardvarks, orangutans, and all other mammals will fight or flee, as well as share food, given a set of circumstances that requires them to do a basic "I need to think this through." Also, standard computational systems nowadays are set up to do some basic reasoning.

3. *Consciousness or Conscious Mind*—the ability to recognize oneself as an actor in some event, think about one as a self who is thinking, form beliefs about the past and future, imagine things that could not be directly experienced by the senses, and experience a range of emotions that are more than basic pleasures and pains, all of which require a brain with a fairly big frontal lobe.

We know humans have this ability, whether or not some animals (or even aliens out there in the universe, or androids we may create in the future) have this ability is difficult to determine.

If pressed, most people would say that if a thing has at least perceptual awareness, then that thing has a mind. Notice that, although an amoeba has a basic stimulus-response mechanism, it does not seem to have perceptual awareness (so, it probably does not have a mind), and the same goes for a lot of other species in the various biological kingdoms like bacteria, fungi, and plants. Insects could be considered a borderline case where they may or may not have mind. All vertebrates seem to have perceptual awareness, so they probably have minds. Pet fish, sharks, lizards, snakes, frogs, mice, cats, and dogs, as well as little children, easily recognize when it's feeding time, for example, so these animals all seem to be perceptually aware of what's going on around them.

But, there seems to be a big difference between a marlin's mind, a mouse's mind, and a man's mind (more alliteration!). Basic reasoning and consciousness are qualities of a mind, too, but most people would *not* say that a marlin, or even a mouse, is conscious the way a man is. The fact that humans are able not only to speak, write, theorize, and create works of art, but also to solve quadratic equations, construct space shuttles, erect cities, and uphold civil and moral laws to benefit the weaker members of a society all seem to be evidence of the fact that humans are conscious.

Figure 15.1 represents circles of the types of mind we have spoken about, as well as examples of vertebrates that exhibit that particular type of mind. There are things that we can all agree don't have minds—like tables, lamps, the Sun, trees, and (possibly) ants—which are outside of the circles. Also we have drawn the circles nested in one another to indicate the fact that Perceptual Mind is the least complex form of mind, with Reasoning Mind building upon, and being more complex than, Perceptual Mind. Finally, Conscious Mind builds upon, and is more complex than both Perceptual Mind and Reasoning Mind. So humans like our surfer dude in the figure have Conscious, Reasoning, and Perceptual Mind, while cats, mice, chimps, and artificially intelligent beings—like computational systems—have Reasoning and Perceptual Mind only, and frogs, snakes, sharks, and zombies (as we would argue) have Perceptual Mind only.

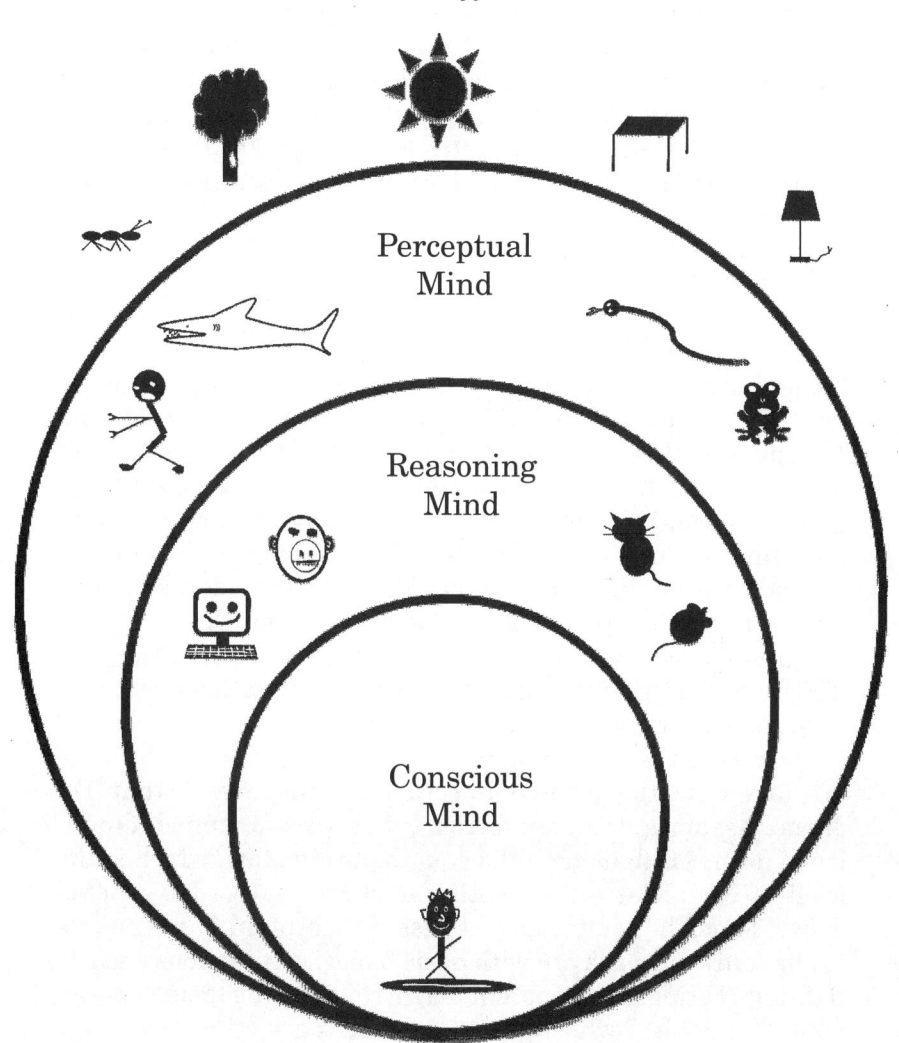

People for the Ethical Treatment of Zombies (PETZ) 183

FIGURE 15.1 Types of Minds

Where would a zombie fit in here? It seems like zombies are akin to sharks and other merely perceptually aware animals that move (almost) relentlessly in the direction of their prey so as to feed. However, while sharks are commonly known as "Mindless Killing Machines," they are really probably better described as "Conscious Mindless and Reasoning Mindless But Not Perceptually Mindless Killing Machines." Sharks seem to have Perceptual Mind, and zombies seem to have this kind of basic mind, too. (Also, sharks and zombies aren't machines, which, by definition, *really* are mindless.) You'll notice in Figure 18.1 that we put a crooked, creeping, carnivorous zombie (more friggin' alliteration!) as an example of something with a Perceptual Mind, too.

Brains . . . Must Have Brains!

Modern brain science can help us answer the question of what kind of a mind a zombie has in *The Walking Dead* series. In the TV episode, "TS-19," Rick Grimes and the band of survivors head to the CDC in downtown Atlanta, hoping that someone there has some idea of how to fix the zombie outbreak. There, they find a single survivor, Dr. Edwin Jenner, living underground in a bunker and attempting to figure out the zombie plague, as the fuel powering the facility runs out. Jenner shows the group a video of a Functional Magnetic Resonance Imaging (fMRI) scan of a brain that dies of the zombie infection, and then comes back to life a few hours later.

Now here's the interesting part. When the human brain is overtaken by the zombie infection (to the extent that Dr. Jenner assumes it *is* an infection), it revives in a much-diminished form. All that comes back is the brain stem, which is the level of complexity of a reptile or shark, as we have noted above. Thus, the zombie has, at best, a Perceptual Mind, and its brain's only concerns are with basic biological functions such as fighting, eating, and reproducing—reproducing being irrelevant to zombies, who reproduce by biting victims who they don't then immediately consume.

Us and . . . All of Them

So, it seems to be a *no-brainer* that zombies should be shot on sight—usually in their much-diminished brain—to prevent those

God-forsaken evil things from eating *our own* brains! Most people feel toward zombies the way they feel toward sharks, and so far we have shown why, given that zombies are very much like sharks with their primitive brains and perceptual minds.

And there's moral positions that we can point to in the history of Western philosophy that straightforwardly justify the killing of sharks and zombies, even for the fun of it. According to a family of moral theories that can be called *anthropocentric* (the Greek word *anthropos* means "human"), moral status derives from, and depends upon, complex forms of conscious rationality, including the ability to conceptualize the world in a mutually understandable way.

This kind of view is one of the oldest in Western philosophy and has been advocated by almost every major philosopher (and other thinkers) in Western history. It also has enduring popularity for us humans, obviously, since we're the only kinds of things that can engage in complex forms of conscious rationality! Also, this view of morality goes hand in hand with the view that humans are the most important, valuable, or sacred kinds of biggest-brained things in the universe.

There are many problems with anthropocentric moral theories, but one in particular is significant. Any anthropocentric view—almost by definition—seems straightforwardly *biased* in favor of humans, which itself (the bias) could be considered immoral from the start! On the anthropocentric view, it makes sense that humans would not only deserve full rights and privileges, but also deserve to be treated "most morally"—so to speak—since humans are the ones with the biggest brains and the only kinds of things that can conceptualize the world in a mutually understandable way! To heck with animals and their thoughts, feeling, and interests! Forget the environment and the planet! These things don't count morally anyway! Or, they count only insofar as they serve our interests as the big-brained bosses of this planet.

And zombies? Anthropocentric moral theorists would have no problem: keeping some animal or zombie as a useful pet, say, as a means of protection of person or property; killing an animal or zombie outright for sport or just the fun of it; testing lethal drugs on the animal or zombie for the purposes of helping humans or just to see what happens; making a cool animal-skinned or zombie-skinned briefcases to sell at the flea market.

One example of a zombie as a useful pet can be seen when Rick and the survivors meet Michonne, a badass ex-lawyer who is deadly with a samurai sword. She shows up to the group's new home—an abandoned prison—leading two zombies behind her in chains. Apparently one was her ex-boyfriend. Michonne still has a use for him though, since the smell he gives off discourages other zombies from attacking her as she travels. It's as if the zombies are like junkyard dogs, or some other kind of guard dog that one might have in their home or walk around with in a bad neighborhood for protection. A guard dog's primary purpose is to be a useful protector of someone or someone's possessions. As soon as Michonne is admitted to the safety of the settlement in the prison, however, we learn the extent to which she sees these zombies as mere tools to be used for her own defense: she kills them right on the spot (and shows us how good she is with her sword)!

Many anthropocentric moral theorists would not have a problem with Michonne's actions since pets are animals and would only be shown some moral consideration on the basis of their relationship with their owner. The word *owner*, however, points out that this moral consideration hardly amounts to a status equal to that of humans. Pets are still property, still owned by their master, and by and large can be treated as the master wishes. And if animals are to be shown some moral consideration, then animals have some right to be treated well even if they are property.

All of Them and . . . Us

The desire to show animals some moral consideration—especially given what occurs in the typical factory farming process—is what prompted a set of moral views that can be called *utilitarian*, which are almost completely opposed to the anthropocentric view of morality. According to utilitarian views, moral status derives from, and depends upon, the capacity to feel pleasure and pain, and one should always and everywhere maximize pleasure and minimize pain as much as is possible. So, bringing the most pleasure to most is the moral thing to do, while anything else is immoral. Another way to think about this is that there are certain living things that have an "interest" in merely living out their lives unbothered, unmolested, and unharmed, and the moral thing to do is to respect the *interests* of any living thing.

This kind of view hasn't been popular with anthropocentricists, as you can imagine, since animals having a Reasoning Mind and a Perceptual Mind would be considered on a par with humans having a Conscious Mind. Also, this view of morality goes hand in hand with the view that humans are *just as* important, valuable, or sacred as *any other* kind of living, self-interested, pleasure-and-pain-experiencing animal in the universe. The most influential contemporary utilitarian arguments come from Princeton University philosophy professor, Peter Singer. Singer argues for what he calls the *expanding circle*, which is basically the idea that morality ought to continue to expand ever wider, until all beings capable of experiencing pleasure and pain—with interests—get the moral consideration they deserve.

Now, if a zombie can experience pleasure and pain, then it has an interest, and it can be harmed; therefore, it shouldn't be harmed needlessly. If it's coming right at you to eat you, that's one thing, and killing it seems right to do in the same way that killing Jaws is right to do when he attacks. But killing a zombie just for the sport of it, for example, would be morally wrong according to most utilitarians, just like killing any animal for sport would be.

It Gets Even Deeper, Dude

The standard utilitarian approach to animal ethics is fascinating because it almost always provokes a reaction: some think it goes too far, others think it doesn't go far enough. Those who think it goes too far believe there *is* something special about being human, something (like rationality or consciousness or self-awareness) that we don't share with the animals that specifically entitles us to a kind of moral consideration that is cheapened if it included lesser forms of life. Such critics often mock these proposals by questioning why one stops at just animals (and usually the cute mammals, at that!). Why not give rights, privileges, and moral considerations to sharks, insects, and trees, too?

Though the last sentence is intended to mock proponents of the expanding circle by questioning its boundaries (how far should it expand?), it's *exactly* the position taken by those who want to apply moral considerations to things beyond people and animals with more complex nervous systems. Aldo Leopold's *land ethic*, for example, emphasizes the functional unity of ecosystems and attempts to give moral consideration to them in the interest of benefiting all the participants. This means that one ought to cultivate an almost spiritual reverence for forests, rivers, and even the ground itself. It's not as far-fetched as it sounds. People often care deeply about their homes and communities and invest a great deal of energy into maintaining and beautifying them. If you think of your environment as your home, then the motivation carries over.

A similar view, called *deep ecology*, was advocated by Arne Naess. Deep ecology views the entire Earth as an organism, and questions the morality of a civilization that thinks of the Earth as a source of resources to use and exploit for its own benefit. Both deep ecology and the land ethic have reasons for extending moral consideration (though not always the same *kind* of moral consideration) to plants and inanimate objects, and both condemn the thoughtless exploitation of natural resources.

Figure 15.2 represents our version of Singer's expanding circle of things deserving of a moral status, rights, and privileges. Notice how Figure 18.2 looks similar to Figure 18.1, further emphasizing our point that mind and morality are interconnected with one another. If zombies were real, they would likely be things that could be morally harmed, probably starting with some version of a land ethic, but maybe even on some utilitarian moral positions, too.

PETA, PETZ, and Preserves

As you can imagine, plenty of utilitarians, land ethicists, and deep ecologists have a moral problem with killing animals for sport, killing animals to eat, and killing animals for experimentation. Singer's utilitarian arguments from the 1970s have been incredibly influential for animal protection groups all around the world, including People for the Ethical Treatment of Animals (PETA). There are even some land ethicists and deep ecologists who have a moral problem with zoos, aquariums, and keeping animals as pets! So, no wild lions kept in zoos, no "mindless killing machine" sharks kept in aquariums,

FIGURE 15.2 The Expanding Circle

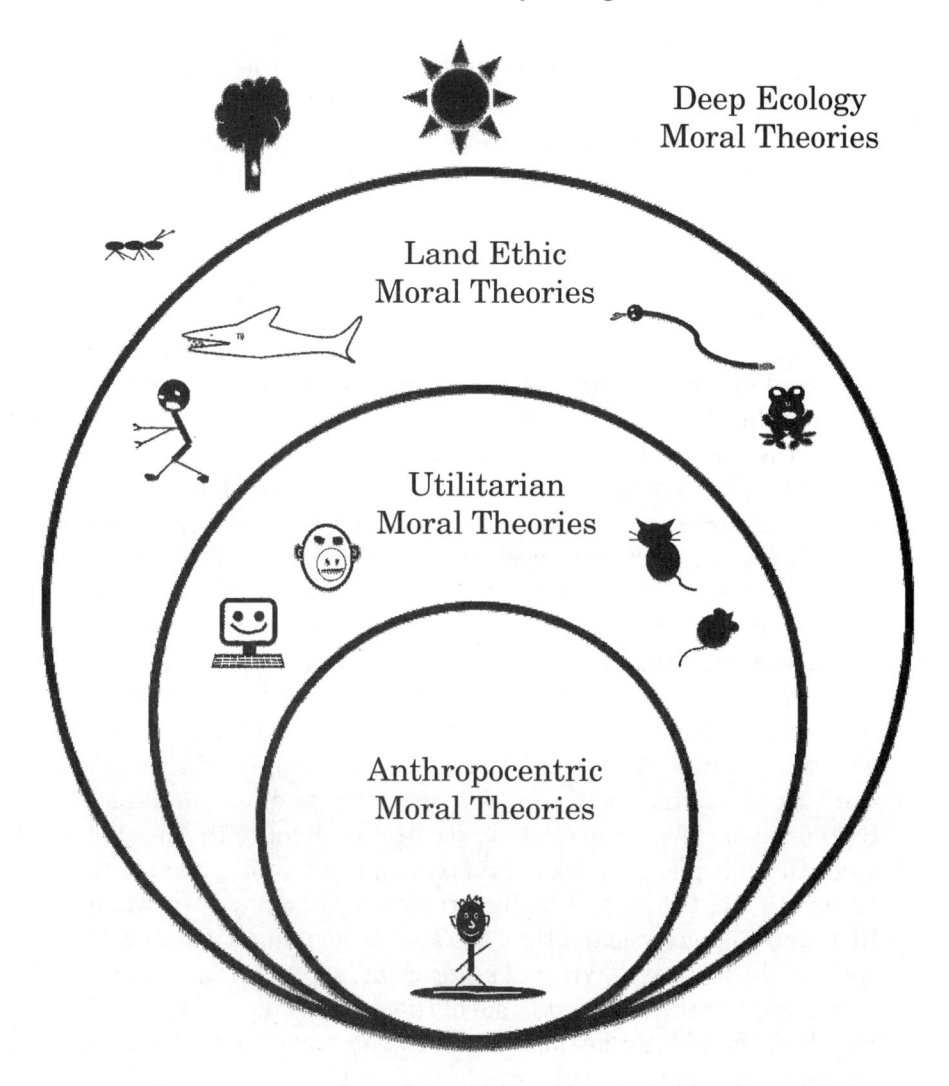

Deep Ecology Moral Theories

Land Ethic Moral Theories

Utilitarian Moral Theories

Anthropocentric Moral Theories

no naturally wild, but tamed, cats or dogs as pets, and—if they existed—no zombies in zoos or as pets either. Animals and zombies (with their shark-like existence) have an "interest" in merely living out their lives unbothered, unmolested, unexploited, and unharmed, and the moral thing to do is to respect the interests of these living things.

Since no moral theorist we have spoken about would deny that humans have a moral right to defend and protect themselves, any living thing that may cause harm to humans has to be respectfully dealt with in a way that does not cause the living thing harm. So, even though a zoo or an aquarium might not be the place to keep some living thing, and humans have to co-live with other living things at times, it's ultimately up to us to set up environments, or preserves, where living things can live out their lives unmolested. Part of this has to do with not invading their spaces in the first place. But sometimes, animals and other living things encroach upon our already-established habitats.

So, the fact of the matter is that we need to set up reservations and places of preservation for those animals that may be dangerous to us, according to many anthropocentric, utilitarian, land ethic, and deep ecology moral positions. That's why there are even places designated in ocean waters for the preservation of sharks. The same would go for zombies, then, with something like a zombie preservation area.

In fact, something like this occurs in *The Walking Dead* series with Hershel, a farmer that Rick and his band of survivors encounter due to the accidental shooting of Rick's son Carl. Hershel and his family welcome Rick and his band, and the survivors even consider living at the farm with Hershel since there is plenty of room and extra people would be able to help with the farming. A major problem arises, however, when Rick and his party learn that Hershel is keeping a number of walkers in his barn. While it's not clear why at first, it later becomes clear that at least some of them were once members of Hershel's family. By keeping them in the barn (and therefore on his property) they still sort of are family.

Rick is outraged because he believes that they are, first and foremost, zombies (duh!) and are a serious threat to the safety of the farm. Hershel disagrees, not wanting to stop thinking of them as people and holding out hope that so long as they remain "alive" there is hope that they might someday "turn back" to being human. In the show, he is not so explicit about his hope that they might "turn back" but argues instead that they be thought of as sick people rather than inhuman monsters. In the episode "Secrets" we see that Hershel thinks they are entitled to personhood and uses an analogy to mental illness saying "A paranoid schizophrenic is dangerous too, but we don't shoot sick people." Hershel is reluctant to even adopt the term 'walker' to refer to zombies, and admonishes his daughter to not call them walkers either. This is only one of several conflicts between Rick's group and Hershel's, but it is a pivotal one, as we will see.

The group has spent a great deal of time at Hershel's farm, in spite of serious disagreements, because they have been searching for Sophia, a little girl who became separated from their group. The debate comes to a head in the episode "Pretty Much Dead Already" when Shane, in a rage at the thought of living near confined walkers, breaks open Hershel's barn and goads the other members of Rick's party to mow them down with gunfire as they escape the barn. Hershel is horrified, but ultimately seems resigned to accepting what's happening. Finally, when all the zombies have been killed, one final one comes out: a zombie Sophia. Rick has felt such remorse over losing her, that he finally seems to understand Hershel's position, thinking of her as a zombie means admitting she's lost even though she's standing right in front of him! Still, he rather quickly (albeit painfully) comes to exactly that conclusion, and shoots the zombie Sophia in the head.

It seems that in *The Walking Dead*, the main reason people ever extend any moral consideration to zombies in any form or fashion is that they *used to be people*. More than that, they used to be people who were important to other people, and hence we're inclined to try to keep them alive and unharmed in spite of the danger they pose. This motivation, however, is straightforwardly anthropocentric as well as egotistical from the perspective of the utilitarian, land ethicist, and deep ecologist. It is a personal decision on the part of the former family members, lovers, and friends of those who became zombies to try to preserve some aspect of their relationship with them.

One Last Thing

There is one important (and infamous) example from the books that borders on a genuinely unethical *mis*treatment of zombies while keeping them alive: it involves a character called *The Governor*. The Governor (whose actual name is Philip) got his name because he was in a position to give himself a grandiose title just for the hell of it. More accurately, he is the mayor of a small, rural town called Woodbury, which is relatively safe from the zombies due to the proximity of an abandoned National Guard armory. The people have built walls to keep the zombies out, and have plenty of weapons with which to fight the zombies, all thanks (so far as we can tell) to The Governor.

But that's not all. The Governor is, to be blunt, a sick freak. He's a sadist who tortures people who visit Woodbury, including Rick and Michonne. He cuts off Rick's hand as part of interrogating him to find out where his group is living, and he restrains and repeatedly rapes Michonne to punish her for her disrespect toward him. Michonne's act of disrespect consists of rapidly killing a death-match opponent and depriving the people of Woodbury of a good show.

You see, The Governor has instituted the practice of forcing outsiders who come upon the camp to fight to the death in an arena whose outer walls are ringed with chained-up zombies. Thus, we see a clear vision of The Governor's character and his immorality; he uses other human survivors for blood sport and other zombies as part of the game, too. As far as we can tell, no one, whether human or zombie, gets much moral consideration from The Governor. No one, oddly enough, except his zombie daughter, who he keeps chained up in his apartment, and whom he seems to continue to kiss (in a manner with some incestuous connotations).

The governor's widespread cruelty, and his showing of pseudo-consideration for his zombie daughter (who he seems to love more as a pet than a person) reminds us of what Immanuel Kant said about cruelty to animals. He says "If a man shoots his dog because the animal is no longer capable of service, he does not fail in his duty to the dog, . . . but his act is inhuman and damages in himself that humanity which it is his duty to show towards mankind. . . . We can judge the heart of a man by his treatment of animals" ("Duties toward Animals" in *Lectures on*

Ethics). So even though Kant is an unashamed anthropocentrist, we still get a satisfying argument for why killing (or torturing or exploiting) zombies indiscriminately, just for the heck of it, is wrong. The Governor's character shows this point as well as anything could, and the other characters struggle to maintain their humanity towards each other after constantly struggling to survive against the zombie threat and the ever-present possibility of death. Ironically, caring about Zombies because they used to be human turns out to be a crucial link to the humanity of the survivors more than even for the zombies.

How could we preserve our humanity and show moral respect for zombies? If there were a way to keep the zombies someplace safe from humans where they could find their own food from other animals—as sharks do by preying on weaker, slower, unsuspecting animals—then that would be ideal. Hershel's motivations are personal and have to do with the fact that the zombies used to be people he cares for, but he's on the right track in terms of a kind of PETZ idea to set up a zombie preserve. The episode "Pretty Much Dead Already" just shows how complex and hard it can be to stick to such noble aims when the world is falling apart.

16
The Only Good Walker Is a Dead Walker

FRANKLIN ALLAIRE

In all my years of being a fan of the living dead genre I have always been fascinated with peoples' inability to kill a member of the walking dead even when their lives depended on it. How many times have we all yelled, "Just kill it!" at the screen?

To me this is a no-brainer (no pun intended)! If I'm trapped in a room with the undead I will not hesitate to kill them because they will not hesitate to kill me. What if it's your undead mom? Could you kill your undead brother? Would you kill your undead spouse? Yes! I've gone so far as to tell family members I won't hesitate to take them down and have asked that they do the same for me.

Imagine my surprise when I learned that the general consensus regarding what people call 'zombies' (I prefer to avoid the zee-word in favor of 'living dead', 'undead', 'walkers', 'geeks', and the politically-correct 'living-impaired') is that they are animal-like and, therefore, have some moral value. What!?! Who would have thought that there are people out there who feel the undead have moral value? It seems so strange that something so common-sense would draw people in to an applied ethical discussion. It also stands to reason that the undead, like any other creature human beings may take for granted, should be given their due consideration. So I was thrilled to be given the opportunity to offer the counter-point that walkers have no positive value and that we can kill them indiscriminately without feeling bad about it.

Kill or Be Killed

One of the common threads that link all undead apocalypse comics, movies, and television shows such as *The Walking Dead* is the need to kill of those who have been become walkers. It's possible, that you find yourself in a situation like Rick's where shooting walkers is your only way to get to safety. Perhaps you're sitting around the campfire with Dale and are approached by a herd of walkers. Inevitably, as one of a handful of lucky (or perhaps unlucky) survivors, you must beat, stab, burn, or otherwise incapacitate walkers, even those who were friends and family.

This need to kill—or re-kill—walkers on a daily basis can be unsettling. Some may advocate for restraint from indiscriminate killing, for example limiting slaughter to life-and-death situations. In a politically correct apocalyptic world there may be people who advocate for walker's rights and the ethical treatment of the undead, like Hershel. So does killing a walker deprive them of any rights they may have as a walker? Regardless of the situation, killing walkers raises some moral and ethical issues. Is killing *any* and *all* walkers justified or unethical? Do walkers have a right to life and pursue their dreams and goals? Or does killing them violate what philosopher and animal-rights activist Tom Regan refers to as the *respect principle*—we are to treat those individuals who have inherent value in ways that respect their inherent value.

I believe, that walkers have no moral value and that the only good walker is a dead walker. Since we are not currently living through an undead apocalypse we have the luxury of pondering whether killing walkers is right or wrong. However, if a dozen walkers were bearing down on your family and friends this luxury would go out the window in favor of a heavy, blunt, wieldable object.

At the heart of this debate are two philosophical concepts—ethics and personhood. Moral philosophy explores whether the organisms, in our case the undead, have some moral value necessitating the living to treat them humanely. Personhood examines facets of the human condition that make us uniquely human, separate us from other living species (such as cats, dogs, and Venus flytraps) and whether or not the living dead possess the awareness necessary to qualify as people or even animals.

Ethics of the Living and the Undead 101

Before we can determine whether an action is immoral, we need to have a basic understanding of where morality comes from. Moral philosophy is a branch of philosophy that is essentially a search for a litmus test of proper behavior. Glenn's employment of the golden rule—Do unto others as you would have them do unto you—is a classic example of a normative principle within ethics. Glenn helps Rick, a complete stranger, in the hope that someone would one day do the same for him.

According to some moral philosophers, moral values are not handed down to us from on high, but are based on human desires. The motivation behind human actions varies widely from inherent selfishness to our universal capacity for benevolence. Regardless, moral values stem from cultural evolution and society's needs. This results in what look like universal moral truths. For instance killing and stealing is pretty much on everyone's do-not-do-list.

If you'd told Rick prior to his coma that one day he would beat a walker to death in front of his neighbor's house he probably would have locked you up. The concept of both a walker and killing it just doesn't fit into that reality. Hence when Rick kills his first walker in "Days Gone Bye" he is both shocked and disgusted with himself and with the result of his action. However, it's not long before takes out two more walkers (Leon Basset and Hannah the bicycle girl) with only slight hesitation. Since moral values are humanly created and bound by cultural norms, values tend to change as the culture changes over time or as circumstances change.

So how do you determine what's right or wrong? Individuals and groups determine moral values through a process of weighing principles. Sometimes this process is conscious. Most of the time, however, it happens without our being aware of it. It's what Jeremy Bentham calls act-utilitarianism. We tally the consequences of each action we perform and thereby determine whether an action is morally right or wrong. We address a laundry list of principles by asking ourselves questions. Our answers tell us whether we (both the individual and society) think an action is morally acceptable.

Let's suppose you're standing outside and a walker is lumbering towards you. The questionnaire running through your mind might include:

- What is a consequence of killing this walker that is beneficial to myself?
- What is a consequence of killing this walker that is beneficial to the rest of society?
- Does killing this walker help those in need? (principle of benevolence)
- Does killing this walker assist others in pursuing their best interests even when they can't do so themselves? (principle of paternalism)
- Does killing this walker violate the law? (principle of lawfulness)
- Does killing this walker violate its freedom over its own actions and/or physical body? (principle of autonomy)
- Does killing this walker violate its right to due process, fair compensation for harm done, and fair distribution of benefits? (principle of justice)
- Does killing this walker violate its rights to life and free expression?

The first two questions are easy for us to answer. Are there personal and social benefits to killing any walker? Yes! If I kill a walker, *any* walker, that's one less walker that could potentially infect me or anyone else.

Killing walkers also takes care of the principles of benevolence and paternalism particularly if there are children in the group of survivors. Additionally, in *The Walking Dead* there doesn't seem to be any functioning government. So lawfulness, at least legally speaking, is not an issue. Questions regarding autonomy, justice, and rights could be harder to answer.

In order for rules, laws, or ethics to work there has to be reciprocity—give and take—between all members of the society. Traffic signals work because we all recognize and understand that green means "go" and red means "stop."

Do walkers share our values? Who knows? Thus far in *The Walking Dead* it appears that walkers are only interested in attacking the living. While one could question whether the undead are moral creatures, the greater philosophical question is whether the undead are *aware* of their capacity to be moral or immoral creatures and are therefore *capable* of performing moral actions. Herein lies the chink in the "walkers have moral value" argument. It stems from an *assumption* that we are discussing *human beings*. Although there are similarities between humans and walkers, there are also many differences and the nature of the being must be taken into account.

Friend, You Need Glasses, It Was a Walker

Walkers may look a bit like people, but are they? Certainly at one time all walkers were once people. But after being bitten they died. It just so happens that in *The Walking Dead* universe they can come back. People tend to assume that "human" means genetically human. If that's the case then walkers are subject to all the moral rights and privileges that humans possess since they are genetically identical to their previous living incarnations.

We, however, are interested in looking at humans in the moral sense with the implication that we are members of a moral community into which philosophical heavyweight Immanuel Kant included angels, God, and other non-human rational beings. As members of a moral community we're bound by the commands of morality and possess the rights and duties accompanying such membership. Simply being genetically human is neither necessary nor sufficient for being human.

There's no doubt that pre-walkers (human beings), while alive, are moral creatures meaning they are aware that a moral code exists. Whether they follow it or not is another discussion altogether. What concerns us here is the walkers' *personhood* after it has been resurrected, to use Dr. Edwin Jenner's description in "TS-19." Personhood refers to those qualities and feelings we acquire throughout our lives that make us human beings. American philosopher Mary Anne Warren proposes a thought experiment involving an imaginary space traveler having to decide whether alien beings have the right to be respected, the right to be treated morally, or the right to life. We would easily modify such a thought experiment to suit our needs here.

Let's suppose an alien space traveler visits *The Walking Dead* universe. If you can find a copy of *The Walking Dead*,

Issue #75, you can see what this *might* be like. What criteria might they use to determine if the undead are worthy of being respected and possibly protected? Warren cites five criteria they might use to determine personhood: consciousness, reasoning, self-motivated activity (regardless of whether that motivation comes from selfishness or benevolence), the capacity to communicate, and the presence of self-concepts and self-awareness. While this isn't necessarily a checklist it does represent an individual's personhood as the interplay of physical, biological, and metaphysical factors. Additionally, some of these characteristics are more essential than others. The point is, however, that a being lacking all five criteria can't possibly be considered capable of being a member of a moral community.

Gray Anatomy

Physically walkers aren't much different from the living. We experience this through Rick's eyes on several occasions early in "Days Gone Bye." First he confuses a walker-child for a living child. Later, Rick accuses Morgan Jones of murder for killing a walker he took to be a man. Duane and Morgan then explain to a confused and incredulous Rick that what he thought was a man was really a walker. Given the fact that Rick has no idea what has happened to the world it's easy to see how he could make that mistake. After all, except for some gashes, discoloration, and the occasional lost limb walkers pretty much look like us on a really, really, bad day.

Biologically, walkers are a bit more different from us. Whereas we are born, walkers are made. Walkers reproduce only by infecting someone. Although walkers and the living eat, there is no evidence that walkers eat for sustenance. Nor is there any evidence that walkers even possess a functioning digestive system, let alone other systems absolutely necessary for survival.

As the playback of TS-19 showed, after a period of no activity the brain reactivates albeit on the most primitive level. The barely functioning nervous system is a key piece of personhood because it's responsible for the transmission of impulses to and from the brain. In other words, it's how we *feel* things. Tickle us, do we not laugh? Prick us, do we not say . . . "Ouch"? This is evidence that our brains are receiving and sending messages to the rest of our body. A walker's brain is active at the most basic level, which is barely enough to create movement and to interpret certain stimuli. We've seen that walkers can at least see, hear, and smell. However, walkers don't appear to feel pain.

Rick and the other survivors encounter walkers missing limbs, parts of their faces, and even whole sections of their bodies, yet they don't demonstrate any awareness of their injuries. Nor do these injuries inhibit them from wanting to attack the living. Hannah, the bicycle girl Rick encounters twice still wants to attack Rick despite the lack of the entire bottom half of her body. In addition, the first walker that Rick kills in "Days Gone Bye" takes a few hits to the head to go down. If someone hit you in the head with a bat, wouldn't you call off the attack? I know I would. Even my dogs let me know when I play a little too rough with them. Whether it's a disconnection or complete non-reactivation, a walker's brain doesn't register the pain a living and fully functional organism would feel.

Of Mice and Men and Walkers

The brain plays a metaphysical role as well. The resurrection event activates only the most primal portions of the brain. There is only instinct driving a walker. Kant refers to this type of individual as the purely sensuous being—one who is entirely subject to causal determination. This type of individual is incapable of rational thought, applying impartial judgment, and following moral codes of conduct. As Kant puts it, we do not morally fault the lion for killing the gazelle, or even for killing it own young. In his philosophical opinion, animals are irrational and are acted upon by the environment as opposed to humans who are rational and are capable of acting upon their surroundings.

In the past, this principle has been applied to animals leading to the extraordinarily inhumane treatment of animals (as in animal experimentation). Looking back to Warren's criteria for recognizing moral community members, we can recognize that animals do possess some of the traits necessary for moral treatment. This includes capacity to feel pain as well as the ability to communicate.

We've already described walkers' nonchalance when it comes to their own "injuries" but what about the ability to communicate? Walkers have no language. At least none we can easily recognize—something that saves Rick's life after Duane hits him in the head with a shovel. The ability to express oneself seems to be a key factor to personhood for both human beings and animals with the ability to speak just one method of communication. Think of all the non-verbal communication that occurs between humans including both conscious and unconscious gestures and body language.

Animals also seem to display a variety of communication methods. Granted, some of our interpretation of animal communication mistakenly attributes human-type intentions where these don't really exist, but it's obvious to me when my dogs are happy, sad, hungry, or need to go out and pee. George Romero's *Land of the Dead* hypothesizes that the undead evolve to develop communication. This would certainly be an interesting development in the world of *The Walking Dead*! But in the comics and the TV series there isn't even a hint of this happening.

While it appears that some walkers, such as Morgan's wife, may retain some residual abilities (such as using tools, turning door knobs, or walking up and down stairs), there is no evidence that there is any higher level thinking among the walker population. Walkers seem to be missing one of the most critical pieces of the brain that distinguishes humans and animals from walkers. The part that *thinks*.

Key Cognitive Ability #1: Planning Ahead

One facet of thinking is our ability to plan ahead. Cultural philosopher and anthropologist Ernest Becker cited this cognitive ability—conceptualizing reality in terms of causality and conceiving of future events—as crucial to the survival of highly intelligent species. We see evidence of this throughout the first six episodes of *The Walking Dead*. Rick's gift of a walkie-talkie to Morgan in "Days Gone Bye," distracting walkers with the alarms from stolen cars in "Guts," and Glenn's elaborate plan to retrieve the bag of guns in "Vatos" expresses the human ability to plan ahead.

The idea of having a "plan" especially in a hazardous situation, like a city crawling with walkers, seems like a no-brainer. This trait gives us the ability to predict future events as well as plan and therefore control certain aspects of the foreseeable future and is an indication of, as Kant puts it, a reasonable and rational mind. Because we cannot know fully what action is best we choose between alternate courses of action. For example Rick, T-Dog, Morales, Glenn, Andrea, and Jacqui could have tried to run past hundreds of walkers with guns blazing and bats swinging. Instead they chose to slather themselves in Wayne Dunlap-walker's guts so they could walk past the walkers.

This is one of the distinguishable features between walkers and humans. From what we've seen on *The Walking Dead* there seems to be no forethought or planning when it comes to walker attacks. Instead, they wander around and happen to come upon a group of survivors as in the attack on the survivors' camp at the end of "Vatos." Or someone is unlucky enough to stumble upon a group of walkers as Rick does on horseback in "Days Gone Bye." Unlike the survivors, the walkers don't plan. They don't lay traps. They don't think about their next source of food. They can't figure out how to cut themselves down from a noose. They stumble, shuffle, and crawl to their next meal wherever and whenever that may be.

Once again human beings are not the only species that have the cognitive ability to plan ahead. Watch any animal special on National Geographic or the Discovery Channel and you'll see animals like bees, lions, and dolphins planning ahead to ensure the survival of their group. While it isn't at the level of human planning, this is a major factor that makes walkers distinctly *un*animal-like. Consequently, walkers should not be treated as animals because they don't display behavioral patterns consistent with higher-order animals. Perhaps they could be considered on the level of viruses, bacteria or at most cockroaches. How guilty do you feel chlorinating your water or putting out roach bait?

Key Cognitive Ability #2: Reflection and Self-Consciousness

Although both humans and animals share the ability to plan ahead with other members of the animal kingdom, the ability to reflect upon ourselves seems a particularly important characteristic of the human species. Both Becker and Kant note that this ability is both a blessing and burden as it allows us to look inwards to contemplate our own rightness or wrongness. And we may not necessarily like what we see.

Other creatures, including animals, are *acted upon* by the world. Having the ability to reflect and choose the principle to guide our actions makes us *actors* upon the world. It is the development of individual self-consciousness that gave humans beings the real possibility of rising above the constrictions of nature itself. We exercise our will and our reason as determined by the duties of membership within a moral community. The fact that we can reflect and choose between alternate courses of actions introduces the possibility that there can be better or worse ways of achieving our ends and better or worse ends, depending on the criteria we adopt. Walkers, like animals, clearly lack this ability to reflect upon themselves and their actions. Walkers (re)act out of pure instinct only.

Will You Use a Gun, Club, Ax, or Shovel?

The evidence here leads us to conclude that walkers are *not* human beings. At least not in the way that *we* are human beings. Nor are they animals, at least in moral status. If they are alive, they are *merely* alive without an awareness of themselves or the world around them. They lack any type of higher-level reasoning ability or self-awareness, don't have the capacity to reflect upon themselves in an open-ended manner, and are completely incapable of rational thought. Nor do they have the ability to think rationally about their motivations as well as the morality and consequences of their actions. Walkers are not members of a moral community and walkers have no duties towards each other or humans. And, as Mary Anne Warren notes, only creatures with duties have rights (legally and morally) since rights are a consequence of being a member of the moral community. Creatures with no possible moral duties, such as walkers, have no moral rights.

Therefore Rick, Lori, Guillermo, Andrea and other survivors shouldn't have any qualms about killing a walker just as they wouldn't have any qualms about killing their vegetables when they cook them alive. The undead are subject to the causal nature of the universe but are not the originators of the causes the way human are. All of the moral philosophical views we've expressed here assume a human or animal morality. Since walkers are neither human nor animal, any and all universal moral or ethical truths don't apply.

I'm Sorry This Happened to You

In "Days Gone Bye" Rick, Morgan, and Duane encounter the Leon Basset–walker, someone Rick didn't think much of. Before shooting him in the head, Rick comments that he can't leave him like this (as a walker). Later, on his way to Atlanta, Rick finds Hannah-walker. Prior to shooting her he apologizes saying, "I'm sorry this happened to you."

We can infer from Rick's attitude and statements that being a walker is a fate worse than death. Andrea certainly would agree, which is why she shot Amy once she was resurrected. Shooting a walker, therefore, may be the right thing to do since we're helping someone to not be a walker.

But it's not always that easy. In a poignant moment towards the end of "Days Gone Bye" Morgan has his walker-wife in the crosshairs but he can't bring himself to shoot her. If the living dead don't have any moral value, why do we hesitate to kill them? Why do some people insist the living impaired have moral value when they clearly don't? It comes down to the fact that we're not wholly rational beings and from time to time we give in to our non-rational impulses. Kant refers to this as the duality of the human situation. We know that walkers aren't us, but they were us before they were bitten.

As a result we tend to project and assign human traits (emotions, motivations, and morality) to non-human, non-rational things such as animals and plants and even inanimate objects (a favorite T-shirt or pair of sneakers). But we're not talking about an animal, plant, or object to which we randomly assign human traits. Walkers used to be people. Which makes it hard to kill them. Sometimes they are former people we once knew and loved. That makes it harder. Is Morgan's walker-wife still his wife? Clearly she isn't. The parts of her that he fell in love with (personality, charm, humor, passion) are gone. And although those parts of his wife are gone, Morgan continues to project or impose those qualities onto her in an irrational way.

Walkers are not smart. They're not fast. They're not co-ordinated. They don't reason or plan. And they will not stop or hesitate to kill the living. But *our* hesitation is their greatest advantage. Therefore we must remain vigilant and unemotional when it comes to killing walkers. The minute we hesitate to shoot or stab the brain of a walker, even one we knew, will be the end of us.

17
I Don't Think Those Rules Apply Anymore

ADAM BARKMAN

In "Guts," Andrea tells Rick about her sister Amy's love of mermaids. Staring down at one embossed on a necklace in an abandoned store, Andrea asks Rick if he thinks it would "be considered looting" if she were to take the necklace, to which the former cop quickly replies, "I don't think those rules apply any more, do you?"

In this case, and in countless others, the old rules or laws are challenged because of radically altered circumstances. However, in both the TV series and the comic books, it's never very explicit what kind of rules or laws are being challenged. The question that needs asking is whether all laws are subject to change, or just some.

To answer this question, we need a clear distinction between what some call the natural law or the universal moral law, and its extension or application, both in individual ethical matters and in laws of state.

The Natural Law

The natural law is the sum of general moral principles or "v-rules" (as virtue ethicists say) which all rational beings have the ultimate capacity to discern. Hindu philosophers call this law *Rita*; Confucius, The Way of Heaven; Plato, Goodness; the Stoics, *Natura*; and Kant, the Categorical Imperative—but all meant roughly the same thing by it: a set of basic moral principles that are self-evident as soon as the terms are properly understood.

"Do no harm" is a self-evident principle, but these terms aren't obvious. Is this statement an absolute statement or a general, all-things-being-equal, statement? If taken as an absolute statement this isn't self-evident at all, and is, in fact, patently false: when I trip, punch, tie up or even kill a man who is attempting to kill my wife, I am harming him, and few would think this wrong. So, the words "Do no harm" must mean *generally* or *all things being equal*. For example, if, for *no reason except for the sheer fun of it*, a person cut down a tree, dissected a frog, or killed a person, we would say that such a man is *obviously* a villain. However, if there were other considerations (and there usually are) such as that I needed the tree to build my house, I wanted to test a drug on the frog to help cure cancer, or I killed a would-be murderer to protect my child, then we have moved from the realm of self-evident, foundational truths to the realm of argumentation. Self-evident principles are obvious, beyond doubt when the terms are properly understood and, like moral virtues, good in and of themselves. But arguments that *use* moral principles are fallible, debatable, and less valuable than the self-evident principles themselves.

It's one thing to talk about the natural law, and it's another to say what it looks like in detail and practice. This is crucial since while it's easy to be skeptical about an uncreated moral law "out there," it's another to be skeptical of principles that are as self-evident to the mind as $1 + 1 = 2$. So while the truths of these principles will be clear when the terms are properly understood, it does require some work to understand them.

One basic principle is that of general beneficence or the sacredness of life. At the core of this principle is the notion that equals should be treated as such. We see the principle generally forbidding the harm of others in Lao Tzu's *Tao Te Ching*, which states, "Since they do no harm to each other, virtue flows," and the principle generally commanding us to love all humanity in Cicero's "Men were made for the sake of men that they might do one another good."

We all know intuitively that all things being equal it's better not to harm a thing than to harm it. It's a villain who enjoys torturing animals for fun; it's a monster who rapes to satisfy his own pleasure. In *The Walking Dead*, Issue #82, Morgan alludes to this principle when he tells Carl, "We get so focused on getting what we need that we stop caring about other people. Maybe it's what we have to do to get by, but it takes away a piece of your soul every time." And when Glenn saves a tank-entrapped Rick and is later asked why he saved him, Glenn says, in keeping with this principle, "Call it a foolish and naive hope that if I'm ever that far up shit creek someone might do the same for me" ("Guts"). The point: when general beneficence flows, shit creeks don't build up as fast.

Another principle is special beneficence or just preference for those closest to one's self. All things considered, a person acts well or justly to favor his or her family and friends over and against others. It's self-evident that if I have one unit of food and have before me my own daughter and another man's daughter, *all things being equal,* I should give the unit of food to *my* daughter: if the two girls are identical in every way except that one happens to be my daughter, then I *ought* to favor the one who happens to be my daughter.

In Issue #7, when Rick offers to let Tyrese and his daughter sleep in the RV with Rick and his family, Lori is upset with her husband for what she perceives to be his neglecting his moral duty to protect his family from this new potential threat, saying, "Don't be so trusting, Rick." Similarly, in "Wildfire," Morales says that he and his family won't go with the others to Fort Benning, explaining, "I gotta do what's best for *my* family." As I said, this principle, as with all other principles are "all things being equal," meaning that they need to be weighed against other general principles in order to determine in a particular circumstance what to do.

Another principle is that of piety or proper respect for one's superiors—be it for one's god, ancestors, rulers, elders, parents, and so on. Confucius insisted, "The services of love and reverence to parents when alive, and those of grief and sorrow to them when dead: these completely discharge the fundamental duty of living men."

All people know it as basic that, all things being equal, children should respect and obey their parents and teachers. If this weren't the case, then we'd have five-year-olds who wouldn't eat their veggies, go to bed on time, or even stay in their beds at night (preferring to chase walkers?). The fact that we think parents have the *moral right* to restrict their child's freedom strongly suggests the child has the *moral duty* to obey (always, of course, stipulating *all things being equal,* and not, for example, speaking of cases where the parent commands the child to do something immoral). Guillermo, the custodian-turned-leader of an abandoned hospital, demonstrates a proper sensitivity to this principle staying behind to help the elderly when others "took off, just left them here to die" ("Vatos").

Related to this are general duties to posterity, nature, and those who are weaker or in lower positions. It's self-evident that, all things being equal, the strong should help the weak. We all know that we'd be acting immorally if, *all things being equal*, we polluted the environment so that there would be few trees and animals left for future generations. We have a duty, of course to the environment (which is "weak"), but also to the unborn human children, who are also weak: to harm the weak for no reason, or to fail to help them when there's no reason not to, is immoral. There are countless examples of this principle. "Those who oppress the young and cheat them because of greed," the Buddhist scriptures declare, "are themselves reborn *katap tanas* [rotten bodied ghosts] to feed on birth-impurities,"[1] and the Egyptian *Teaching of Amenemope* says in all seriousness, "Laugh not at a blind man nor tease a dwarf." Rick adheres to this duty to the weak when he returns to, and puts out of her misery, the legless zombie-woman, telling her, "I'm sorry this happened to you" ("Days Gone By"), and does so again when he protects the walker-bitten Jim from being outright killed, declaring, "Jim isn't a monster or some rabid dog. He's a sick, sick man." ("Wildfire").

You get the idea: the natural law reveals itself in general ways to all people. But how does it apply specifically to individuals? What if I want a really beautiful mermaid pendent for my sister, but I can't purchase it? Is stealing wrong when money isn't valuable, and the only thing the shopkeeper wants is a pound of flesh to feast on?

Applying the Principles

When Andrea asks Rick if he thinks it would be okay if she were to take the mermaid necklace from the store in walker-infested Atlanta, she can be seen as asking not only whether it

---

[1] *Buddhist Scriptures*, p. 11.

would be illegal if she were to take the necklace but also, and more basically, if it would be immoral, unjust, and, in our sense of natural law, unnatural to do so.

Although some believe that "Do not steal" is a general command of the natural law, this should probably be seen as a secondary, derivative or deduced principle. Prior to the command not to steal is the principle of general beneficence; that is, foundational is the general command of general beneficence or "do no harm," and then, when we consider context and other factors, we deduce or derive the command not to steal. When one person takes what belongs to another person without the other person's consent, the first person fails to treat the second person with proper beneficence, in effect treating the second person as if he or she weren't an equal. To make this clear, most of us wouldn't consider it stealing if a starving person (a superior) took food from a mere animal (an inferior).

In addition, what makes the command "do not steal" derived is that it's connected to two statements about human nature—statements which can, with minimal work, be grasped by a careful, truth-seeking person, but are not themselves self-evident. The first statement argues that all human beings are rational souls, spirits, or persons and, in this respect, are equal, even if they are unequal in countless other respects such as positions of authority or in terms of ability, beauty and so on. The second statement argues that human beings can—at least as things now stand—own things (for if all ownership were illusory, then the word "steal" would lose all meaning).

The first statement could be criticized by someone like Aristotle who declared most barbarians "natural slaves" and women "incomplete men" (both lacking the rationality of Greek men), or the cannibalistic "hunters" in *The Walking Dead* comics who see their quarry as less human than they (Issues #61–66). To this, I'd reply that Aristotle seems to have confused the value of the rational soul with spiritual or rational function (the perceived inferior intelligence of non-Greeks and women), and hence was lead astray, while the cannibalistic hunters appear to have taken the principle of general beneficence ("value life," including one's own life) and applied it *only* to themselves (to love themselves at all costs), which gave them false justification for hunting and killing other humans who would normally be preserved under such a principle.

Why We Need Virtue

Virtue is central to applying natural law. The virtuous person is someone who gathers together all the relevant moral principles and factors in a particular case, and then discerns what the proper course of action is: in such cases, we no longer speak of "all things being equal" but rather "all things considered." This kind of discernment is what Aristotle calls "practical wisdom." It weighs, balances, and discerns.

When we meet the cannibalistic hunters in the *Walking Dead* comic book, there seems to be two laws in conflict: "Preserve one's own life" and "Don't kill innocent people." The only way that the hunters can preserve their own life is through killing innocent people, namely their children, so they can eat them. But what is more morally admirable: Giving some food of your own to a child in need, which ultimately would violate the preservation law, or killing an innocent person to eat them, which would violate the don't-kill-an-innocent law?

It seems as if sharing food would be the moral thing to do (even though they can't do it in this circumstance). So in this context, self-sacrifice, starving to death, may be morally preferable to killing and eating innocent people. The natural laws are easy to understand, but knowing how they apply in each case isn't so easy. A virtuous character can help with this because a courageous person might be able to face the fear of dying, without being tempted to break the law against killing innocent people. Wisdom would be needed to determine the difference between shooting down a plane full of innocent people which might be used in a terrorist attack, and letting the terrorists accomplish their mission.

The general mood of apocalyptic literature, and *The Walking Dead* in particular, is often that ownership and personal property are exaggerated concepts that are folly in the mouth of the furnace, or, in our case, the mouth of the walker. While we might sympathize with the view that shows at times the vanity of worldly possessions (apocalyptic literature is great for idol-smashing), a strong view that there are no property rights at all is problematic in a world of imperfect people since it's ripe for abuse. The strong could take an unfair or better portion of what might legitimately or naturally belong to the community of people.

When human beings initially found themselves on Earth, none had an absolute claim to the Earth and so the goods of the Earth—setting aside for the moment animal rights and so on—properly belonged to the community of humans. Yet, because imperfect people didn't share communal goods justly, it was—and still is—up to human beings to decide how to share or divide up the goods, and an individual's share of the goods is what we call personal property. Thus, while personal property is a concept derived from a more basic concept, namely, the community of goods, it is a legitimately derived right.

All this, then, makes stealing morally prohibited. So what can be said about Andrea and the necklace? If she were to take it, would she be stealing—would she be acting unjustly? Because the original owner of the necklace (and his or her heirs) are very likely dead or worse, the necklace can reasonably be thought to belong to no one now and so whoever were to take possession of the necklace now would have a legitimate claim on it, properly appealing to "the right of first claim."

But what if Andrea found, and claimed for herself, four units of food (where a unit is indivisible) and Rick, for example, found none? Moreover, what if Rick—let's say he is surrounded by walkers—had no reasonable means of finding and claiming his own food? If Rick were to take any of the food held by Andrea, would he be stealing? I would say that he wouldn't be stealing for the following reasons.

Since moral duties usually (but not always) imply corresponding moral rights, and since the principle of general beneficence makes it a duty to do good to human beings, a moral right to life—in the same general sense as the duty to preserve life—may reasonably be inferred. In other words, Rick, just as much as Andrea, has the same basic claim to food and survival, and so for Rick to take two units of food would be simply for him to appeal to the principle of general beneficence and the notion that equals should be treated as such—the food ultimately still belongs to the community and justice demands proper distribution, where proper distribution likely means equal distribution.

However, if Andrea had five units of food, then I think Rick *would* be stealing if he were to take three units since even though both Rick and Andrea equally have the right to food and survival, Andrea has the additional right of first claim (a right subordinate to the right of survival, but a right nonetheless) which would tip the scale in her favor if the survival of the two of them were in question. Of course, this reasoning only works all things being equal. If we were to factor in that Rick is a larger man than Andrea and probably needs more food to survive or if we were to factor in Rick's greater survival value to the group, then things might look a bit different. But such are the complexities of applying the natural law to particular situations.

Legislating the Natural Law

Things are no less complex when it comes to relating the Natural Law to the laws of state, that is, when constructing actual laws. Although it's universally agreed upon by those who acknowledge the natural law that it is a foundational element in the construction of actual laws, it's not always agreed how much of the natural law needs to be factored in when making laws of state. Why make all murder (a prohibition derived from general beneficence) illegal, but not make it a crime to fail to be patriotic at all times, where patriotism is a command derived from the principle of just preference to those closest to one's self? Or again, why is it a crime to lie in court, but not a crime to lie to one's parents?

The answer resides in the difference between an individual and the state. While individuals are called to discern and enforce the natural law in all its particularities in respect to the scope of the self, the state is merely charged with discerning and enforcing public justice. Thus, while a just individual will both privately and publicly love his country (even if he is, in both circumstances, also critical of it), the state will only be concerned with patriotism insofar as a failure to be patriotic would harm the public, such as in the case of treason. The same goes for lying to one's parents and lying in court (that means you, Carl).

And so, because stealing is not merely a private matter but also a public matter most governments make it illegal. But what about the United States? Obviously before the zombie apocalypse, stealing was a crime, hence Andrea asked Rick if it "would be considered looting" if she were to take the mermaid necklace. But does the United States government still exist and have authority in *The Walking Dead* universe?

I argued that if Andrea were to take the necklace, she probably wouldn't be acting immorally since the necklace likely belongs to no one. Nevertheless, what I assumed there is that there is also no government which, even if the original owner of the necklace were dead, might possibly require Andrea to surrender the necklace to them as the proper possession of the commonwealth. This, I should add, would almost certainly be the case of the Governor and his city or even the Alexandria Safe-Zone Community and its territory. If the government were still functioning, then its actual laws would also be functioning, and so stealing would still be illegal and thus if Andrea were simply to take the necklace (as opposed to using it for survival purposes), it's possible that she would still be acting illegally and, insofar as the Natural Law requires us to show respect for those above us—here, the laws of the land—Andrea might thus be considered immoral for taking the necklace.

However, at least thus far in *The Walking Dead* it seems clear that there is no longer a "United States of America" with its legal laws and legal authority. Rick doesn't stop the abusive Merle Dixon because Rick is a *cop*, but rather because he is a *good man*, saying, "All I am any more is a man looking for his wife and son" ("Guts"). It's precisely because the laws of state have broken down that some, such as Carol who proposes a polygamous marriage between herself, Rick and Rick's wife, Lori, saying, "We don't have to follow the old rules, we can make new ones" (Issue #27).

She imagines that there is no longer any binding morality—morality being, as with the laws of state, merely a social construction. But the natural law and its principles are prior to the laws of the land and, as we have seen, are not merely the basis of just actual laws but are ever-binding on individuals. So even when the laws of state are no more, the natural laws still exist. It's this reasoning that justifies things like breaking the laws of the state, when those laws are immoral. Stealing is wrong even if there is no government on Earth to enforce this command; however, in the case of Andrea and the necklace, it's likely that she isn't breaking any legal law nor, for that matter, any natural law, since it wasn't *owned*.

The Good, the Bad, and the Evil

In Issue #61, Father Gabriel calls the walkers "abominations" and fully endorses their destruction. His language is biblical—the same language used to denounce those who violate the natural law, such as murderers, liars, and thieves. While it's true that walkers are unnatural in the sense of being "against God's design," Father Gabriel commits a mistake by lumping "bad" things with "evil" things. A bad thing is simply something that isn't functioning according to its general design plan, whereas an evil thing is, strictly speaking, something willful which chooses to act against what is natural or just.

Cancer is bad, defaced paintings are bad, spilled whiskey is bad, but it would be odd to call cancer, defaced paintings, and spilled whiskey evil. And the same is true for walkers: they are bad, but not evil; they are unnatural in one sense, but they aren't violating the moral principles of the natural law (since they have no ability to choose). The Governor admires the walkers and says "they are no different" than humans insofar as "they want what they want" (Issue #28). But this says more about what happens to a human being who willingly ignores the natural law than it does about walkers and humans themselves, for a human being who willingly ignores the natural law reduces himself to the level of a walker, where hunger, strength and the mood of the group rule supreme.

Such humans become the walking dead. As many in the *The Walking Dead* universe still recognize, to be human—really human—we need law and we need virtue, not only to keep individuals on the path to true happiness, but also to underpin actual laws which aid individuals and nations as they strive for the same goal.

18
Dead Ends

ELIZABETH RARD

Hannah, her husband Andrew, and her two children are preparing to flee the city, which has become overrun with walkers. Andrew knows that his neighbor Palmer has a truck, and he knows where the keys are. So he hurries next door, to get the keys off of Palmer's dead body, in hopes to secure transportation to the safe zone being set up in Atlanta ("Everything Dies").

Andrew never really hesitates over the morality of taking something that doesn't belong to him. Palmer is dead, and his children and ex-wife are in danger. But should he hesitate? If it was wrong for him to steal the truck before the zombie apocalypse, why is it suddenly okay for him to do it now?

One might be able to spin lots of different theories about why it is wrong, but they all revolve around moral values. The question is: do these moral values exist objectively, or are they something invented by man? If they're objective, the apocalypse, whatever its form, will not change the fact that doing X is wrong. If they're invented by man, then we have the opportunity to revise these moral values, whenever we'd like, and perhaps there really is no reason to be moral people at all, just as there isn't any particular reason for people to speak in English or in some other language.

A Shambling Form

The first half of the second season, is largely driven by the search for Sophia. The philosopher in me can't help pointing out that 'Sophia' is Greek for wisdom and makes up one of the root words of philosophy (*philos*, 'love', being the other).

The search for Sophia drives a wedge between Rick and Shane. Shane wants to leave her behind and move on to someplace safe, where there aren't walkers threatening to storm out of a barn to kill everyone. But Rick wants to stay, at least until they find Sophia, possibly longer. Rick is clinging to a sense of moral obligation, and it's hard not to sympathize with him. How could it ever be morally acceptable to leave behind a little girl lost in the woods? These are the situations that seem to give real credibility to the idea that ethics is objective. It isn't my interpretation of the scenario that determines the rightness or wrongness. Shane is simply wrong and Rick is right. It's as if they were arguing about whether one plus two equals three or twelve. This is called moral realism, because there are *real* moral facts about the world.

One of the earliest and best examples of moral realism is found in Plato's *Republic*. Plato believes that *ideas* are not only real objects, but they are *more* real than everyday objects. He called these ideas the Forms. Plato thinks that these Forms exist because they help explain why our knowledge about things are relatively unchanging, even though the world that we live in is constantly changing.

Hannah, the bicycle girl we see in "Days Gone Bye" and the central character of the Webisodes, changes significantly through time. Once she becomes a walker, her skin slowly greys, she loses her hair, and her body begins to dehydrate. If I said that I know that Hannah had fair skin, I would be wrong, since she doesn't have fair skin anymore. She's changed. But I could say something that has a much more universal truth, that walkers survive so long as their brains are relatively undamaged. Now this truth, is true not only about Hannah, but about all walkers. Why? According to Plato, it's because the truth applies to the Form walker, and all actual walkers are mere imperfect copies of the Form walker. This, says Plato, is how we get knowledge.

The same also applies to morals. For something to be good, it needs to "participate" in the Form of good. The act of staying to look for a lost girl in the woods is good because it participates in the Form good. In fact, Plato thinks that knowledge and the good are so closely linked, that the only reason why people do bad things, is because they lack knowledge of the Form good. If they simply understood things better, they wouldn't do bad things.

Unfortunately there are some serious problems with Plato's way of looking at it. There doesn't seem to be any explanation of knowledge that I know about Hannah. I know that she was a mom. Clearly, Hannah wasn't always a mom, like when she was a child. I certainly don't know that she is a mom from the Form of human being or Form of walker. Sometimes our knowledge changes when reality changes, and Plato's theory can't capture this, since his theory is about a perfect *unchanging* world of ideas.

There's a similar problem for Plato's view of morality as well. Sometimes, when the circumstances change, something that is usually morally right, could become morally wrong. Take the simple case of lying. Usually lying is morally wrong, but 'white lies' don't seem to be morally problematic. If Glenn tells Rick "I'm fine," when really he is a bit upset that his car has some walker guts on it, Glenn has lied to Rick intentionally, but nobody thinks of this as a moral fault. Or imagine that Dale learns that Shane plans on hurting Glenn for no good reason, and that he can prevent Glenn from being harmed by lying to Shane. He should do it, right? But if there is a Form of good, and lying simply doesn't participate in it, then lying could never be good.

What Walkers Are For

Another philosopher who tried to ground morality objectively was Aristotle. Aristotle held that everything has an objective final goal or purpose that must be reached in order for that thing to become perfected. The purpose of a thing is determined by that thing's "characteristic activity" usually something that is unique to that thing.

A knife's characteristic activity would be to cut things, even though it *could* be used for other things. For humans this goal is to develop certain moral virtues that will allow us to act in accordance with our rational soul, controlling our emotional responses to situations that might otherwise control and overwhelm us. For example, bravery represses the urge to run screaming from every walker that staggers our way. Since higher reason is unique to humans, it's our characteristic activity. Walkers would presumably also have a final goal that involves munching on as many living humans as possible.

For Aristotle, in order to be a virtuous individual, you must demonstrate a repeated ability to engage in actions that reflect a balance of emotions and a preponderance of rationality. However, none of our survivors and would-be moral exemplars have consistently demonstrated this ability, suggesting that none of them have formed the habits that Aristotle promoted.

When Carl is shot by Otis early in Season Two, Rick wants to charge off to get supplies even though he is weak from blood donation and his presence is required because he has yet more blood to give. Rick's impulse is rash and demonstrates that his confidence is interfering with his ability to act in accordance with reason. Shane understands that Rick can't leave Carl's side and volunteers to go for supplies instead, demonstrating courage. However, when it's discovered that the barn is full of walkers, Shane responds with anger while Rick shows the virtue of patience, realizing that the barn does not pose an immediate threat but that a confrontation with Hershel may lead to unfortunate consequences (like leaving the partial security of the farm to play hide and seek with more Walkers).

Alas, a virtue theory such as Aristotle's presents several drawbacks for application in a zombie infested world, if not a regular world. First off, if virtue theory is supposed to provide an objective basis, it is a shaky objectivity at best. While all humans share the potential of rationality at least, the right reaction of any given person in any situation is relative to the abilities and position of the person. Aristotle believes that the virtues, although discoverable by reason, are relative to an individual. A temperate amount of food for Darryl, would be an excessive amount of food for Carl. Furthermore, the goal or function of an object is not likely determined by the actions that are unique to that object. Just because I'm the only person who can do something, that doesn't necessarily mean that it is in some way my purpose to do that thing. If I'm the only person capable of creating a new kind of super-powered killing machine, it doesn't in any way follow that I have a moral obligation to create the killing machine, even if I can program it to target only walkers. Moreover, it could be that I can do several things that other people or things can't do. Aristotle thinks that our purpose must be singular, but this doesn't capture the human condition.

Another hurdle for virtue theory's claim to objectivity is that Aristotle believed our acquisition of virtues could only take us so far on the road to human flourishing. We also need luck on our side. In order to become a virtuous person I will need to demonstrate virtues that require a certain social, financial, and even medical standing. If I'm born a slave, or poor, or am handicapped, then I'll be unable to become a fully realized and perfect human being. It seems reasonable to say that we can add "ended up in a zombie infested post-apocalyptic nightmare world" to the list of unfortunate situations that will take me out of the running.

Wittiness and magnificence (the ability to attain honor and material goods) are a couple of Aristotle's virtues that this applies to. While I might be able to remain witty when confronted with a herd of walkers (if Lori gets bit by a walker she will become a MOM-ster), it will be difficult to demonstrate magnificence in my spending choices when the economy has collapsed. And even if the economy hasn't completely collapsed, I could only shop at the mon-store and buy jeans that were men-dead.

Killing Walkers Is Only Natural

Natural law theory continues in the tradition begun by Plato and Aristotle. It attempts to find an objective basis for morality, rooted firmly in human nature, and accessible through that most human of attributes, rational inquiry. Aristotle's final goal or purposes argument lays the groundwork for an ethics of natural law with a claim to objectivity.

When Rick wakes up in the hospital, he has no idea how much the world around him has changed. He's unaware of the existence of walkers, the collapse of government, the death of a large percentage of the world's population, and the fact that squirrel is now on the menu. Many of the rules that have up to this point guided Rick's actions are founded in a consensus among the world's inhabitants. Some of these rules are arbitrary as to which side of an issue they take. If I choose to knowingly drive on the wrong side of the road and my action leads to someone's death it would seem that I am morally responsible for the death. It's wrong to break the law that says I should always drive on the right-hand side of the road when going down a two-way street in Atlanta. However, it would seem odd to say that there is something *objectively* wrong with driving on the left hand side of the street. Instead, breaking the law is wrong because we all have an agreement to follow the rule in order to avoid a consequence that we *believe* to be objectively wrong: that causing an innocent person to die through willful negligence is an immoral action.

When Rick steps outside of the hospital many of the laws and rules that had previously guided Rick's actions have become obsolete. It no longer matters which side of the road Rick, or Dale drives on because it's very unlikely that they will encounter fellow motorists on their travels. If Dale needs to swerve onto the left-hand side of the road to plow down a family of walkers or avoid an overturned semi-truck we would allow that this behavior is permissible. Likewise, if Glenn and Maggie need to take supplies from a store whose previous owners are most certainly zombified at this point, we would not attempt to stop him on the grounds that stealing is wrong because it's against the law.

If moral skepticism's correct and there's no objective basis for morality, then when we eliminate governments, religious institutes, and the general consensus of society, all of our moral prescriptions will evaporate as quickly as our traffic laws. Natural law theory holds that there are some moral rules that are objectively based in nature or human nature and will therefore exist even without artificial laws or institutions. The basic line of reasoning behind natural law theory is that if an action is unnatural for a human being then it will be self-destructive to human beings. Living in accordance with what it is natural for humans to do will be a beneficial, and therefore moral, way to live.

Natural law advocates will often argue that the natural laws are intuitive, or self-evident. If we simply reflect upon them for a while, we will understand that some type of action is wrong. This can be plausible, since intuitively, most people believe that murder, stealing, and rape are morally wrong. But natural law uses this intuitive *feeling* as its *sole* justification for its position. This leads to problems when we encounter someone who does not share our intuitions.

Most people today have a pretty strong intuition that racial discrimination is wrong, and that race is an irrelevant characteristic when it comes to a person's value. But when we meet Merle Dixon, his obvious prejudices speak loudly: he has different intuitions. He doesn't find it self-evident that T-Dog is equal to others, but assumes that, specifically because he is Black, T-Dog is inferior. Hershel has the intuition that walkers are *still* people, though almost everyone else believes otherwise. How could we resolve these moral disputes? Why is Merle's intuitions wrong, and ours right? If we appeal to reason, then it isn't the natural law that makes it right, but rather argumentation.

And sometimes our intuitions are simply wrong. Most of us have had the experience of changing our beliefs about morality at one time or another. The best a natural law advocate can do is to assert that our previous beliefs were "unreflective" intuitions, and when we've given it some thought, we recognize the self-evident truth of the wrongness of discrimination. But this flies in the face of the self-evident nature of natural law since, clearly, some people don't find it self-evident because they believe otherwise. Some natural law advocates might soften the moral rules so that they are change with the context, but how and why the context affects the rules isn't usually based on any particular guiding principle, but on yet more intuitions. Finally, natural law assumes that human nature and morality is static and unchanging like Aristotle's singular final goal. But this assumption suffers from the same problems that we pointed out against Aristotle.

Walker Morality

What if human nature is dynamic and so constructed that it is actually at odds with the sorts of religious and social ethical theories that have become popular over the last two thousand years or so? Would the collapse of traditional values and institutions brought on by the zombie apocalypse then become an opportunity to allow the true nature of humanity to reshape our moral landscape?

Friedrich Nietzsche described the nature, not just of human life, but of all life, in terms of what he called "the will to power." According to Nietzsche, human striving is not motivated by a simple desire to live, but a more aggressive desire to master the world around you and to overcome or reinvent yourself. Science claims objectivity and undermines meaning. Humans are nothing more than a complex collection of matter. Religious morality controls our actions, praising those actions that express the least will to power. We should not try to dominate others but rather we should protect the weakest in society. Philosophy attempts to control the way we think, determining the proper way to use rationality. More money, more power, more people seeing the world through our eyes, a desire to claim objectivity for our beliefs, these are all manifestations of the will to power.

Furthermore, Nietzsche criticizes traditional morality on several key points, including its assumptions about human nature and free will. In order for a person to be held morally responsible for their actions they must have free will. It would not be appropriate to blame me for knocking someone down if a walker ran up and pushed me into that other person. Likewise, when Otis shoots Carl, Rick is unable to truly blame Otis because he was ignorant of the fact that by shooting the deer he would also be shooting Carl. We don't hold Otis morally responsible for his actions in this situation because he did not intend Carl to be injured. He had no reason to believe that a human child might be standing on the other side of the deer. So Otis didn't make a choice to shoot Carl.

Nietzsche makes the point that if we don't actually have free will at all, if all of our actions are beyond our control, then we cannot hold people responsible for their actions. Nietzsche argues that our actions are determined by a complicated causal system but that ultimately our actions are determined by the type of person that we are. Nietzsche thought that everyone has a fixed psychological makeup that completely determines the kind of person we are. All of our actions are then causally determined by a combination of external factors and our reactions, caused directly by our personality type, to these external factors. The modern systems of morality are designed to control the actions of some through a system of blame and guilt

The moral systems of our time, according to Nietzsche, are institutions of what he called a slave morality—a moral system designed to protect and glorify the weak and suppress the powerful through guilt and obligation. A new version of slave morality can be seen in the first half of Season Two of *The Walking Dead*. Hershel and his followers at the farm have been capturing and keeping walkers in the barn in order to remove the harm without having to hurt the walkers. The reasoning here is that walkers are sick humans who are attacking others through no fault of their own. Nietzsche was critical of a slave morality that would not even allow for the punishment of those who threaten it. Hershel is deeply attached to a Christian way of thinking about moral issues. For Hershel, just because the walkers would harm him and his family is not sufficient reason to kill them. Before the end of the world this tendency might have manifested as a liberal position towards crime, preventing criminals from committing further crimes is the only justification for imprisonment, so we shouldn't commit the evil of punishment for punishment's sake.

Hershel has taken this tendency to an extreme level. We cannot execute walkers, even though they would rip our bodies to shreds given a chance, because they are blameless in their actions. This is not to say that the walkers themselves are players in Nietzsche's power struggle, but that they are being used as a means of control. Those who are strong and fearless, willing to fight back in the face of a herd of walkers, are being labeled cold-hearted for their willingness to remove the walker threat using the most permanent solution available. Hershel, the old, kindly, southern gentleman is able to keep Rick and Shane in check by imposing his will to power on to them, forcing Rick and company to re-evaluate how they view walkers.

When we first meet Maggie she seems to be controlled completely by slave morality. The only Kool-Aid to drink is Hershel's, so she views the killing of walkers as morally problematic. However, after Glenn saves her from an attack by a walker she begins to question her position that walkers should be protected if the cost is the safety of the group. After Shane opens the barn and releases the walkers she appears to support the decision to kill the walkers rather than attempt to recapture them. Up until this point Maggie has found comfort and safety from her inclusion in the group at the farm, even if the safety is an illusion supported by the pity that traditional morality encourages us to spare for the walkers. By making them into an object of pity rather than a fierce threat to survival, those at the farm can feel a sense of moral superiority to Rick's group even while relying on Rick and Shane to make the hard decisions.

Beyond Good and Zombies

Nietzsche's theory that there are different fixed types of people is problematic for any morality that relies on human nature for a claim to an objective basis. As Nietzsche points out ethical systems claim universal application because they offer a system that will benefit all those they control. These systems assume that human nature is homogenous to the point that one ethic is appropriate and beneficial for all. However, as Nietzsche argues, humans vary largely in their capabilities and potential. The essential nature of humanity is then that it has more than one essential nature. Depending on your nature the conditions required for your flourishing will differ greatly. Some individuals are weak and slow. Flourishing for them will be comfort and safety. These individuals are the ones who practice slave morality. (Although its easiest to understand master and slave morality in terms of physical strength, Nietzsche believed that it was mental and political strength that was far more potent than physical strength.)

But Nietzsche identified another type of person. Some individuals have the potential to achieve true excellence, and for these individuals there should be a different morality appropriate to their nature. These individuals will be characteristically solitary and life-affirming. They will seek out responsibility that allows them to exert their own will over their lives and the lives of others. These individuals will be noble and will refrain from pettiness. Evaluations of good and evil, for Nietzsche, are merely causal mechanisms. They are implemented in order to maximize pleasure and happiness. But pleasure and happiness are the goals of the lower type of humans. These higher humans can realize a level of excellence that pushes humanity forward, but only if they are unrestrained by slave morality. It is excellence, not happiness, which Nietzsche holds as the highest goal.

Nietzsche thought that those who struggled to move beyond conventional ethical systems and rise above the heard were what he called "overmen." Such individuals, who do not dwell on their mistakes and regrets but rather look to themselves for value and justification, might view a zombie apocalypse as an opportunity rather than a disaster. These are the Overmen that Nietzsche thought would be our philosophical descendents. They would take a hammer to traditional values in order to discover what is worthy of preservation. This is not to say that they are immoral but rather that they are beyond the traditional rules and moral systems that the herd relies on for guidance. Nietzsche describes the Overman as being "happy, powerful, and triumphant." They fully express their will to power through adoption of a system of morality which relies on the honor and nobility of an authentic individual, rather than manipulation and control of the good and evil of the slave morality.

When Carl is shot by Otis, Shane sets out to find medicine and supplies that might save Carl's life. After retrieving the supplies, Otis and Shane find themselves confronted with a seemingly unending barrage of undead walkers. Shane tries to get himself as well as Otis out safely but when it becomes clear to Shane that it's not possible for both to escape he quickly makes the decision to sacrifice Otis in order to save himself and Carl.

This action would be condemned by both a traditional Christian ethical system and a typical pre-apocalyptic legal system. While natural law theory would recognize that survival might be counted among human goods it may also conclude that there is a mismatch between the aim of survival and the means of killing an innocent person such that reason will tell us that killing of an innocent is always a flawed action. Shane did not kill Otis for no reason, nor was his motivation to cause harm. His justification is rooted in his own desire to triumph and save a child's life that he values higher than that of Otis. He is strong and he believes that he can protect the group, or at least those worthy of survival, in a way that someone like Otis could not. He accepts the way the world has become and understands that a new morality is required if humans are to triumph over walkers. Through his actions and his unapologetic approach to situations he is discovering and defining his own set of values, ones that will dictate his actions but which Shane does not feel the need to explain.

One characteristic of those who create and practice a master morality is an ability to move beyond regret and guilt. To create something beyond ourselves, we have to move beyond our own sense of guilt, as well as the artificial remorse that we are pressured to feel by conventional slave morality. When Shane returns without Otis he seems to be struggling with twinges of regret over his actions. He seems to channel this response into a need to confrontationally criticize the behavior of anyone hesitant to make a sacrifice for the group. He more than once voices the opinion that the search for Sophia should be ended because it puts the group at risk.

Shane opens the barn doors, forcing the others into a situation where they must kill the walkers, against Hershel's rules. It appears that Shane is overcoming his last attachments to traditional moral institutions, and the Hershel's slave morality. He's creating a new morality forged by post-apocalyptic world, his own drive to survive, and desire to exercise his power over others. He forces the group to join him as he redefines morality for a new age of mankind: The Walker Age.

The Eternal Return of the Walkers

The zombie apocalypse offers the opportunity for a paradigm shift in morality. All of the old institutions have been erased and the goals of humanity have been simplified. These old institutions were an expression of the will to power but they were tools to control and diminish humanity. Humans have been deprived of the opportunity to create their own values. Most of us have accepted our diminished roles without a struggle, but as the walkers rip the flesh from our bones they are also ripping away the infrastructure that has made it so easy for humanity to ignore it role in the creation of our own purpose.

As many of the unimportant goals of the pre-zombie world fall away we are left with a need to redefine humanity and morality with respect to our new singular purpose. Before the apocalypse, we could strive for noble goals like philosophy and the bettering of all humanity. Now survival presents itself as the obvious function for the new world. Shane's actions are largely motivated by a desire to keep the group alive. He is abandoning traditional slave morality and he is attempting to exert control over those around him but there is nothing noble about his methods or goals. He is acting out of fear and anger, he rages against the way the world has become and does not embrace the opportunity to create something stronger than what came before. Nietzsche thought that we must embrace the world as it is, cruel and meaningless, and take our joy from the knowledge that we would choose the world given the choice. Rick alone seems to be searching for a purpose beyond survival. He is finding joy in the way the world is, post zombie.

For much of the first half of Season Two Rick seems to shy away from any decisions that require him to establish a solid ethical position, either traditional or revisionary. He agrees that the search for Sophia is a threat to the group but feels responsible for her disappearance. Rick is uncomfortable with a barn full of walkers but takes a diplomatic approach to the situation in an attempt to remain in Hershel's good graces.

Even Rick's reaction to the news that Lori was sleeping with Shane elicits a response that at first glance seems detached. His reasoning about Lori's 'affair' actually displays hints of an ethic that goes beyond the traditional. He reasons, very practically, that Lori thought Rick was dead and that the world was ending. When Lori realized that Rick was alive she immediately broke off relations with Shane. Rick does not judge Lori's actions in terms of right or wrong. Rather he admires her strength in surviving and keeping their son safe. He is beginning to see the benefit of their suffering. The pain that Rick and Lori have been through together has strengthened their relationship.

It is characteristic of master morality that we abandon the temptation to equate all things pleasurable as good and all things painful as evil. When Carl awakens briefly, before the bullet has been removed, the first thing he does is to recount the beauty of the deer. The agony he now suffers pales in comparison to the beautiful moment that he experienced. Rick finds in his son a new perspective on his situation. It's not the pain that he endures, it's the strength he gains and the joy that he finds in spite of the pain. Rick cannot cry for the way the world is, he must embrace it. His insistence that Lori should have the baby, even though it will not have memories of a world without walkers, is an embrace of the way the world is, a realization that Rick and his family can create meaning for themselves even if they have lost the comforts that played so prominently in their former lives.

It is characteristic of the higher individual that they seek out great responsibility, not simply because they desire the material benefits that accompany power, but because they have a desire to live a life in accordance with their own will. Rick has played the role of reluctant leader from the beginning. At first he fell into the role almost by default. He would suggest an action and the others would agree with him. Ever since the arrival at the farm, though, Rick has been in a possession where he must eventually choose to fight for his power, or to allow Shane to overtake the group and shift the priorities to a more utilitarian position.

As of the middle of Season Two, neither Rick nor Shane have established themselves as being entirely in line with the higher individuals of Nietzsche's master morality. Rick places great value on Carl and his safety. Nietzsche thought that an Overman would be a solitary individual, not allowing for emotional attachment to other individuals, seeing people as mere tools. Shane is definitely a better candidate for this trait. He sacrificed Otis because it allowed him to achieve his own goals of survival and supply retrieval. He wanted to abandon the search for Sophia because she had become inconvenient. But Shane seems to find no joy in his existence. He sees only the pain of the world and does not love the world as it is for the existence it allows him. His pain is not constructive as it is for Rick.

In the end the only nature that is fixed is that of the walkers. They are the ultimate herd and there is no diversity among them (other than how intact their bodies happen to be). Traditional moralities for humans rely largely on the assumption of one human nature. These moralities are typically reinforced by the institutions of our societies. However, when walkers have removed these institutions we are given are perfect opportunity to re-evaluate the values of humanity.

If it is true, as Nietzsche says, that our nature is naturally of two kinds then we must allow for a new morality to govern those who cannot flourish under traditional morality. We must admit that there may be a goal above that of happiness to match those humans who rise above the hordes of humans and walkers alike.

19
Babes in Zombie Land

TAURIQ MOOSA

Amidst the violence and horror of the zombie apocalypse, an entirely ordinary and usually joyful event occurs: Lori is pregnant. For us as readers, we know there might some good reason to be doubtful as to why it should be automatically joyous: the father's identity, the lack of stability, and the constant zombie menace. But there's a further problem we ought to consider that has direct implications for our real world: *Should Lori have the child at all?* And, indeed, why should anyone have children even in our world?

What makes Kirkman's world interesting for us, as readers, is to contemplate what we can learn about ourselves, in our current world. Indeed, Rick notes this when he says to himself, "Thinking about the good times makes all this seem so much worse."

The world of Rick and Tyrese, Andrea and Michonne, serves as a useful testing ground for our morals. It allows us to consider the ethical implications of our actions. We can rightly ask: Why have children in a zombie-infested world, where danger is in every fold of shadow? Why do *we* continue life? Why do *we* have children in our own, supposedly safer, world?

Is Killing Always Wrong?

Maybe we should deal with an easier question first. Should the survivors keep surviving at all? What reasons are there to continue living? It may seem strange or obvious but until we have answered it, with good justification, we cannot know we're right. True, it wouldn't be much of a survival-horror story if the survivors were suicidal or pessimistic. We don't want to read a zombie apocalypse book where *everyone* commits suicide, like the family Rick comes across in Issue #2, just before he takes their horse. But just because it would make boring reading doesn't make surviving right, it just makes it entertainment— which can hardly be a good justification for surviving (especially since *we*, their audience and the ones entertained, are not a factor in their justifications for survival).

In assessing the actions of the characters, we're not *really* judging *them*. Their *actions* and their *reasoning* are what matters, since their actions and reasoning can be done by anyone capable of acting and reasoning.

Consider Carl, killing Shane, in Issue #6. On the surface level we have a young boy shooting and killing a man. This tells us little, so what matters is the young boy's reasoning. We know that Carl acted so as *to save his father from a jealous lunatic*. Looked at in this way, our initial judgment becomes more nuanced, if not completely altered. We might say shooting or killing someone is by definition wrong, but there are too many instances even in our world that would refute such a definition. For example, killing in self-defense, or putting some creature out of its misery as it painfully dies.

Killing isn't the same as murder. The context in which killing takes place is what helps determine the morality of the act. We can't simply say that killing is bad. 'Murder' is, *by definition*, 'wrongful killing'. Murder *is* by definition wrong, just as 'joy' by definition is good. By using the word 'murder' we show that we've already made a moral judgment.

Similarly, many of us accept that the survivors steal to stay alive, so many of us do not think that *by definition* stealing is bad. We have no moral objections since our survivors have good reasons to steal horses, cars, bikes and weapons.

If killing and stealing are not by definition wrong, then this must apply to *all* actions worthy of moral concern. We can't assume that any action is by definition wrong. Our focus therefore is on an action that appears obviously good or beneficial: surviving. To be consistent, we must ask: if killing can be good and justified, perhaps surviving can be bad and *un*justified?

The Source of All Horror Is Right in Front of You

There appears to be nothing approaching hope in the landscape of *The Walking Dead*. Governments have failed, most people are dead, or worse, undead, and there is no security when it comes to food or shelter. It's an open battleground for the strongest, the smartest and the devious. It's precisely this kind of place that the philosopher Thomas Hobbes described as "the state of nature" out of which "civilized" humans arose; a place where human life was "solitary, poor, nasty, brutish, and short."[1]

The state of nature is a place where each individual looks after himself, using others only to obtain desired ends, even if it meant hurting them. This is encapsulated by an idea Hobbes refers to: that man is a wolf to his fellow man. Hobbes speculated that humans were naturally selfish, but had learned to form a society in order to live better lives.

When he wakes up in hospital, Rick immediately seeks his family. This is not the state of nature Hobbes depicted, since, we're bringing the morality from our *current* world into the landscape of brutality that is *The Walking Dead*. When Rick finds his family, he sees them amidst the company of fellow survivors, each looking out for the rest. This is slightly different in the television-series, where there are members who are deliberately uninterested in being part of the group due to their selfish ends. They are the men carved out for Hobbes' world.

Here we have an excellent reason why Rick did not simply inject himself with an overdose of morphine when he woke from the hospital, realizing the world had ended: he wanted to find and protect his family. Yet families had taken it upon themselves to *not* continue surviving as a whole, committing suicide together. When we encounter these gruesome scenes with Rick, we should not be revolted that families did this (we might be revolted by the blood shed but not by the motivation). We understand there are situations where living or continuing to be alive is not a viable option such as ones where there will be immeasurable pain that will conclude with death in the short-term.

---

[1] This description must not be confused with some Hollywood celebrities.

If we care for someone, we do not want that person to experience great amounts of pointless suffering. This is certainly the reason we can sympathize with parents in *The Walking Dead* who took it upon themselves to kill their children. These parents did not kill their children because they liked killing or simply wanted to harm their children. They did it for the same reason parents agree to turn up their children's morphine level to lethal levels in hospitals: though the child dies, the child is no longer suffering and there is no risk of them suffering in the future.

The survivors are in a similar situation as dying patients. They would face a world devoid of the order they've lived with. They would face great suffering, constant fighting, all for a world that doesn't appear to have a chance of returning. Even if we think trying to maintain the human species is a good thing, it's unlikely they could breed enough to compensate for the amount of people dying or dead already. They seem the last vestiges of the human species destined to become extinct. All this pointlessness and suffering could be avoided if they painlessly killed themselves. Of course they can find meaning in fighting, they could carve out a meager existence through forging new relationships and so on. But inevitably, they will die and probably be the last people—all the while having fought and fled, from zombies, humans, and other beasts.

Even in our world today there are plenty of reasons people commit suicide: physical or emotional pain, boredom with life, loss of meaning, and so on. Suicide is the certain 'last door', after which no suffering or pain or meaninglessness can ever slip through. Albert Camus famously said: "There is but one truly serious philosophical problem, and that is suicide."

Ask yourself why *you* don't commit suicide. Like most people who are reading this, you're probably somewhat comfortable, have friends and loved ones, talents, goals, hobbies and so on. There are things you want to do, places you want to see. This is what we might call the *Common Perception of Reality*: it's generally favorable and there is no reason to commit suicide. Life is quite wonderful.

That's why people hate pessimists who say life is actually more filled with suffering, disappointment, emptiness, meaninglessness and so on. Many people think pessimists are just upset, misguided people, no better than whinging teenagers that have yet to have joy or refuse to acknowledge joy in their lives. Yet one can proclaim life is filled with suffering and disappointment and not be a bore, a prude, or a cynic. What matters is a realistic conception of life. So just how different is our world from the zombie-landscape, from Hobbes's state of nature?

It's not so different. All over the world we have wars, famines, poverty, natural disasters, diseases, violence and other atrocities on a daily basis. Few people truly have a comprehension of the sheer amount of misery in the world. We know of horror occurring even in suburban households (recall Josef Fritzl who appeared to be an ordinary father but was a lunatic who kept his daughter in a dungeon and raped her regularly for years). We might be living comfortable lives, but we would be foolish to deny there exists massive amounts of suffering.

Even in comfortable lives, there is a lot of suffering. Random acts of violence or horror can occur quite easily. We know the dangers of car accidents which cause deaths of many innocent people, children included. But even people who do not experience car accidents, horrible fathers, or bad families will have to suffer watching loved ones die, be it parents or friends. Almost everyone will endure such suffering, as well as experience loss and regret at actions either performed and, equally, actions *not* performed—through cowardice or weakness of will. There will always be the girl that was never asked out, the job never taken, and so on. These are the things that also bring suffering and you will more than likely experience it.

The true terror, fear and dreadfulness of the horror genre is best seen if we realize that horror is not a glimpse into someone's dark imagination, but a bridge into corners of everyday life most of us would rather not think about. If we create something horrific that is so bizarre that no one knows what it is, the chances are that it would remain bizarre—not scary. In order to carry terror, there must be some connection, we must formulate a way to comprehend it with those same moral tools we take everywhere (including the landscape of *The Walking Dead*).

Our world is not a calm, happy, beautiful place. It's filled with horror and suffering. We share capacities for pain, horror, fear. Thus we can comprehend what it's like to be abandoned, alone, terrified. Whether it's a monster or a man—and today we know one can be both—we understand terror. People die and suffer every day, often for reasons of utter stupidity, like corruption, or, worse, for no perceived reason at all, like car accidents or natural disasters.

Our world, therefore, is not so different from Kirkman's nightmare. Like Dante, we can ask where else did Kirkman get his horror story except everyday life? Sure, we're not fighting zombies. But there are many people, fighting to stay alive, facing thuggish armed militants probably in some war, invading and raping and pillaging their town, village or city. Which is worse: co-ordinated thugs, ready to do horrible things to you and your family or a mindless, herd of mindless humanoid creatures?

Zombie attacks are like animal attacks, they're unfortunate when they happen, but they're not the horror of thugs raping you or your family, killing your neighbors, and burning your village to the ground. It's obvious that the thugs are worse and, what makes it more so is that the thugs exist right now.

Just because we don't experience such an environment, or such threats, does not mean someone else isn't or hasn't. For many people, a zombie apocalypse would be an improvement. In such a world, one possibly worse than Kirkman's, why do we bother continuing? Of course people might say, "Sure, the world is terrible, but just because it's terrible doesn't mean I should kill myself."

How Consistency Slaughters Morality

The survivors' world might be awful, filled with the dead, the undead, and evil governors but that doesn't appear to them to be a reason to kill themselves. After all, they have faced these and haven't slashed their wrists or shot themselves *en masse*. Perhaps there are some reasons they could attempt against their horrible situation to continue regardless.

These reasons need only be *superficially* persuasive to be accepted by many people. They might strive to continue fighting to improve the lives of others. They might want to help those struggling to survive and those who want to survive. There might be *more* suffering in the world if most people committed suicide, since those who remained and wanted to live would not have help—though this would put the burden on living on those who precisely do not want to live. And so on.

In our world, we might say something similar. Most people do not want to commit suicide, they probably want to live as long as possible. It's a reason that's as good as any. Instead of committing suicide, would we have other moral obligations? Easily, we should do what we can to improve the situation that made us consider suicide: the suffering in the world. If we're not in the position of suffering, like many impoverished people in Africa and India, then we're probably in a position to *help* them. We would be like Rick and his band of well-armed survivors: we have the means to help those who require it. If Rick and his band committed suicide, those who are helpless could not defend themselves and would continue to suffer.

This places quite a burden on us, though. If we can help, if our lives are not filled with suffering, if we are financially comfortable, we should donate or do something with our time to help those who require it. Suicide might be counterproductive since it prevents an able-bodied person from contributing to reducing suffering in the world. There might be good reasons for that person to commit suicide—say, she's in pain—but excluding such legitimate reasons, those who can do something, *should* do something.

This points to another contrast where the survivors are better than us: it takes a zombie-apocalypse to get people on their feet helping others. We see such things every day, when a natural disaster occurs and money floods in due to the attention of the event. But perhaps the greatest on-going wrong in the world, the continual oppression of women, especially in poorer or highly religious communities and countries, continues largely devoid of the attention of disaster relief efforts. This does not mean we should ignore aid where it is needed—it means that we must be consistent! Why does a flood warrant the attention of so many people, but not the continual denigration of half the species? What about the ongoing AIDS epidemic, hunger and suffering of children in Africa?

Consistency therefore takes a Michonne-like sword swing at common morality. If we're not consistent in our reasoning, whether moral or otherwise, then there's little point in reasoning, at all. Consistency matters since it informs us about the quality of our reasoning. If our theories are not consistent, then it is good reason to reject them as we would the explanations of a crackpot detective spinning theories inconsistent with the evidence.

If laws weren't consistent in their application, we would claim that they were unfair or unjust because people wouldn't be treated equally. Consistency is built into science and medicine: we know a drug works if it consistently works. In moral reasoning, therefore, consistency matters, to judge the quality of the moral theory or action in question.

If the main reason the survivors can justify their ongoing survival is to help others, as Rick does with Morgan (and vice versa) and, eventually, the group does with Tyreese and his family, and if our world is similar to Kirkman's, then we appear to have a moral duty to be *consistent* and reduce suffering where *we* can, too.

The Worst Thing Zombie-Survivors Can Do

In comics, movies, or TV series, one of the most drastic revelations is when a character reveals she is pregnant. It's difficult to say why, but usually there's a scandal involving who the father is, whether they can look after the child, whether an abortion should be performed, and so on. The major pregnancy of *The Walking Dead* is Lori's, since it's heavily implied that the child is Shane's, who is deceased in the comic, but very much alive in the TV series. Rick knows this, but quickly dismisses the importance of the father, since what matters is looking after the child. The boisterous Glenn and his lover Maggie also have hints of wanting to have children. This is especially so when the survivors reach the relative safety of the prison.

In Issue #41, Maggie and Glenn are in bed discussing their newly wed status. Maggie informs Glenn that people are wondering why they have a baby's crib in their bedroom. Glenn asks if she's pregnant already. Maggie says she could be, but in a way suggesting she *wants* to be. Glenn informs her it's not possible, since he's been careful. Maggie asks him why he's been careful. Glenn sits up slightly, and asserts that it's too dangerous to have a family now. Indicating the prison, Maggie says they're safe. Pushing forward she asks, What if the prison is in fact the safest place available and they don't ever find another place? If that's the case, does it mean, Maggie asks, that they should never start a family?

Perhaps in a normal environment, if the world were not filled with zombies, Glenn might be excited to start a family.

Certainly that's what he's implying. His reasons for not wanting children rest in the fact that the world is not safe.

It's hard to conceive of anything worse for survivors to do than to *make* children to suffer along with them. Not only will this become another human being who will suffer the horror of the world, possibly face death, but will be an added burden to the other survivors with their increasingly depleting food supply. What reasons could there be for making another mouth to feed and another body to protect from the relentless tide of zombies?

The best reason they could offer is to provide another future soldier to protect those in the future who need protecting. But the point of this moral action is to persuade everyone, not a few, to reconsider procreating. This would mean there would *not be any future survivors to protect*.

It appears, therefore, that there are few things more malicious that the survivors could do than to make a new member and a possible new zombie. We might say that Maggie and Glenn simply want to make a family. They're in a position of safety, as Maggie points out. If they don't make a child there, they will never make a child. But what's so wrong with being childless? After all, the child doesn't exist so the child can't be said to be suffering. An absolute guarantee of a child not suffering is to not create him!

Furthermore, we have already seen how Andrea and Dale adopted the orphaned children of Donna and Allen. Here, Andrea and Dale *have* become parents without adding another mouth to feed, and actually helping *existing children*. And surely children who actually exist matter more than some fantastical dream or desired children of potential parents? If what matters to Maggie and Glenn is being part of a family, why can't they adopt a child or children who no doubt require such love and attention? Sure, there might not be any children around the Prison, but there might be children alive, in the world, since they have come across other survivors before.

It's not good enough to say the children must be genetically related to Maggie and Glenn to count as deserving of love. There are plenty of people in our life who are *not* blood-related—from lovers to friends to aid workers—but deserve our love, attention and care. Indeed, the millions of families with adopted and foster children attest to this. Again, we need only think about Dale and Andrea. Besides why does genetics matter? Who cares whether the children are related by blood to the two? There are also plenty of examples of parents who do not love their biologically-related children. Being biologically-related does not mean that by definition you will end loving someone, nor is it an indicator that you should. Just because someone is related by blood doesn't mean they deserve your love or respect. Everyone, including parents need to earn respect. Genetic relationships do not grant special powers or abilities on anyone. Historically, people realized a royal bloodline was no indication that the person was genetically superior to the rest of us, nor would they, by definition, make a better leader.

Even if Glenn and Maggie are not able to find children to adopt, since adoption agencies did not survive the zombie apocalypse, they still have a moral obligation not to have children. Moreover, I'm sure Glenn and Maggie have other dreams that simply will not be fulfilled, like returning to a life like they had before the zombies. Hopes and dreams are not moral obligations, but the life that we secure for our future children is our moral obligation.

Notice, though, that this applies to us, too. Consistency demands that if we make a moral judgement about Glenn and Maggie's obligations to be parents, that it would apply to us, too, so long as there aren't relevant differences between our world and Kirkman's. This means that couples who want to have children need to think carefully about their reasons for doing so. After all, there are a myriad of dangers for the child: stillbirth, genetic abnormalities, and environmental harms. Expectant mothers might be able to protect their child from cigarette smoke and alcohol, but how do they protect the children from poverty, racism, gang violence, discrimination, and other ills of our modern world? Our world is just as dangerous as Maggie and Glenn's world. This means the argument against Glenn and Maggie having children *apply to us, right now*.

Adopting a New Ethic

If what matters is having a family or being a good parent, we can aim such action toward *existing* children. Non-existent children can't suffer, but at this moment, there are plenty of orphaned children who *do* require love and care that are available to be adopted by us in our world; of course, given Kirkman's world it is harder for Glenn and Maggie to adopt but that doesn't lessen the overall moral importance of pursuing that line of parenting. Our world has not got an infinite supply of resources, so, like the survivors, we must ask why we should add to overpopulation if we want to care for a child? Part of that population consists of children *whom we can care for.*

We might think that richer countries are not in such a horrible state as Kirkman's world. But that's short-sighted: you need only consider war-torn, poverty-riddled landscapes if you want something to match or best Kirkman's landscape in horror terms. *Your* environment might be better, but that only means you then have a stronger obligation to help those who don't live in it. You can bring children *out* of such horrible environments, as many celebrities are fond of doing (and for which they deserve our support, if they do it for the benefit of the children. This is consistent with the same reason the survivors have for continuing: helping others. Here we can reduce the suffering in the world by helping existing children, since they are the ones who are suffering now.

Indeed, people who live in comfortable settings are like survivors with food, guns, and shelter. Imagine that these well-fed, secure survivors come across a camp of abandoned children fighting off hordes of zombies. It seems obvious that these well-off survivors have a duty to help these children. Why, then, would such a moral duty not apply to currently well-off citizens of richer countries, in terms of children living in poorer countries? It's obvious that these children require help. All evidence points to the beneficence that adoption has; in fact, it seems more effective than simply throwing money at communities when you can actually help an individual or many individuals via adoption, active volunteering or both. But of course many people will reserve the time and effort for children who are not yet born (and therefore are non-existent) because they will be biologically related. Yet, like the survivors who come across abandoned children, it would seem awfully crass to say that these children are not allowed to join your camp because they do not have the matching DNA. This is racism at the most specific level; a prejudice against all those who are not related to myself.

These may seem like strange sentiments but, again, if we apply our reasoning and agreement with Glenn that the zombie landscape is no place to raise a child, why should we think any differently about our very similar world? Furthermore, our obligations should not be ignited by sudden, extreme events which only a shine a sudden burst of realization because of their immediacy. Prolonged agony becomes merely the heartbeat of the world and we ignore it. Yet, it remains agony, suffering and, therefore, a problem. But non-existent children can't suffer. The orphaned child however *does* exist and suffering only affects existing entities.

Too Much?

What we've looked at so far seems to test how willing we are to adhere to consistency if only to keep up the duty of ethical thinking. We've seen that sound criticisms of the survivors apply equally to our *world* and our*selves*; we've seen ideas of right and wrong turned on their heads, with killing being moral and having children as *immoral*; we've noted that if our judgement of characters is such because of the harsh world they live in, it is little different for our world since there are many aspects which are worse in our world. We've noted that the true horror behind this genre is not the fantastical elements but how much it reflects our world.

We can explore the darkest parts of humanity from the comfort and safety of our homes, anchored by the idea that we need only close the book or turn off the television to escape the nightmare—knowing full well that some people have experienced, are experiencing, or will experience similar suffering due to the monstrous nature of many human beings or the sheer brutality of an uncaring universe.

The Walking Dead is a useful background on which to test our assumptions, to probe our thoughts, to display our intuitions. Like a lab, the zombie-apocalypse world allows us to put our moral thinking under a microscope, to see how it plays out when put into this wriggling character and that. Now, we've reached some tentative conclusions but like all things done in lab, we have to take our conclusions back into a place that, for many, is worse than anything a horror writer can create: our current world.

20
What's Eating You?

WAYNE YUEN

Zombies are frightening for all sorts of reasons, their poor hygiene, their brutal single-mindedness, not to mention their dietary needs, namely us. So when the end of the world comes in the form of zombies, we should be afraid of them. But if *The Walking Dead* teaches us anything it's that zombies aren't the only thing we should fear. More often than not, what we have to fear isn't the zombies, but other people. Nothing is more frightening than desperate human beings.

In the "Fear the Hunters" story arc (*The Walking Dead*, Issues #61–66), Rick and company encounter a group of survivors who have turned to cannibalism to survive. Eventually Rick, Andrea, and Abraham put a violent end to their cannibalism, but only after Dale's legs are amputated and eaten by the cannibals, with the rest of him being saved for a later meal. It's a horrifying end to a central character, and it feels right that the cannibals are executed for what they have done.

But did Chris and his band of cannibals really do anything morally wrong? Most people's immediate reactions are, "Of course cannibalism is wrong!" But then again, most people have sympathetic feelings for people on the edge of survival, cannibalizing the dead to survive. It's almost impossible to talk about cannibalism without mentioning the movie *Alive*. The movie is based on the true story of a group of plane crash survivors, trapped on the Andes mountains, who resort to cannibalism to stay alive. Did they do anything wrong? If not, what's the difference between Chris and his band of cannibals, and other cannibals that we find heroic?

The Meat of Morality

These are clearly ethical questions, and when trying to answer ethical questions it helps to have some kind of framework for making ethical judgments. Without some kind of theoretical framework, people's ethical judgments tend to drift based on emotion and intuition. Ethical judgments based on emotion and intuition tend to be inconsistent. We might say that cannibalism is okay in one circumstance, like in *Alive*. and wrong in another sense, as in the "Fear the Hunters" arc. This leads people to believe that ethics is purely subjective, that what is right and wrong is based on a person's opinion alone. But this view—ethical subjectivism—fails on many levels.

Probably the most obvious way that it fails is that rarely are people willing to be consistently subjectivist. For example, if you believe that murder is wrong, according to your own opinion, than you're justified that it is wrong. However, I am equally justified in believing that murdering is morally acceptable, since it's my opinion that it's right. What kind of rational defense can you pose against me when I decide that I would like to murder and cannibalize you? The only way that we can give a rational defense is to abandon ethical subjectivism and appeal to some kind of moral framework.

So what kind of moral frameworks are there? Plenty, but the two most dominant ones are known as Utilitarianism and Kantianism.

Utilitarianism states that something is morally acceptable so long as it produces more net 'utility' than any other options available to us. 'Utility' is usually taken to mean 'happiness', but sometimes it can mean other things like satisfying our preferences, which may not always make us happy. So under Utilitarianism, the consequences of an action determine the moral worth of that action.

Kantianism states that an action is morally acceptable so long as it does not use a person as a means to an end, but rather treats people with respect and dignity, and that it is an action that can be consistently applied as a law of behavior amongst all people. Under Kantianism, the character of the action and its logical consistency determine its moral acceptability.

Here's a quick example of both theories in action. In the TV series, Rick decides that he must go back and retrieve his guns from the city and search for Merle, a decision protested by Shane, Lori, and Morales. So, was going back to rescue Merle the morally right thing to do? A utilitarian could argue that it was the right thing to do, since the group having more guns would benefit the group in the long run. This is in fact one of Rick's arguments.

However, another utilitarian might argue that Rick should ignore Merle, since if he is successful in retrieving him, Merle would only increase the tensions within the group because of his bigoted attitudes, making more people unhappy. On the other hand, a Kantian would say that Rick can't leave Merle behind since doing so would not be treating him with the respect and dignity that all people ought to be shown.

Had it not been Merle, but Lori or Carl who had been left alone in the city, Rick would not hesitate to rescue them. This action, saving people because they deserve respect and dignity, must be consistently applied as a law of behavior for all people. When Rick tells Daryl, "We don't kill the living," after Daryl has suggested that they kill Jim before he turns into a walker, Rick is making a universal principle that should apply to everyone because of the respect and dignity that they're owed.

Utilitarianism and Kantianism don't always agree, but when they do, we have very good reason to think that something is morally permissible. When they don't agree, the best thing to do is to try to determine which theory captures the most morally relevant ideas that pertain to the situation at hand. Is the outcome more important than a principled approach? Utilitarianism might be our choice. But sometimes the outcome takes a back seat to the actions that are being recommended, and so a principled approach would be better.

When Amy's dying, there's certainly a danger of a walker harming members of the group. The utilitarian thing to do might be to force Andrea away from Amy's corpse so that the group can ensure that Amy will not reanimate into a walker. But that act seems particularly heartless to Andrea's grieving process, so a Kantian approach of letting Andrea grieve, trusting in her to do the right thing when Amy does reanimate, is the right course of action.

Finally, people might disagree about what a particular theory recommends. One utilitarian might calculate the outcome one way, while someone else another way. Two Kantians might disagree about what it means to treat a person with respect and dignity, or what counts as a person at all! Moral theories aren't perfect tools, but they are far better than relying on whimsy, mood, or emotion. Both the moral theories I've mentioned take values that are at the core of morality and build a rational framework around them to justify moral judgments.

The Cannibalism Conundrum

With these frameworks in mind, we can turn our attention to cannibalism. For most people, it's a pretty straightforward idea, human beings eating human beings. But this definition of cannibalism won't do for a philosophical investigation. It only takes a little thought before we're bogged down with questions like, "Is it cannibalism for me to swallow my own saliva?" After all, your saliva inevitably has cells from your mouth in them, that you would end up digesting. If this is cannibalism, we are all cannibals from the day we're born. So what counts as cannibalism?

Let's stipulate that cannibalism, for the purposes of this argument, is when one human being eats human flesh, not excretions or other cells that would be lost to normal wear and tear. So kissing a lover, biting and swallowing your fingernails, post nasal drip, swallowing a tooth (it's not flesh), drinking urine, or sucking on a cut would not make you a cannibal (although it might make you a vampire). You would be a cannibal if you bit off the tip of your tongue and swallowed it, ate a filet made from a human corpse, or turned the tables on a walker and sunk your teeth into it. I think this definition covers what most people would consider cannibalism so that we don't have to investigate trichophagia (a disorder characterized by the impulsive desire to eat your own hair) and more mundane forms of auto-cannibalism. (Under a loose definition of cannibalism, we would be cannibals because of the routine operation of our immune system.)

So is cannibalism morally wrong? In a plane crash scenario where we have plenty of dead bodies to eat, and no food, a utilitarian could very easily justify cannibalism. It would make more people happy if I lived, than if I died. Specifically it would make me happier, even if the vast majority was really squeamish or grossed out when they hear of my method of survival.

The dead are not going to lose a lot of happiness from being eaten, since they're already dead!

A Kantian could justify cannibalism as well, since we didn't kill the person specifically to eat. Why is this important? Kant says that people, or perhaps more precisely persons, are owed moral consideration. A human's rationality, their ability to live in accordance with moral rules (even if they choose not to) is what grants them that respect. Since dead bodies can't reason, they aren't (so a Kantian might argue) owed the same kind of dignity and respect that living human beings are owed. So utilitarianism and Kantianism seem to be in agreement, that if we find ourselves in a survival situation, with dead bodies, we can eat them.

This however, doesn't mean that cannibalism of dead bodies *in general* is morally acceptable. When Carl shoots Shane, the survivors don't decide to eat Shane's corpse. It isn't even considered. The survivors are in a position that they don't need to cannibalize human beings to survive. They've been foraging food from abandoned houses and the environment via hunting and scavenging. Moreover, eating Shane would probably upset many people within the group, including Rick, even though Shane just tried to kill him. This is why we don't eat dead bodies in general. If I were to show up at a wake with fork, knife, and bib in hand, it wouldn't *just* be unusual or distasteful, but my actions would be upsetting to others in a significant way. This clearly wouldn't be maximizing anyone's happiness, except maybe my own if I really enjoyed human meat (and under utilitarianism, we have to maximize utility overall, not just my own) nor would it be treating the mourners with respect and dignity.

You might be thinking that there is something really inconsistent in what I've just argued for. If eating the dead would not treat mourners with respect and dignity, then why would it be any different, morally speaking, if I were at the funeral parlor, or if I were a survivor of a plane crash? In both cases, learning that your loved one was eaten by another would probably be upsetting and a little disrespectful to the ones left behind. The key difference is the *need* in one situation versus the *desire* in the other. Denying me the ability to eat human flesh in a survival situation devalues my own dignity by making me a mere tool to the preservation of another's dignity.

Morally Bad Hunters

We never learn that much about Chris and his band of cannibals in the comics. Through a couple of speeches, we learn that they're really terrible hunters of wild game, which leads them to start hunting human beings. It's heavily implied that Chris's group turned on themselves first, eating their children, in order to survive. Are the hunters moral monsters? When Chris is defending himself and his group to Rick he says:

> "I want to make this abundantly clear—we don't do this because we *want* to. It's important to me that you know that. There aren't a lot of us left—living people. If there were *anything* else we could do to get by—we'd do it. There isn't. Food is scarce. . . . if we weren't doing this we'd starve to death. I hate to say it, but it's me or you. . . . And whenever that's the situation—it's very easy to choose *me*."

Chris and his group's situation sounds a lot like the survival cannibalism that we've examined before. Let's imagine the beginnings of their cannibalism which have two distinct possibilities.

The first possibility is that Chris' group is wasting away from starvation and reasonably enough, one of their children dies first. The group facing certain death, decide that they eat the dead child in order to survive. This gives them enough strength to forage some more and find enough food to build up their strength. If this is what happened, and we really don't know that it isn't, then Chris' group hasn't done anything morally wrong. Cannibalism in a survival situation, seems to be morally permissible from our previous reasoning. The second possibility is that Chris' group was wasting away from starvation and they decide to kill a child to stave off starvation. Even if this is not how things happened, this case more closely mirrors Dale's kidnapping and subsequent cannibalization.

Is there anything wrong with the second scenario? There does seem to be some morally problematic things with it. First, who they are eating was killed to be eaten, rather than died from some other cause, then eaten. This is clearly a case of murder, the killing of an innocent person. Although it usually goes without saying that murder is wrong, some analysis is needed to explain the wrongness here versus cannibalization of already dead body.

First, the act of killing the child, or Dale if it had been allowed to progress that far, reduces happiness. The child could have lived and in all likelihood wanted to live. The alternative of letting someone die increases happiness slightly, since it never cuts short anyone's life. Killing the child also reduces, by one, the things in the world that *could* contribute to maximizing utility. If we could choose between killing a child or a killing a rabbit, we should kill the rabbit, since the child has more potential to maximize utility. The child has the capacity of generating more utility because of its complex desires, such as hoping the future will have fewer walkers. The rabbit can't plan for the future in the same way that a child can, for example. But if this weren't the case, say the child suffered a severe brain trauma that left the child vegetative, the rabbit would suddenly have a greater capacity for generating utility than the child, and the rabbit might be the one we choose to let live.

Under a utilitarian conception, no person's happiness is worth more than another's. Choosing the child's life over random chance of who starves to death first, preferences everyone else's life over that child's life. It isn't fair to the child. Nor does killing the child give respect or preserve the child's dignity as a person. So from a Kantian perspective what they did was wrong as well.

The wrongness is multiplied in the case of Dale. Not only is Dale used as a source of food for the survival of others, thus not respecting or preserving his dignity, but he survives it! He gets to experience the terror of understanding what has happened to him and what they intend to do to him in the future. Whereas the child's life is simply cut short, Dale's life is prolonged, which allows him to suffer longer. This significantly reduces the amount of net utility, and opens up the possibility of the hunters *repeatedly* disrespecting Dale. It's ironic that Chris admits to being a bad hunter because it is never more apparent that they are bad hunters than in their treatment of Dale. Regardless of how one morally views hunting, good hunters, both in the moral sense and in the skilled sense, strive for "clean kills," where the prey suffers as little as possible. The hunter's treatment of Dale seems to purposefully extend the suffering of their prey as much as possible.

So even if the hunters began their cannibalism in an ethical fashion, by eating only those who have already died, they do not continue a morally acceptable form of cannibalism. Their egregiously disrespectful actions to Dale rightfully earns them the title of moral monsters, perhaps on par with or surpassing the other distinctly monstrous character of *The Walking Dead* series, The Governor.

One might argue that Chris and his group had no other choices, they had to hunt others in order to survive. Chris says it plainly enough, "If there were anything else to get by . . ." If Chris is correct then perhaps he gets a free pass on our moral judgment. After all, it makes little sense to hold someone morally responsible for something that they couldn't help but do. If I must digest my own cheek cells every day, then I can't be held morally blameworthy for being a cannibal, since I can't avoid doing it.

But this is line of argument fails. With only a little imagination we can think of countless ways of surviving in the apocalypse. We could, by the force of hunger, risk befriending a group of survivors like Rick's, instead of trying to eat them. We could try hunting walkers and being a zombitarian-kind-of-cannibal. Speaking as someone who is a vegetarian for ethical reasons, zombitarianism sounds like a morally preferable option to hunting wild game, so long as you are not the cause of the person dying in the first place. They're already dead (twice dead actually), and arguably they have no moral worth.

Or we could simply choose to starve to death. Continuing to live is not a moral obligation. Sometimes morality demands that we sacrifice our lives for the sake of a greater good, to prevent harm, or to do what is rationally compelled by our moral obligations. To say that survival is a good reason to throw out ethics, is like saying, "I'm exempt from being moral whenever my life is threatened." If this were true, police officers would be exempt from morality by the nature of their profession, but we expect these people to be subject to the same morality as everyone else. No doubt, our moral obligations may change when our lives are threatened, as we've seen with survival cannibalism, or in more common cases like self-defense. However, I don't believe there is a plausibly consistent reason that would allow us to murder when we're starving.

Do unto Others . . .

When Rick and company confront the hunters, they systematically kill and burn each of them. Rick's life wasn't in danger, especially with Andrea sniping from the forest. Was he justified in killing the hunters? Rick's justification was that they needed to be punished. A post-apocalypse execution was the only thing that the hunters could possibly deserve. Was this justice? I raise this question because of how a Kantian might respond to this. Immanuel Kant, the founder of Kantianism, argued that the death penalty was needed, since it was the only way for us to punish people for the ultimate crimes, namely murder. This seems like a rare case where Kant himself seemed to recognize that the situation of a moral act affects the morality of it instead of insisting on universal laws on everyone.

Killing people is okay when we're killing guilty people. But why punish at all? Punishment for Kant was a way for us to fully show the equality between people. If Chris, as a rational human being, believed it was okay for him to hunt down and kill other human beings for food, then that is an action that can be consistently applied as a law of behavior amongst all people, according to Kant. If Dale was good as a steak, so is Chris. This is precisely what Rick was suggesting when he tells Chris that he just might have a taste.

Zombies eat humans. That's partly why they frighten us. Cannibals in many ways are more frightening than zombies, since zombies eat humans mindlessly. Cannibals *choose* to eat humans, which make them all the more frightening. Heroic cannibalism happens in survival situations, where survivors eat the dead because that is their only source of food. Heroic cannibalism *must* be morally acceptable cannibalism. All other forms of cannibalism, be it unnecessary cannibalism, murdering for food, plain curiosity, or the specific desire for human flesh (which, outside of isolated cannibal tribes like the Korowai in New Guinea, is the most common form of cannibalism[1]) are difficult to justify morally since they inflict great amounts of harm on to the one being eaten, and violates the dignity that they deserve as rational persons.

---

[1] Armin Meiwes famously solicited for and found a victim on the Internet in 2001.

We Are the Walking Dead!

FRANKLIN ALLAIRE is a PhD student in Educational Foundations in the College of Education at the University of Hawai'i at Mānoa. His interests include epistemology and identity theory/salience. In his spare time he enjoys running, photography, and preparing his survival shelter for the inevitable undead apocalypse. Should he be bitten and turn, Franklin has made his wife, family, and friends promise to take him down immediately otherwise they will forfeit inheritance of his Star Wars figures and likely become victim to his uncontrollable ontological zombie rage.

ROBERT ARP has interests in philosophy of biology, ontology in the information science sense, and philosophy and pop culture. Without his coffee in the morning, he IS the walking dead.

ADAM BARKMAN is Associate Professor of Philosophy at Redeemer University College (Canada). He is the author of *C.S. Lewis and Philosophy as a Way of Life* and *Through Common Things* and is co-editor of *Manga and Philosophy* and *The Philosophy of Ang Lee*. Teaching Plato and Confucius, Barkman is sometimes deceived into thinking people are smarter than they really are—but Jesus and Nietzsche were, apparently, both right: most people are sheep, which is why in every zombie apocalypse, only twenty people in the world survive.

ASHLEY JIHEE BARKMAN teaches English and Philosophy at Redeemer University College. She holds a Master's in English and in Theology, both from the University of Toronto. She contributed chapters to *30 Rock and Philosophy* and *The Big Bang Theory and Philosophy*. Prior to the highly anticipated Y2K crisis, Ashley was ready for the end with gallons of water and canned food stocked up in her basement; a decade later, she gets to live the end (thankfully) vicariously through *The Walking Dead*.

DAVE BEISECKER is an associate professor of philosophy at the University of Nevada, Las Vegas. A specialist in the philosophy of mind and language, he has written several articles on the conceivability argument against materialism (aka "the zombie argument"), and has even gone so far as to claim in *The Journal of Consciousness Studies* to be a zombie himself, albeit of the relatively benign, philosophical sort. More recently, he has connected zombies of the philosophical sort with those of the cinematic sort in an article, "Nothing But Meat? Philosophical Zombies and their Cinematic Counterparts." He was infected with the zombie virus while doing graduate work in George Romero's beloved hometown of Pittsburgh, where his dreams to join the ranks of the Living Dead on a Romero set went tragically unfulfilled. He now aspires to parlay his contribution in this volume into a stagger-on role as one of Kirkman's walkers.

MICHAEL DA SILVA studies law at the University of Toronto. His primary philosophical interests include social and political philosophy, ethics, and philosophy of law. His previous popular culture and philosophy publications include erudite studies of *Arrested Development* and *30 Rock*. He worries that publishing his works may tip off the undead about the presence of brains in his head and is thus glad that Walking Dead zombies don't discriminate, eating all sorts of fleshy goodness.

ROBERT A. DELFINO is Associate Professor of Philosophy at St. John's University, New York. He received his PhD from SUNY Buffalo where he studied under Jorge J.E. Gracia and Barry Smith. He recently wrote a chapter on the relationship between science, metaphysics, and theology, in the book *Science and Faith within Reason* (2011). Getting scientists, philosophers, and theologians to agree on anything often seems more difficult than surviving a zombie apocalypse.

STEPHEN BRETT GREELEY teaches English literature and composition for The City University of New York at the College of Staten Island, where he also received his MA in English Literature. He has written two as-yet-unpublished books and spends a great deal of time staring at Telperion and Laurelin, the pear trees outside his window, while thinking about how to convince people magic and ghosts are serious subjects. As an avid urban hiker, when the city goes zombie, he will be safely hidden in the Staten Island Greenbelt, eating berries and slow chipmunks.

RICHARD GREENE is a Professor of Philosophy at Weber State University. He has co-edited *Zombies, Vampires, and Philosophy*,

Quentin Tarantino and Philosophy, and *Dexter and Philosophy*. He also does research on skepticism. Richard would not have stopped Andrea from killing herself (but only for purely selfish reasons—she's annoying!).

GORDON HAWKES is an independent scholar in Kelowna, BC. Unbeknownst to all his family and friends—even his wife—Gordon is a real life philosophical zombie. Despite lacking consciousness, Gordon acts and speaks no differently than a typical human being. When he's not writing or studying philosophy, he appears to enjoy reading classic literature, watching old movies, and going for long runs. (He just has no subjective inner experience of any of those things.) His materialist friends deny the possibility of his existence, a fact that would hurt him deeply if he possessed any feelings.

JEFFREY A HINZMANN is a graduate student at the University of South Florida. He has been working on his PhD for so long, he is pretty sure he is one of the walking dead. During his natural life, he said a thing or two in *30 Rock and Philosophy*. As of now, his life, career, and future all seem to hover in that limbo between life and death where all things zombie belong. He's okay with it, though, he's the life of the undead party.

BRANDON KEMPNER, fearing the zombie hordes, fled from the East Coast to New Mexico. There, he hoards books, teaches American literature at New Mexico Highlands University, and waits for the fall of humankind. Once that happens, he hopes to start the very first zombie university, and in preparation has published articles on 9/11 fiction, *The Sopranos*, *Mad Men*, and Afrofuturism.

GREG LITTMANN is a wandering, moaning corpse in an advanced state of decomposition. It is employed as a professor at Southern Illinois University, Edwardsville, where it roams the halls, teaching Epistemology, Metaphysics, Philosophy and Literature, and Philosophy of Mind. Then, when the students' brains are plump and ripe with knowledge, it eats them. In violation of all known biological laws, it has published in metaphysics and the philosophy of logic and has written chapters for books relating philosophy to *Breaking Bad*, *The Big Bang Theory*, *Doctor Who*, *Dune*, *Final Fantasy*, *Game of Thrones*, *The Onion*, *Sherlock Holmes*, *The Terminator*, Neil Gaiman, and *The Walking Dead*. According to legend, the best defense against Greg Littmann is to cover yourself in a white wine sauce with maybe a little cracked pepper. Mmm . . .

MARTY MCKENDRY holds an MA in philosophy from the University of Toronto, where he studies law. Over the course of his legal career, he has published scholarship on constitutionalism and the rule of law in the context of a zombie apocalypse. He has also diligently developed practical skills with shotguns and incendiaries via the Left 4 Dead video game series. Marty is a veteran of the Canadian Naval Reserve. He intends to use his old unit as a rally point on Z-Day, citing the caches of small arms, provisions, and watercraft.

TAURIQ MOOSA is a tutor in the Philosophy Department at University of Cape Town. He is a Masters Student in Applied Ethics, specializing in Biomedical Ethics at the Centre for Applied Ethics, Stellenbosch University. He has written for numerous publications including *Skeptic Magazine, Free Inquiry, Secular Humanist Bulletin*, the James Randi Educational Foundation and others. He is also a columnist for the popular website 3quarksdaily.com, where he pretends that people like Steven Pinker and Richard Dawkins read his work. If he's ever part of a group of zombie survivors, he hopes to be the rational, calm one that gets the girl. More than likely, he'll be the evil one that creates conflict by hoarding resources, shooting a shotgun and screaming like a Hillbilly.

PETER PADRAIC O'SULLIVAN teaches English at San Jose State University.. When he's not teaching college freshmen how to scavenge for food in a zombie wasteland, how to improvize spring-loaded decapitation traps with common household items, and how comma splices are merely run-ons with jewelry, Peter writes prodigiously in whatever genre will have him. While his satire has been published on the website *Revolution Science Fiction*, his crowning achievement is a ball of string bigger than his head, to which he adds string weekly.

DANEE PYE received her BA in Philosophy from UC Berkeley and is now working on a PhD in Communication Studies at the University of Texas at Austin. While her work focuses on the intersections of feminism, rhetoric, and philosophy, she also dabbles in psychoanalysis from time to time. She has researched topics as varied as *Suicide Girls* and *Coraline*, has Nietzsche under her skin, and secretly thinks every important literary work would be better with zombies.

ELIZABETH RARD is mainly interested in logic. By day she teaches philosophy. She moonlights as a zombie slayer and her weapon of choice is her trusty chainsaw. Elizabeth hopes to someday teach at the first integrated zombie-human university, Zomford, after the initial horror of the zombie apocalypse has passed.

RACHEL ROBISON-GREENE is completing her Ph.D. in Philosophy at UMass, Amherst. She's co-edited two books on philosophy and popular culture, *The Golden Compass and Philosophy: God Bites the Dust* and *Dexter and Philosophy: Mind Over Spatter*. Some of Rachel's early morning class students bear a striking resemblance to the folks in Hershel's barn.

JULIA ROUND <www.juliaround.com> has always preferred zombies to vampires (who, like, totally suck). By day she is a senior lecturer in The Media School at Bournemouth University, UK, where she teaches comics and literature and edits the academic journal *Studies in Comics*. By night she dons her Zombie Killing Hoodie and, armed only with a bad temper and knowledge gleaned from too many zombie movies, stalks the seafront dispatching the undead and anyone else who gets in her way. All other hours are devoted to publishing thinly disguised rants in academic journals on cult media and literature. She is writing a book analysing the impact of the English Gothic tradition on contemporary British and American comics.

SI SHEPPARD is an Assistant Professor of Political Science at Long Island University, Brooklyn, the ideal place to be in the event of a zombie pandemic. The campus is built like a fortress on top of a self-contained city block. Overpass walkways link multistory buildings big enough to support roof gardens and cisterns. On-site generators offer emergency power. Medical and other supplies are laid in. Yep, reckon we'll hole up here for a while.

KYLE TAYLOR is a second year student at St. John's University, New York. When not talking about zombies he enjoys sailing and whitewater canoeing from his home in upstate New York. His career aspirations are as broad as they are many, but one thing's for certain: he'll never stop doing what he's passionate about . . . unless there is a zombie apocalypse.

JASON WALKER was on the verge of finishing his dissertation at the University of Wisconsin at Madison on the rule of law as the product of emergent order. The rise of the zombies and subsequent collapse of civilization could have put this outcome in doubt, but he now resides with his wife in the Alexandria Safe-Zone, where he plans to empirically test his thesis. He only hopes his fellow survivors are okay with sparing electricity for his laptop, and that carrier pigeons can successfully transport his completed dissertation back to Wisconsin. He respectfully requests that readers refrain from punny jokes about his last name.

WAYNE YUEN teaches philosophy at Ohlone College. He is co-editor of *Neil Gaiman and Philosophy: Gods Gone Wild!*, and has written deeply profound essays on topics such as: *The Terminator, Buffy the Vampire Slayer, The Golden Compass,* and *Avatar* among other things. He also maintains the Zombietarianism page on Facebook. He's promised his wife that if she becomes a zombie he will keep her in the backyard as a well-treated pet.

Index

a priori, 142–44, 146–47, 151
Adlard, Charlie, 11, 13
Adorno, Theodor, 161
afterlife, 5–6, 51, 97, 101
Alive, 244
anarchy, 83, 130–36, 140, 164. *See also* government
Aquinas, St. Thomas, 40, 168
Aries, Philippe, 169–170
Aristotle, 168, 211–12, 219–223

Becker, Ernest, 202–03
Bentham, Jeremy, 197
Berkeley, George, xi
Bismarck, Otto von, 138
Blackmore, Susan, 11
Bloomberg, Michael, 175
Bobo Doll Experiment, 98
Boethius, 40
Bradbury, Ray, 174
Brooks, Max, 116, 155, 164
Butler, Judith, 108–09, 116

Campbell, Bruce, 51, 73
Camus, Albert, 120–28, 144, 158, 234; and absurdity, 120–21, 124–28; *The Plague*, 121–27; and Sisyphus, 124–25, 127–28

cannibals: humans as, 92, 94, 97, 130, 211–12, 243, 246–251; zombies as, 51, 68, 251. *See also* morality
Carroll, Noel, 69–71, 75
Center for Disease Control (CDC), xi, 10, 33, 43, 63, 73, 113, 123, 126–27, 129, 170–71, 184
Chalmers, David, xii–iii, 6, 10–14
Cicero, 208
civil society, 82–83, 85, 90, 94–95, 233
Confucius, 102, 207–09
consciousness, 3, 9, 11–15, 26, 56, 59–60, 120, 181–82, 188, 200; animal, 19–23; lack of, 4, 19–23, 72; rationality and, 185; of self, 203–04; states of, 10; system and, 27. *See also* mind
Cracked, 81

death: fear of, xi, 50–51, 168–69; and life as mutually exclusive, 41–42; as prerequisite for becoming a zombie, 19–20; respect for, 54, 61. *See also* horror

Dennett, Daniel 12–15, 23; and zimbo, 13
Descartes, René, xiii, 5–6, 8
Dostoevsky, Fyodor, 144
Drezner, Daniel W., 131
dualism, 5–7, 9, 15

English Civil War, 86
Enlightenment, 97, 169–170
epistemology, 31–32; of zombies, 33–36
equality, xii, 55–56, 84–85, 110, 213, 238, 242, 251; and gender, 97, 99, 101, 106–07, 115. *See also* feminism, gender
existentialism, 141–154, 156–166; and angst, 158–59; and authenticity, 124–25, 146, 149, 159–164, 166, 227; and humanism, 142, 144–45, 150, 153; and the Other, 163–65
experience: of being a zombie, 13–15, 20–23; bodily, 18–19; of fear, 23

Federal Emergency Management Agency (FEMA), xi
feminism. 97–101, 106, 114. *See also* equality, sex and gender difference, 98–99, 102–03
Fido, 31
free will, 54, 59–60, 142, 145–46, 148–152, 158, 162, 175, 224
Fromm, Erich, 174, 176
functionalism, 22–24

Galileo, Galilei, 169
gender, 107–116; as performative, 108; and primitive clan, 109–110; roles, 110–11; and social conditioning, 113. *See also* feminism; equality
God, 40, 51, 89, 101, 124–25, 141–45, 151, 153, 159, 169, 199; wrath of, 170–71
government. xii, 82–87, 94, 147–49, 198, 214–15, 222; authoritarian, 93, 174–75; lack of, 131, 135, 147, 221, 233; and punishment, 85, 94–95; role of, 82. *See also* anarchy

Hamlet, 51
Heidegger, Martin, 144
Hobbes, Thomas, 82–86, 90–95, 233, 235; and *Leviathan*, 84, 94–95
horror, 68–70, 235–36; paradox of, 69, 71; and suffering, 234–242. *See also* death
humanity, 55, 77; residual, 53–55, 58–62, 164; walkers as non-human, 199–205. *See also* personhood

impossible beings, 41–42, 45–46, 50–51
instinct, 21, 34
intentionality, 9, 202

Jackson, Peter 27

Kant, Immanuel, 40, 54–57, 59–64, 192–93, 199, 201, 203, 205, 207, 244, 247–251
Kierkegaard, Søren, 144, 159
King, Stephen, 164
Kirk, Robert, 3
Kirkman, Robert, vii, 3, 12, 69–71, 76, 78, 83, 106, 141–46, 149–153, 166, 236, 238–241

Index

Land of the Dead, 31, 83, 202
Lao Tzu, 208
legal rights, 57, 198, 204
Leopold, Aldo, 188
Lewis, C.S., 172
Locke, John, 82–95
logical possibility, 11–12
Lord of the Flies, 131

Machiavelli, Niccolò, 130
materialism, 7, 10–11, 15, 85, 145, 174–75
mind, xii, 5, 7–9, 25–27, 40–45, 180–83, 203; conscious, 59, 181–83, 187; as the "I," 5–6; and experience, 9; and mindlessness, 14, 19, 21, 34–35, 44–45, 172, 180, 184, 190, 236; perceptual, 181–83, 185, 187; reasoning, 181–83, 187; residual, 59. *See also* consciousness; instinct; neocortex
Moore, Tony, 11, 13
morality, 144–45, 155–166, 196–99, 208–216, 218–230, 236–38, 244; anthropocentric, 185–86, 193; and cannibalism, 246–251; and deep ecology, 188, 190; and dignity, 40, 54–60, 244–49, 251; and duty, 54, 56–57, 59–62, 64, 104, 209–210, 213, 238, 241–42; of having children, 238–242; and killing, 231–32, 249–250; post-, 139–140; and treatment of zombies, 179–188, 198–206; and virtue, 207, 212, 219–221. *See also* natural law; realism; utilitarianism

Nagel, Thomas, 72, 127–28

natural law, 207–216, 221–23, 227; virtue and, 212–13. *See also* morality
neocortex, 7, 20, 44, 48. *See also* mind
Nietzsche, Friedrich, 144, 223–230; and slave morality, 224–26; and will to power, 223–24
Night of the Living Dead, 27, 30, 70, 131, 155, 165, 167
nihilism, 158

personhood, 191, 196, 199–202. *See also* humanity
philosophical behaviorism, 22
Pinker, Steven, 6
Plato, 207, 218–221
property, 82, 85, 87–95; personal, 212–13; protection of, 185

Qin Shi Huang, 130
quasi-living, 42, 48–50

realism, 129–133, 137–38, 140; moral, 218. *See also* morality
Regan, Tom, 196
religion, 124, 144–48, 159, 169–170, 223–24, 237
Resident Evil, 71, 106, 155, 164–65
The Return of the Living Dead, 27, 29–31
Romero, George, 3, 10, 27, 31, 67, 70–71, 74, 115, 155, 165–67, 202
Rousseau, Jean-Jacques, 172–75
Ryle, Gilbert, 6

Sartre, Jean-Paul 141–48, 151, 153, 160

science, 8, 70, 169–171, 184, 238; and free will, 175; and knowledge, 8, 224; and religion, 169–170
sex. *See* feminism, gender
Shaun of the Dead, 27, 31, 77
Singer, Peter 39, 187–88
social contract, 83–88, 94, 113
Socrates, 39
sovereign, 82–86, 93
soul, 4–6, 40, 44, 77, 101, 156, 161, 166, 209; rational, 211, 219
speciesism, 39
state of nature, 82–87, 92–95, 233, 235
suicide, 60–63, 120, 123–24, 158, 232–37

Tilly, Charles, 133
28 Days Later, 31, 155, 164–65
28 Weeks Later, 165

utilitarianism, 180, 186–88, 190–91, 197, 230, 244–46, 249. *See also* morality

vampires, 74–76
Vargas, Manuel, 48
vatos, 112
virus, 48–50, 155, 165–66, 203

The Walking Dead (comics): Issue #1, 91, 157, 159; Issue #2, 148, 232; Issue #3, 100, 105; Issue #5, 149; Issue #6, 150, 232; Issue #7, 209; Issue #11, 142; Issue #14, 165; Issue #15, 165; Issue #16, 134; Issue #17, 135, 159; Issue #18, 136; Issue #19, 159; Issue #22, 158; Issue #23, 134–35; Issue #24, 102, 159–160, 162, 164; Issue #26, 143; Issue #27, 161, 215; Issue #28, 137, 216; Issue #29, 137; Issue #30, 136; Issue #34, 138; Issue #36, 138, 140; Issue #41, 158–59, 165, 238; Issue #43, 161; Issue #54, 136; Issue #55, 165; Issue #56, 158, 160; Issue #57, 159, 161; Issue #58, 4, 160–61, 163; Issue #60, 157; Issue #61, 152, 159, 211, 216, 243; Issue #63, 92, 211, 243; Issue #65, 93, 211, 243; Issue #66, 159, 162, 211, 243; Issue #67, 160; Issue #71, 139; Issue #75, 139, 200; Issue #76, 132; Issue #81, 6; Issue #82, 208; Issue #84, 140; Issue #90, ix; Issue #91, 5
The Walking Dead (TV episodes): "Days Gone Bye," 34–36, 46–47, 50, 58, 109, 146, 148–151, 157, 164, 168, 197, 200–05, 210, 218; "Guts," 34, 36, 43, 46, 48, 53, 61, 87, 103, 109, 202, 207, 209, 215; "Pretty Much Dead Already," 47, 128, 191, 193; "Save the Last One," 13; "Secrets," 191; "Tell It to the Frogs," 100, 103, 110–11; "TS-19," 7, 19, 33, 44, 49–50, 56, 127, 158, 165, 170, 184, 199; "Vatos," 62, 90, 103, 111, 127, 173, 202–03, 210; "What Lies Ahead," 113–14; "Wildfire," 18, 43, 49, 62–63, 104, 115, 121, 158, 209–210
Warren, Mary Ann, 199–204
Weber, Max, 133
White Zombie, 30–31, 155, 165

Zombieland, 77, 82, 155

If the Earth can have natural ice ages, can it have natural freak heat waves? This would explain what is currently happening to the world. What if records don't go far enough back, and the last freak heat wave was just before temperatures plummeted into an ice age.